DIALOGUE AND CONFLICT RESOLUTION

Dialogue and Conflict Resolution

Resolution

Potential and Limits

Edited by

PERNILLE RIEKER AND HENRIK THUNE
Norwegian Institute of International Affairs, Norway

Routledge
Taylor & Francis Group

LONDON AND NEW YORK

First published 2015 by Ashgate Publishing

Published 2016 by Routledge
2 Park Square, Milton Park, Abingdon, Oxon OX14 4RN
711 Third Avenue, New York, NY 10017, USA

First issued in paperback 2017

Routledge is an imprint of the Taylor & Francis Group, an informa business

British Library Cataloguing in Publication Data
A catalogue record for this book is available from the British Library.

The Library of Congress has been applied for

ISBN 13: 978-1-138-09859-6 (pbk)
ISBN 13: 978-1-4724-3883-6 (hbk)

Contents

List of Contributors

John Ashworth has worked continuously with the churches in Sudan and South Sudan ever since 1983 in a range of fields, focusing for the past 15 years or so on peace and reconciliation. He is a Fellow of the Rift Valley Institute and has been a Visiting Scholar at the Kroc Institute, University of Notre Dame, but sees himself primarily as a practitioner and not an academic. Ashworth's most recent book: *The Voice of the Voiceless: The Role of the Church in the Sudanese Civil War 1983–2005* (Nairobi: Paulines Publications Africa, 2014).

Målfrid Braut-Hegghammer is Assistant Professor at the Norwegian Defence University College and MacArthur Junior Faculty Fellow at the Center for International Security and Cooperation, Stanford University. She completed her doctoral dissertation at the London School of Economics in 2010, which focused on the nuclear programs in Iraq and Libya. She has been a pre- and post-doctoral fellow at the Belfer center, Harvard University (2008–10), and a Stanton Junior Faculty Fellow at Stanford University (2012–13). She has published scholarly articles in *International Security*, *The Middle East Journal*, and *The Nonproliferation Review*.

Georges Fahmi is an El Erian Fellow at the Carnegie Middle East Center in Lebanon. He holds a doctoral degree from the European University Institute in Italy (June 2013). Fahmi obtained both his Bachelor and Master degrees from Cairo University, Department of Political Science. His research interests include religion–state relations in the Middle East, democratization, and religious movements.

Jakub M. Godzimirski holds a PhD in social anthropology from the Polish Academy of Sciences and Letters (1987) and an MA in social/cultural anthropology from the University of Warsaw (1981). In 1995 he joined Norwegian Institute of International Affairs (NUPI), where his main areas of research have been Russian foreign and security policy, energy policy and developments in the post-Soviet space and in Central and Eastern Europe. Godzimirski has conducted several studies on Russian foreign and security policies focusing on the role of Russia in post-Soviet conflicts (Crimea, Chechnya, Georgia, Abkhazia, South Ossetia, Moldova and Transdniester), Russia's relations with other actors (OSCE, NATO) and on

Russian energy policy. He has published on political and social transition in Central and Eastern Europe, energy security, and issues related to migration and diaspora.

Sverre Lodgaard served as director of the Peace Research Institute in Oslo (PRIO) 1986–92, the United Nations Institute for Disarmament Research (UNIDIR) 1992–96, and the Norwegian Institute of International Affairs (NUPI) 1997–2007, and is now senior research fellow at NUPI and associate fellow of the Today Institute for Global Peace and Policy Research, Hawaii. He is engaged in projects on nuclear disarmament/non-proliferation and European security, and chairs a Middle East working group on the Arab Spring, Turkey and Iran. Lodgaard's most recent book is *Nuclear Disarmament and Non-Proliferation* (Routledge, 2011).

Frida Nome is a doctoral candidate at the Norwegian School of Theology and a researcher at NUPI. She has studied Arabic at a Palestinian university, and has worked with the international observer corps in Hebron and for the Norwegian Embassy in Damascus. Nome has been active as a researcher since 2005, basing most of her academic work on fieldwork in Syria, Lebanon, Israel, Palestine, Turkey and Iran, and has written extensively on topics related to the MENA region. She also served as a senior advisor to the Norwegian Foreign Ministry's Section for Peace and Reconciliation, August 2009–August 2011.

Pernille Rieker is a Senior Researcher at NUPI, and holds a doctoral degree from 2004 from the University of Oslo. Her research interests are related to international security, European integration, regional security and external governance as well as national foreign and security policy with a special focus on the Nordic countries and France. From 2005 to 2009 Rieker headed the Department off International Politics at NUPI. She has also worked as a senior advisor at NordForsk (2009–10). She has published several books and scholarly articles in *European Security*, *Journal of Integration*, and *Security Dialogue*.

Michael Semple is a Visiting Professor at the Institute for the Study of Conflict Transformation and Social Justice, Queen's University Belfast. He conducts research on conflict transformation and the role of non-state armed actors, with a focus on the Taliban movements of Afghanistan and Pakistan. Semple has extensive experience of Track One and Track Two dialogues in successive stages of the Afghan conflict. He has served in Afghanistan as a political officer with the UN mission and as deputy to the EU Special Representative.

Ole Jacob Sending is Research Director at NUPI. His research focuses on global governance, with a particular focus on the role of international organizations and non-governmental organizations in conflict and emergency settings. Current projects include studies of humanitarianism and armed violence in urban settings, and the dynamics of recognition within transnational policy networks. A two-time Fulbright Award recipient, Sending has been visiting scholar at Stanford University (2002) and at UC Berkeley (2008/2009). He served as a senior adviser in the Policy Analysis Unit in the Norwegian Ministry of Foreign Affairs from 2006 to 2008. His work has been published, *inter alia*, in *International Studies Quarterly*, *European Journal of International Relations*, and *Millennium*. He is co-author, with Iver B. Neumann, of *Governing the Global Polity* (University of Michigan Press, 2010), which won the 2012 International Political Sociology Book Award. He is currently working on a volume on the politics of expertise in global governance, to be published by the University of Michigan Press.

Paul Saurette (PhD) is Associate Professor at the School of Political Studies, University of Ottawa. He holds degrees from the University of Manitoba, York University, the London School of Economics and Johns Hopkins University. He is the author of *The Kantian Imperative: Humiliation, Common Sense, Politics* (University Press of Toronto, 2005), as well as a range of articles on political thought, international relations, political communications, ideology and the media. Saurette has also worked as a researcher and consultant to various non-academic organizations, including government agencies, independent think-tanks and research institutes, charitable foundations, political candidates, and private-sector companies such as McKinsey & Co.

Henrik Thune is a Senior Research Fellow at NUPI and head of its Middle East Programme. He holds PhD and Masters degrees in international relations from the University of Oslo and the London School of Economics and Political Science. Thune has served five years as a diplomat in the Norwegian Ministry of Foreign Affairs, and has lengthy experience of work with peace and reconciliation processes, on First and Second Track initiatives. From 2009 to 2012 he was project manager in the Secretariat of the Norwegian Foreign Minister. Thune is currently conducting research on inter-state relations in the Middle East, Norwegian foreign policy, and the role of the news media in international relations.

Acknowledgements

This book project began as a research project initiated at the Norwegian Institute of International Affairs (NUPI) in 2011 in cooperation with Chatham House and funded by the Norwegian Ministry of Foreign Affairs (NMFA). The project involved a series of workshops in London and Oslo, and resulted in a NUPI report edited by Pernille Rieker and Ole Jacob Sending. This report stimulated fruitful discussions about dialogue and its usefulness as an efficient foreign policy tool. The NUPI team in the project therefore decided to continue the work and prepare a book on this topic. After a period in the NMFA, working in the secretariat of the former Norwegian Minister of Foreign Affairs, Jonas Gahr Støre (who also has been particularly engaged in this issue), Henrik Thune returned to NUPI and agreed to serve as co-editor of this book.

We are grateful for financial support from the NMFA and its Section for Peace and Reconciliation. We would also like to thank Alexis Crow, former expert at Chatham House, for initiating the project in 2011 together with a team of NUPI researchers. At NUPI, Karsten Friis, Vegard Walther Hansen, Mikkel Frøsig Pedersen, Ole Jacob Sending and Ståle Ulriksen have been involved in the early stages of this project. We would like to thank all the authors for their collaboration and for contributing with thought-provoking chapters that shed light on the many aspects of dialogue as a foreign policy tool. Our thanks go also to Ulf Sverdrup, NUPI's director, and to two anonymous referees for providing valuable comments. And lastly, we are deeply grateful to Susan Hoivik for language assistance and to Lilly Pijnenburg Muller for assistance in preparing the manuscript in accordance with the Ashgate guidelines.

Chapter 1

Introduction

Pernille Rieker

Dialogue has become one of the new buzzwords in international politics today. Small states in particular are increasingly stressing the importance of dialogue and mediation. For instance, Jonas Gahr Store, former Norwegian Minister of Foreign Affairs, has expressed a view that has become shared among many diplomats and scholars of foreign affairs: '... engaging in dialogue with a group and its members is not the same thing as legitimizing its goals and ideology. Used skilfully, engagement may moderate their policies and behaviour'. He refers to this approach as 'principled realism' – an approach that attempts to find solutions that both improve the world and recognize the constraints of the current global order (Store 2011).

While there has been growing interest in the potential for dialogue as a tool for conflict resolution, it is still not clear what is really meant. The term is used in several different ways in the scholarly literature and the empirical discourse. 'Dialogue' is often used as a synonym for more formal negotiations between two or more parties in a conflict where the aim is to reach a negotiated agreement; further, it is commonly used to refer to the more informal processes ('back-channel diplomacy') of communication among opposing parties, leading up to such negotiations; and thirdly, the term is used quite extensively to describe the broader peacebuilding processes, grassroots initiatives, and bottom-up policy approaches that aim at avoiding the escalation of a conflict or crisis, but which rarely have an explicit ambition of reaching a concrete negotiation phase.

In addition to these diverse understandings, the role of dialogue also differs according to the context or the specific conflict in question. Of special importance here are factors like power relations and the existence and role of a third-party actor or facilitator. While these factors have been addressed in the literature on the potential and limits of negotiations (Jönsson 2005), few (if any) contributions have systematically explored the potential and limits of less formal dialogue processes. With this book, we aim precisely to fill that gap by focusing on such processes – those leading up to more formal negotiations, or the broader peacebuilding processes. All these informal processes hail *dialogue* as a progressive force in fostering mutual understanding and resolving conflicts. It is therefore central to the rhetorical vocabulary of foreign-policy actors. But, we ask: can dialogue carry such a burden? Does dialogue really resolve conflicts? And, if so, – under what circumstances and conditions?

This book critically assesses the role of dialogue as a political tool for solving deep-rooted conflicts among states and between conflicting parties within formally recognized territorial borders. Our ultimate objective is policy-oriented: to contribute to a more nuanced and better understanding of the potential and limits for dialogue as a tool for conflict resolution in deep-rooted conflicts and crises.

Dialogue in Deep-rooted Conflicts

Establishing dialogue between parties that may not be interested in talking with each other – and where a breakdown in communication is part of the problem, owing in no small part to conflicts over fundamental values – presents particular challenges.

The quality of any form of communication hinges on the context of communication and on the ability of the parties to present their message in a manner that is understandable – in other words, that messages can be coded and de-coded to avoid misunderstandings. Central here is how the parties to a conflict define the cause of a conflict and possible ways of addressing it. As we shall see, what is often lacking is precisely such a shared framework within which the causes of a dispute can be assessed and discussed. Instead, the actors create mutually exclusive causal narratives and deep emotions that serve to drive the parties further apart. For the sake of analytical precision we have chosen to focus on dialogue in case generally seen as 'hard' ones: high-intensity international conflicts, or crises with high stakes. We define a 'crisis' as a set of interlinked events where i) there is uncertainty on the part of actors about how best to advance their interests; ii) there are clashing values and interests, with high stakes involved; and iii) the actors are unsure about the facts of the situation and about the strategies of the other actors.

On this basis, we decided to study the following cases: the Russo-Georgian conflict of 2008 and the ongoing Russo-Ukrainian conflict that started in 2013; the conflict(s) between Western powers and Libya under the Gaddafi regime; nuclear (back channel) diplomacy and the conflict between Iran and the Western powers over Iran's nuclear programme; recent religious tensions in Egypt and attempts at interreligious dialogue; the attempts at dialogue between the Kabul regime and the Taliban in Afghanistan, as well as the dialogue between North and South in Sudan.

In each of these case studies we aim at answering three inter-related questions:

1. What was the character of the dialogue between the actors prior to, during, and after the 'peak' of the conflict/crisis?
2. To what extent has the dialogue been successful?
3. What determines whether the dialogue can succeed?

Studying the behaviour of states during times of crisis – in a situation of not only conflicting values but also uncertainty about intentions of the other – can offers a good vantage point from which to assess the strengths and weaknesses of dialogue as a foreign-policy tool.

The Different 'Tracks' of Diplomacy

As hinted at above, we also need a better understanding and clarification of what is meant by 'dialogue in international politics'. To be sure, the concepts of *dialogue* and *negotiations* are both essential elements of diplomacy. *Dialogue* seems to comprise the more informal communication between parties at different levels (at the political level and at the level of civil society). *Negotiations and bargaining*, on the other hand, generally refer to a more formal process initiated between two parties (often states), aimed at reaching an agreement or negotiated settlement.

This means that dialogue may be referred to as both 'Track I' and 'Track II' diplomacy. These terms were first coined by William D. Davidson and Joseph V. Montville in their article entitled 'Foreign Policy According to Freud', which appeared in *Foreign Policy* in 1981 (Davidson and Montville 1981). According to these authors, Track I diplomacy is what diplomats do in terms of formal and informal (back-channel) negotiations between nations; Track II diplomacy is a specific kind of informal diplomacy, in which non-officials (academic scholars, retired civil and military officials, public figures and social activists) engage in dialogue, with the aim of conflict resolution or confidence building. This kind of diplomacy is often applied in deep-rooted conflicts or crises where there is the risk of the conflict escalating out of control (Davidson and Montville 1981: 145).

More recently, a third category of diplomacy has been introduced: 'Track III', referring to be dialogue initiatives undertaken by local grassroots organizations or international development agencies and the like. With this has come a greater focus on more informal dialogue processes in the scholarly literature as well.

While Track I diplomacy involves diplomats and applies *outcome-oriented* approaches, Tracks II and III involves civil society and are more focused on the *process of confidence building* than concrete outcomes (Reimann 2004).

The distinctions between the three tracks are shown in Table 1.1.

Table 1.1   The Three 'Tracks' of Diplomacy: Actors, Measures
and Objectives

Tracks of diplomacy	Type of actors	Measures	Objectives
Track I	The state; officials and political leaders; diplomats and formal mediators	Short-term, actor-oriented. Facilitation and negotiation Soft measures like fact-finding mission, negotiations assistance, economic assistance. Coercive measures. Use or threat of sanctions and military enforcement	Outcome-oriented
Track II	Private persons, former diplomats, non-governmental organizations, academics institutions, religious organizations etc.	Medium-term, indirect processes Non-coercive measures From cultural exchange to negotiations between non-official representatives.	Process-oriented
Track III	NGOs and local organizations	Long-term peace-building. Grassroots activities	Process-oriented

While these distinctions might be helpful for creating an overview, there are also some obvious limitations with such a categorization. In practice, diplomacy, dialogue and negotiations tend to be highly more complex processes that include more actors, measures and processes than shown by this simplification.

It is important to note that the robustness of dialogue – as a tool for conflict resolution – depends crucially on how it functions and shapes actors in different settings. Much hinges on whether dialogue aims to promote understanding, whether it aims to change actors' identities and interests, or whether it (merely) seeks to avoid escalation and the use of violence. Moreover, the motivations for engaging in a dialogue can differ. In some cases actors may engage in dialogue for instrumental or tactical reasons with no commitment to peaceful resolution of the conflict. In other cases, the UN Security Council may have imposed dialogue on the parties, without their having sufficient commitment to achieve further confidence building or an agreement of some sort.

Dialogue Situations where the Aim and Motivations Differ

It is also important to note that the distinction between the two diplomatic 'tracks', mentioned above, is far from clear-cut in practice. In fact, some types of informal dialogue situations are often facilitated by diplomats; if such dialoguing proves successful, more formal negotiations are likely to follow. Thus, one interpretation of 'dialogue' sees it as the process leading up to more formal negotiations. In turn, that means that some of the literature on negotiations might be useful for studying this type of dialogue. Here we should note the distinction between distributive and integrative approaches (Zartman 1988). Whereas the distributive approaches are far from a dialogue situation in the sense that they praise a zero-sum view where the goal of negotiations involves claiming one's share of a 'fixed amount of pie', integrative theories and strategies have more in common with dialogue: that they look for ways of creating value, or 'expanding the pie', so that there is more to share between parties as a result of negotiations (Alfredson and Cungu 2008: 15). Perhaps the best-known example of the integrative approach is the 'Harvard Negotiation Project' which builds on the work of Roger Fisher and William Ury. They frame negotiation as a three-phase process, where efficiency depends on how negotiators treat four essential elements: *interests, people, options and criteria* (Fisher and Ury 1981). These four elements have, in a later edition of the same book, been refashioned into seven elements or steps of negotiations (Fisher and Ury 1991).[1]

While the integrative approach is also a strategy for Track I diplomacy, we may assume that this phase often is preceded by a phase of a more informal dialogue or some kind of 'back-channel dialogue'. There might also be cases where Track II diplomacy actually goes over into a new phase, which can be analysed as a form of integrative negotiation process. Thus, the borders between the different types of processes are not always so clear-cut; in some cases, we might usefully combine insights from the literature on diplomacy, negotiation and conflict resolution, for a better understanding of the potential and limits of dialogue as a tool for conflict resolution. In this book, Track

---

1 *Step 1: Identifying interests* (may be both implicit or explicit and may differ from positions – identifying interests may show that there are win–win potentials); *Step 2: People* (separate the people from the problem, trust, diplomacy, creating personal relationships); *Step 3: Alternatives* (crucial for both parties to recognize their Best Alternative to a Negotiated Agreement – BATNA); *Step 4: Identifying options* (this may promote creative thinking and expand problem-solving capabilities); *Step 5: Criteria/legitimacy* (agreeing on mutually acceptable criteria); *Step 6: Commitments* (all parties must respect the commitments made); *Step 7 Communications* (good communications skills, such as being an active listener and learning to deal with difficult emotions).

I diplomacy is therefore also used to describe the 'back-channel dialogue' undertaken by diplomats.

Additionally, there are cases where dialogue has no ambitions of leading up to a negotiation phase, but is seen as a way of promoting understanding and trust. The aim of such a process is then rather to prevent a more violent conflict or to avoid the escalation of an existing conflict. These processes are often facilitated by one or several third parties, and are frequently conducted more or less clandestinely. As the chapter by Thune and Nome shows, this type of dialogue processes is complex: indeed, it could include the whole peacemaking apparatus aimed at creating confidence and trust among the parties at various levels of civil society. While Reimann (2004) and others would include this in the category of Track II and Track III diplomacy (depending on the actors involved) that is process-oriented rather than outcome-oriented, Nome and Thune are sceptical about using such general and all-embracing tags. They prefer to call this *non-party conflict diplomacy*. This approach differs in that it refers to 'the attempts of a third party actor – a state, international organization, NGO or individual – to engage one or more contending parties in dialogue to find a peaceful solution to an armed conflict, without using coercion and with no direct interest in a specific outcome' (p. 31). While Nome and Thune agree that this type of dialogue is process-oriented rather than outcome-oriented and emphasize the importance of the neutrality of the third-party actor, they are less concerned about distinguishing between the actors and referring to these processes as different 'tracks': 'most mediation efforts are Track I and Track II at the same time; not separate initiatives or processes – one official and the other unofficial – but often purposely combined' (p. 33). However, even if the different tracks of diplomacy are combined, it might still be useful to distinguish between outcome-oriented and process-oriented approaches, as well as the power relationship between the opposing parties (see below).

Dialogue and the Role of Power

Dialogue situations differ also with regard to the power constellations involved. A dialogue between more or less equal parties will have a very different dynamic than one where the power relation is asymmetrical. While the former type may have at least the theoretical possibility of ending up as a Habermasian ideal-situation of communicative action (Habermas 1981) even if this is difficult in deep-rooted conflict, this is highly unlikely in cases of asymmetrical power relations.

Either way, a successful dialogue process always implies some sort of willingness to learn and be persuaded by the force of the better argument. This means that 'soft power' or the power of attraction might be relevant here. Joseph Nye (2004) has identified three distinct types of power: hard, economic and soft. Whereas the first two seek to coerce or induce in order to obtain the behaviour desired from another actor, *soft power* involves 'getting others to want the outcomes that you want'. Threats and force are the 'currencies' of hard power, and payments/sanctions of economic power, but 'policies, values, culture and institutions' are the currencies of soft power. While hard power entails the ability to force preferences on others, soft power 'rests on the ability to shape the preferences of others' which in turn requires good communication skills.

Thus, the foreign policy tool of dialogue seems to fit quite well with the concept of soft power. This is a tool that traditionally has been favoured by smaller states, and by larger actors with fewer hard-power resources (like the EU), but has also become increasingly accepted as a fruitful approach for more powerful actors (for example, the USA). On the other hand, it is more difficult to be convincing as a credible soft power when that actor also has considerable hard power and economic power.

Dialogue is somewhat of a paradox in world politics: while dialogue is a defining feature of diplomacy and is frequently called upon to ease tensions and avoid conflicts, it can also be seen as a sign of weakness, precisely because it implies the willingness to change one's position and be persuaded by the arguments of the other side (Kagan 2008). Since this is a central characteristic of dialogue (although different types of dialogue focus on different kinds of instruments), it may be important for communication to be conducted in secrecy. This may help to make it easier for the parties to speak more freely and consider various different options or measures.

Is Dialogue Always a Good Thing?

'Dialogue' often has positive connotations. But is it always a good thing? Dialogue with counterparts from the same culture, where actors typically share a set of values that can enable communication and promote conflict resolution, can be difficult enough. Dialogue in the international realm, amidst conflicting value systems and with no overarching authority to sanction an agreement, is even more difficult. There is often a lack of trust, even outright suspicion, and frequently – as shown in the cases presented here – no real interest in reaching consensus. As Jennifer Mitzen has observed, commenting on Habermas' theory of communicative action, 'strangers might not see consensus as desirable; they might not recognize one another as capable of communicative consensus at all, much less be willing to listen and reflect on each other's arguments' (Mitzen 2005: 404). In addition, there are other dimensions that may either facilitate or constrain the dialogue situation. The following three dimensions are crucial to any type of dialogue: *secrecy versus openness*, *domestic legitimacy*, and *emotions*. These dimensions are discussed in greater detail in the three concept-oriented chapters in the first part of this volume.

Secrecy Versus Openness

Because dialogue implies a willingness to be persuaded by arguments, it has the power to undo and remake any existing social consensus. As such, it may also lead to violence, as argumentative processes face a potentially slippery slope. Without constraints to keep actors committed to resolving their disagreements discursively, arguments can spill over from the conference table to the street, or even to the battlefield (Mitzen 2005: 401). Much of what goes on in seeking to resolve conflicts takes place behind closed doors: indeed, secrecy is often a precondition for getting the parties to meet at all. While secrecy may lead to positive results in some cases, there are also limits to this approach. First, secret talks do not have the same communicative horizon as do public ones. Thus, despite the vulnerability of public dialogue, it may also actually facilitate compromises – not simply through a process of deliberation and the force of the better argument, but due to what Jon Elster terms the 'civilizing force of hypocrisy'. 'Publicity does not eliminate base motives, but forces and induces speakers to hide them' (Elster 2011: 111).

In other words, even though adversaries in a dialogue say one thing and do something very different, the public-ness of their statements may – over time – force them to align deeds with words, lest they be considered hypocritical. However, as Elster also recognizes, this effect of hypocrisy is not always civilizing; moreover, there may be cultural factors that prevent compromises for other reasons. As an example he mentions societies with strict codes of honour. Here, even an individual who does not want to take revenge might be forced to do so, to avoid the contempt to which he would otherwise be exposed (Elster 2011). These insights, emphasized by both Elster and Mitzen, indicate that the civilizing force of hypocrisy, or what Mitzen calls the 'forum effect of talk', works in the long run, whereas secrecy seems to be a precondition for initiating talks and achieving progress in the short run.

The Importance of Domestic Legitimacy

Any leader, whether democratically elected or authoritarian, needs support from core constituencies in order to survive. As described in Putnam's model of two-level games (Putnam 1998: 434): 'domestic groups pursue their interest by pressuring the government to adopt favourable policies and politicians seek power by constructing coalitions among those groups'. At the international level, 'national governments seek to maximize their own ability to satisfy domestic pressure, while minimizing the adverse consequences of foreign developments' (ibid.).

It is easy to think that this logic is valid only in democracies, but even authoritarian regimes need a certain degree of support among the home population (Eriksen 2006). This means that analyses of intercultural negotiations must take both levels into consideration, also in negotiations with non-democratic parties. As we shall see, shifts in the distribution of power at the domestic level can have significant impact – positively or negatively – on the dynamics of the negotiations under analysis here.

The Importance of Emotions

Dominique Moïsi (2009) holds that the feelings of fear, humiliation and hope are central to the types of conflicts analysed here. He argues that the West has been dominated by a culture of fear – fear of the 'Other' and of foreign cultures – in its anxious quest to maintain global dominance. In the Arab and Muslim world, a culture of humiliation is in operation, which feeds into Islamic extremism, leading to hatred of the West. Meanwhile, much of Asia has been able to concentrate on building a better future, creating a culture of hope. These moods, of course, are not universal within each region, and there are some areas, like Russia and parts of Latin America, that seem to display all of these simultaneously.

Peter Coleman (2011) has picked up on the centrality of emotions, arguing that when emotions overshadow how the actors define what the conflict is about, the much-lauded integrative approach will simply not work. Conflicts that are fuelled by emotions, he argues, are highly destructive and make up an estimated 5 per cent of the conflicts that are held to be intractable. Saurette and Thune discuss the role of emotions in greater detail in their chapter in the first part of this book.

Defenders of the integrative approach in the negotiation literature, like Roger Fisher, would say that one should always negotiate. Fisher gets support from Jonas Gahr Støre, the former Norwegian Foreign Minister quoted above, concerning the more informal processes of dialogue. Støre has argued that 'engaging in dialogue with a group and its members is not the same thing as legitimizing its goals and ideology. Used skilfully, engagement may moderate their policies and behaviour' (Støre 2011). Coleman (2011) would concur here, while also noting that dialogue is no panacea and that addressing the emotional aspect is crucial. Others, like Robert Mnookin (2010), would hold that there are also times when one should engage the enemy on the battlefield rather than at the negotiations table. He argues that one should not engage with actors whose values fundamentally contradict one's own, as that may serve to legitimize the former. Both Fisher and Mnookin were called to give George W. Bush advice in 2001 on how to respond to Taliban leader Mullah Mohammad Omar's offer to negotiate. Fisher held that the Bush administration should accept the offer, because one should always try to resolve conflict through a problem-solving approach to negotiation based on the interests of the parties. By contrast, Mnookin argued that the offer should be refused, as there was no point in negotiating with the Taliban at that time, because of the limited chances of success, combined with the risk of weakening the integrity of the Bush administration. These two positions rest on fundamentally different conceptions of what dialogue is and what it can achieve. Against this backdrop, it becomes important to assess empirically how and to what extent dialogue – in isolation or combined with other factors – may help to shape outcomes.

Structure of the Book

The chapters in the first part of this book discuss the meaning of dialogue and the ideas of dialogue in world politics in greater detail. Here the intention is to examine some of the more theory-oriented underpinnings and conceptual boundaries of dialogue as a concept. Three chapters show the different ways of conceptualizing the concept of dialogue and the role it plays in international conflict resolution. Ole Jacob Sending begins by discussing the relationship between dialogue and diplomacy. He argues that dialogue may play different roles in modern diplomacy and identifies and discusses five ideal types of this relationship: dialogue as *communication*, dialogue as *problem solving*, dialogue as *justification*, dialogue as *transformation* and, fifthly, *dialogue as mediation*. He argues that these categories are helpful because they move us away from a generic and normatively charged conception of dialogue towards something that is empirically researchable (p. 15).

While Sending starts out with a general understanding about the relationship between the interlinkage between the concept of dialogue and diplomacy, in Chapter 3 Henrik Thune and Frida Nome follow up with a broader view on how dialogue concerns what they describe as a global 'peacemaking apparatus'. While Nome and Thune see dialogue as a potential problem-solving mechanism of some sort rather than a medium or a justification, they include far more actors and processes than solely diplomats and their diplomatic efforts. They argue that 'conflicts have become arenas for a 'swarming' of third-party actors and a multitude of integrated mediation efforts and channels that fall outside the current terminology'. From this empirical observation they criticize the distinction between the different diplomatic tracks, arguing that dialogue is instead an inherent part of the entire global peacemaking apparatus. Their chapter concludes with a discussion of the potentials and pitfalls of involving third-party actors (or dialogue facilitators) in international conflicts.

In deep-rooted conflicts – the focus of the second part of this volume – emotions often play a crucial role. However, so far the role of emotions has been poorly understood. In Chapter 4, Paul Saurette and Henrik Thune outline the central role that emotions play in international politics and explore the implications this holds for how we understand the potential and the limits of the practice of dialogue in a world of emotional international politics. Arguing that many scholars and practitioners of international politics have systematically ignored the importance of emotions in global politics, they show how emotional dimensions have influenced major historical and contemporary events in international politics and are thus crucial for understanding and navigating in international politics today.

The second part of this volume consists of six case studies that explore different international political crises and conflicts, and assess the roles that various types of dialogue have played. In all these cases, fundamental values were at stake and there has been considerable uncertainty on both sides about the intentions and actions of the other. That said, these cases may be divided into two groups: the first three presents a more outcome-oriented type of dialogue, while the last three are examples of a more process-oriented type of dialogue. Chapter 5 discusses and compares the evolving Russo-Georgian conflict with the more recent Russo-Ukrainian conflict. Jakub Godzimirski argues that although diplomacy dialogue and negotiations failed to prevent the outbreak of these two conflicts, they have played a major part in putting an end to open interstate hostilities and helping to prevent the local conflicts from spiralling out of control.

In Chapter 6, Sverre Lodgaard explores the conflict concerning *Iran's* nuclear programme over the past decade. He shows that, particularly since 2013, diplomacy and dialogue have come to play increasingly important roles in this conflict

The conflict between Western powers and Libya from the late 1990s onwards is analysed in Chapter 7. Målfrid Braut-Hegghammer and Pernille Rieker emphasize that Libyan cases of dialogue are mostly examples of Track I (although back-channel) diplomacy; these talks were outcome-oriented, aimed at transforming bilateral relations for shared political and economic benefits.

The next three chapters present cases of more process-oriented dialogue situations between more or less equal parties. In Chapter 8, Michael Semple analyses the various attempts at dialogue between the Kabul regime and the Taliban in Afghanistan. Dialogue has been a key tool here for over a decade, with the Kabul government and its allies trying to re-create the opportunity that fleetingly appeared in Shahwalikot in December 2001.

Next, in Chapter 9, John Ashworth explores and discusses the conflict between North and South in Sudan, and the role of the churches in the various peace and reconciliation processes. Ashworth emphasizes that dialogue must be home-grown and long-term. Even though the many attempts at dialogue have not yet resulted in a stable peace, he argues that dialogue remains the only real alternative to violence.

The final chapter in this part of the volume – Chapter 10, by Georges Fahmi – discusses the role of dialogue as an attempt to ease religious tensions in Egypt after the Arab Spring. Here Fahmi focuses on three types of dialogue processes between Christians and Muslims, aimed at containing religious tensions after the revolution of 25 January 2011: informal reconciliation sessions, the National Justice Committee, and the House of the Egyptian Family.

References

Adler, E. and Pouliot, V. 2011. International Practices, *International Theory*, 3(1), 1–36.

Alfredson, T. and Cungu, A. 2008. Negotiation Theory and Practice, *Easypool Module* 179. *The Food and Agricultural Organization of the United States (FAO)* [Online]. Available at: www.fao.org/easypol [accessed: 13 August 2014].

Davidson, W.D. and Montville, J.V. 1981. Foreign Policy According to Freud, *Foreign Policy*, 45 (Winter), 145–57.

Elster, J. 2011. Deliberation, Cycles, and Misrepresentation, Paper prepared for the conference 'Epistemic Democracy in Practice', Yale University.

Eriksen, E.O. 2006. The EU – A Cosmopolitan Policy?, *Journal of European Public Policy*, 13(2), 252–69.

Fisher, R. and Ury, W. 1991. *Getting to Yes: Negotiation Agreement Without Giving In*. New York: Penguin Books.

Habermas, J. 1981. *Theorie des kommunikativen Handelns*. Frankfurt: Suhrkamp.

Jönsson, C. 2005. Diplomacy, Bargaining and Negotiation, in *Handbook of International Relations*, edited by W. Carlsnaes, T. Risse and B. Simmons. London: Sage.

Kagan, R. 2008. *The Return of History and the End of Dreams*. New York: Alfred A. Knopf.

Mitzen, J. 2005. Reading Habermas in Anarchy: Multilateral Diplomacy and Global Public Spheres, *American Political Science Review*, 99(3), 401–17.

Mnookin, R. 2010. *Bargaining with the Devil: When to Negotiate, When to Fight*. New York: Simon & Schuster.

Moïsi, D. 2009. *Geopolitics of Emotions: How Cultures of Fear, Humiliation and Hope Reshape the World*. New York: Anchor Books.

Putnam, R.D. 1998. Diplomacy and Domestic Politics: The Logic of Two-Level Games, *International Organization*, 42(3), Summer, 427–60.

Reimann, C. 2004. Assessing the Stat-of-the Art in Conflict Transformation, in *Berghof Handbook for Conflict Transformation*, edited by M. Fisher and N. Ropers.

Berlin: Berghof Research Center for Constructive Conflict Management, Section 1 [Online]. Available at: http://www.berghof-handbook.net/articles/section-i-concepts-and-cross-cutting-challenges [accessed: 11 August 2014].

Store, J.G. 2011. Why We Must Talk, *New York Review of Books*, 7 April [Online]. Available at: http://www.nybooks.com/articles/archives/2011/apr/07/why-we-must-talk [accessed: 11 August 2014].

Zartman, I.W. 1988. Common Elements in the Analysis of the Negotiation Process, *Negotiation Journal*, 4(1), 31–43.

Chapter 2
Diplomacy and Dialogue

Ole Jacob Sending

Introduction

For every crisis that ends without recourse to the use of violence or sanctions, it is often said that diplomacy saved the day. Diplomacy is seen as functioning as a barrier against war – it is what makes it possible for states to resolve their differences peacefully. The idea that diplomacy involves dialogue is central to this view: dialogue makes diplomacy the institutional vehicle for the public use of reason that can temper and transform international politics. But, in this conception, dialogue is a highly generic and normative ideal, and we are left with few tools for assessing whether diplomacy is really about dialogue and how it relates to other ideal-typical forms of interaction said to pervade diplomacy, such as representation (Sharp 2009). Moreover, diplomacy is an integral part of preparation for wars, as when a state is trying to make the case that theirs is just or legal war. Here, too, dialogue is an integral component of diplomacy, as it concerns communication and debate with others about the rationale and legality of using violent means (Hurd 2011).

So how should we understand dialogue in relation to diplomacy? Is it a tool for advancing predefined interests, or is it something which transforms those very interests – or both?

I argue that the role of dialogue in diplomacy can be usefully understood in terms of five main categories: as communication, as problem-solving, as transformation, as justification, and as mediation. These categories are helpful because they move us away from a generic and normatively charged conception of dialogue, and towards one that is empirically researchable (see also Thune and Nome in this volume). Moreover, this categorization brings out how the very meaning of diplomacy hinges on the role and meaning attributed to dialogue. If dialogue is seen as communication, we stay close to the idea of diplomacy as a system for the representation of and negotiation between states. If, by contrast, we view dialogue as transformational, diplomacy emerges in a different light, for it is now seen as capable of changing the interests of states. This implies that we should not take at face value diplomats' own descriptions of their various diplomatic efforts, as there is a symbolic or political profit to gain from presenting diplomatic efforts as being more 'dialogical' than they in fact are. I therefore discuss in the conclusion, albeit briefly, how diplomats use the term 'dialogue' to portray their activities as virtuous and wedded to an ideal of public reason.

Diplomacy

Diplomacy is typically defined as a profession and a set of core tasks, such as communication, representation and negotiation (Satow [1971] 2009). It is also linked quite directly to the art of 'statesmanship'. In Henry Kissinger's *Diplomacy* (1994), for example, it is primarily a lens through which to assess and analyse the history of international politics. There is no shortage of works brimming with empirical detail on the contents of diplomatic tasks, and on the role of diplomacy in managing relations between distinct polities. 'Diplomacy' is generally seen as a peaceful way of managing interstate relations, one that recognizes the differences between states and is geared towards reducing potential friction.

This is related to the sociology of scholarship on diplomacy, with its focus on historical analyses and practitioners' own accounts of their trade. It has therefore been charged that the study of diplomacy has stayed too close to its object of analysis, leading to a relative neglect of theoretically informed studies (Neumann 2012, Jönsson 2002). 'Diplomacy' has a nice ring to it, as reflected in the everyday use of the word in connection with being tactful, treating people politely, etc. It is no coincidence in this context that Adam Watson's (1982) classic study of diplomacy is entitled *Diplomacy: The Dialogue Between States*.

More broadly, diplomacy has been defined as a core institution of international society, and as representing a particular culture. Hedley Bull, for example, defined diplomatic culture as 'the common stock of ideas and values possessed by the official representatives of states' (1977: 316). Neumann has noted that this overly ideational reading misses out on central aspects of diplomacy, key among which are the practices that structure and mediate how diplomacy is performed (2002). Taking a genealogical perspective, Der Derian (1987) treats diplomacy as the 'mediation of estrangement' which has the virtue of enabling a critical perspective since it does not reduce diplomacy to solely what is done by professional diplomats operating as representatives of states (see also Constantinou 1996). But diplomacy can also be seen as a profession, reproduced through the markers of identity and control over key tasks in the hands of recognized diplomats (Abbott 1988). Similarly countering the tendency to approach diplomacy without theoretical reflection, Sharp (2009) has developed a *diplomatic theory* of international politics (see also Sending, Pouliot and Neumann 2015). In this chapter, I seek to contribute to this trend of bringing theoretical concepts to bear on the study of diplomacy (and dialogue), highlighting how the meaning and role of diplomacy hinge on how we conceptualize it in relation to the ideal, or practice, of dialogue.

Diplomacy and Dialogue

The role of dialogue in diplomacy can usefully be categorized into four ideal types: as a *medium or communication* for all types of diplomatic work, as *problem-solving*, as *transformation*, as *justification*, and as *mediation*. Discussing these different ideal-typical relations between diplomacy and dialogue brings out what I see as an important point: namely, that it is exceedingly difficult, and in fact not even useful, to pinpoint and single out *one* relationship between two dominant features or one defining feature of diplomacy. It all depends not only on what we mean by dialogue, but also on what diplomats themselves do: sometimes dialogue is central to their work, at other times it serves to conceal or justify practices that have little to do with dialogue.

Communication

When we treat dialogue as a medium or as *communication*, the character of the dialogue becomes inconsequential. The word is stripped of associations with a commitment to the shared used of reason to reach a new understanding. It is in this sense that Watson defines diplomacy in terms of the 'Dialogue between States', where dialogue becomes constitutive of diplomacy, since as one cannot conduct diplomacy without communicating with others in some way. The transformation of diplomacy as analysed in the literature on 'new' diplomacy takes this feature of diplomacy as a point of departure for analysing how changes in communications technology (fax, email, Twitter etc.) impact on diplomatic practice. For example, the image of the ambassador plenipotentiary with considerable autonomy to determine the best course of action is considerably reduced when the foreign minister is just a phone call away (Frydenlund 2010, Cooper, Hocking and Maley 2008). The role of non-state actors in diplomatic processes, such as advocacy networks (Keck and Sikkink 1998) and epistemic communities (Haas 1992), is here linked to a change in the mode of communication, where the multiplying interfaces between national societies are made integral to the 'new' diplomacy, no longer controlled solely by official representatives of the state. These new actors are, often implicitly, held to bring a stronger 'dialogical' element to diplomacy, as they are seen as mobilizing and bringing the rights and preferences of 'global civil society' to bear on diplomatic processes (Scholte 2004; see also Bartelson 2006).

In this conception of dialogue as a medium, it subsumes diplomacy understood as negotiations, also frequently cited as central to diplomacy. This follows from the fact that diplomacy is about communication and the representation of distinct polities, whose differences and particularities need some type of management or mediation. One of the core skills said to characterize esteemed diplomats, for example, is that of being a skilful negotiator. To be able to get what one wants without upsetting or alienating one's interlocutors is deemed central to what diplomacy is all about. The January 2003 exchange between US Defense Secretary Donald Rumsfeld and German Foreign Minister Joschka Fischer prior to the Iraq War is remembered today *precisely* because it came across as undiplomatic, with Rumsfeld's remarks about the 'old' and 'new' Europe. As several contributions in this volume show, moreover, diplomatic relations between states are often dominated by 'mere' communication, both prior to and during a crisis or war. In Godzimirski's analysis of the 2008 war between Georgia and Russia, for example, there is ample evidence of communication between the parties, also during the war. And in Lodgaard's analysis of US–Iran relations, we also see communication – albeit at a lower diplomatic level, often non-public and mediated through intermediaries (such as Oman).

In sum, dialogue as communication is arguably closest to the dominant view of diplomacy: communication, and dialogue, are means to the end of advancing pre-defined interests and negotiating with others. Dialogue here emerges as a formal description of two-way communication, where the content and the result of the communication may be less important. This is the realm of instrumental calculation and bargaining, where the actors involved have pre-defined interests, where they negotiate and seek to out-smart each other and build alliances to advance their interests, regardless of the substance of the arguments advanced by the opponent. For Kissinger (1994), for example, diplomats *qua* statesmen are meant to mediate between the inside and the outside, fine-tuning national interests with the interests of other states. In this view, the articulation of national interests emerges from the dialogue with other states through the person of the diplomat. The character of this dialogue is not transformative in the sense of being able to change how people understand the world. Rather, it is an exercise in calibration, where the national interest emerges as that which is 'sensible' and 'strategic', given other states' interests, and where this information is simply not available prior to a dialogue with other diplomats. Nonetheless, it is not far from this conception of dialogue as linked primarily to representation and the advancement of national interests, to one in which diplomacy emerges in a quite different light – as helping to defuse tensions and as resolving various types of interstate crises between states, as discussed below.

Problem-solving

If we think of dialogue not in a narrow sense as communication or merely conveying information to another actor, but as a process in which actors can adapt their behaviour and manage their relations, diplomacy can be seen as integral to *problem-solving* between states. Would the Georgian-Russian war have ended after five days if there had been no diplomatic efforts aimed at stopping it? (See Godzimirski in this volume.) How would the debate over, and management of, the Libya intervention have looked if had not taken place within an institutionalized system of diplomatic practice? (See Braut-Hegghammer and Rieker in this volume; see also Adler-Nissen and Pouliot 2014.)

Although diplomacy is typically defined in terms of representation between separate polities, there is a distinct sense in which diplomacy is also geared towards solving problems. It is system for managing relations and frictions between polities, and as such is integral to the maintenance of relations that fall short of the use of force. In this image of diplomacy, dialogue is central, since it helps avoid misunderstandings and can facilitate the establishment of solutions to pressing political problems. There are two distinct ways in which dialogue is here central to the meaning, and role, of diplomacy. First, there is the traditional approach, whereby states meet bilaterally to solve a problem, or crisis, between themselves. The 'hotline' between Washington and Moscow during the Cold War is one example: a mechanism whereby the two states could communicate with each other to help defuse tensions. Similarly, diplomats stationed abroad are expected to collect information and report back to their foreign ministries about big and small conflicts or alignment of interests between states. The single most important rationale for this diplomatic practice is not so much gaining an edge in some specific negotiation, but of being aware of conflicts or divergent interests that may need to be dealt with through diplomatic channels. Dialogue is here something distinct from mere communication: it becomes a crucially important element in avoiding misunderstandings and facilitating shared understandings of the other's position (Sofer 1997). This does not imply, however, that dialogue is here capable of transforming actors' interests, as discussed in greater detail below. But it does imply that dialogue, as more or less regularized communication, can increase states' understanding of their interests and thus help to change their behaviour. In that sense, it may reduce tensions and solve problems. To me, this feature of dialogue is displayed throughout the chapters in this book: dialogue may not in and of itself have ended or prevented a conflict or crisis, but it was a precondition for the establishment of a political solution.[1]

---

1 I do not mean to imply that such political solutions are necessarily just or legitimate: simply that the fighting stopped or tensions were reduced.

Second, dialogue is central to the gradual emergence of governance and collective problem-solving on a par with representation as the core task of diplomacy. Diplomacy is organized around the representation, and therefore also reproduction, of the state as a distinct political unit. But the context within which such representation takes place is increasingly that of governance – of seeking to find solutions to problems that affect many states. The twentieth century saw the institutionalization of a multilateral order, with international organizations at its core, whose rationale has evolved into some form of collective problem-solving – what is often called global governance today (Avant, Finnemore and Sell 2010; Sending 2015). As Jennifer Mitzen has shown, there is a distinct difference between representation and governing: the latter entails an implicit commitment to doing things together – what she refers to as 'collective intentionality' (Mitzen 2013; 2015). In this conception, dialogue is integral to all kinds of diplomatic activity where there is a sense of shared understanding of having to define and act on some border-transcending problem. But here, too, the character of dialogue is not so much responsible for changing actors' understanding or interests as it is central for conducting negotiations about how to govern.

Transformative

Dialogue can also be defined as inherently *transformative* and therefore something which gives diplomacy a potentially progressive force in world politics. It here assumes a role as a solution to a myriad of problems. This we can see in the strategy advanced by Norway's former Foreign Minister, Jonas Gahr Støre, who has argued that however much we may we dislike, hate or want to ridicule or destroy another actor, it is vital to keep on talking – both as a means to prevent a negative spiral and as a tool for building trust and perhaps also new interests (Støre 2011). The literature on the role of advocacy networks and of civil society actors invokes such an understanding of dialogue. Drawing in particular on Habermas (1985), diplomacy here becomes a manifestation of a dialogical process where the force of the better argument may prevail and where there is public use of reason (Archibugi 2004, Price 2002). Thus conceived, diplomacy is a continued dialogue over competing claims in which – over time – some degree of shared understanding can emerge to transform the understandings of all actors party to the dialogue.

In contrast to the image of diplomacy where negotiations may produce a solution that avoids or ends a war, the image of dialogue as transformative attributes the outcome not to the identification of an 'equilibrium' or a solution that all parties can live with. Rather, the solution is here attributed to the fact that the dialogue itself served to transform the understandings of all or some actors – that the 'force of the better argument' prevailed and defined a new set of possible solutions. Many peace and reconciliation processes are interpreted, if often implicitly, in this light: a prolonged process of dialogue generates new and shared understandings of responsibility and mutually beneficial strategies, which culminate in a peace accord or in reconciliation (Powers 2008). As other contributors to the present volume show, however, it is doubtful whether dialogue – in and of itself – can be accorded such causal weight in accounting for such outcomes.

In domestic contexts, dialogue may possibly solve or defuse crises. This is so because there is presumably a stronger degree of a 'shared lifeworld' in the domestic setting; moreover, also because a consensus arrived at through public deliberation is here sanctioned and implemented by the state, which has the resources for enforcing and backing up this consensus. In the international realm, there is no such centralized actor that is able to enforce or underwrite a consensus, so deliberative processes in this realm operate on shaky foundations, where any consensus can just as quickly be undone by a new one through a continued deliberative process (Mitzen 2005).

There is nonetheless one way in which the institutionalized *ideal* of dialogue as central to diplomacy may in fact shape outcomes, even though this ideal is advanced by diplomats for self-serving reasons. Diplomats may use lofty formulations to conceal their instrumentally derived interests, but there are still limits to what can and cannot be said. The ideal of dialogue – as expressed in ideals of a public sphere mediating between the particular and private and public decisions – places constraints on what it is considered appropriate to say and do (Krebs and Jackson 2007). Diplomats, like others, seek to universalize their particular interests. Such structures of justifications have a disciplining effect – what Jon Elster has called the 'civilizing force of hypocrisy':

> Generally speaking, the effect of an audience is to replace the language of interest by the language of reason and to replace impartial motives by passionate ones. The presence of a public makes it especially hard to appear motivated merely by self-interest. Even if one's fellow assembly members would not be shocked, the audience would be. In general, this civilizing force of hypocrisy is a desirable effect of publicity. … Publicity does not eliminate base motives, but forces and induces speakers to hide them. (Elster 1998: 111)

In this sense, dialogue can be transformative 'externally', through the civilizing force of hypocrisy, rather than through the more Habermasian, 'internal' one of transforming understandings and interests. It can operate externally by defining the parameters for what can and cannot be said and changing the assessment of all actors about the costs of either coming across as too self-serving or as hypocritical over time.

Justification

Part of the image of diplomacy as a progressive force is dependent on the role of dialogue: it is because diplomacy is presented as, and often seen as, a dialogue between states that diplomacy emerges as a practice that saves the day, that prevents conflict. In this sense, dialogue is a key *justificatory* tool. There are numerous examples where diplomatic efforts (defined in terms of dialogue and a commitment to find peaceful solutions) have been undertaken at the same time as the warring parties were intensifying their war efforts – such as during the Vietnam War, when US and Vietnamese delegations met in Paris for peace talks while both sides upped their use of force. Similarly, the USA and Britain launched a systematic diplomatic effort to rally support for the invasion of Iraq in 2002/2003, where the idea of dialogue as a meeting of minds committed to finding a shared solution was used as a shield for rather heavy-handed attempts at winning support.

More recently, the justificatory role of dialogue for diplomacy was evident when diplomats met in Geneva in late 2013 to discuss the situation in Syria. Considerable diplomatic work had gone into these preparations: cables, meetings and travel, all aimed at getting the parties to the conflict to meet in Geneva, all brokered by the USA and Russia, and under the auspices of the UN Secretary-General. Listening to the interventions from diplomats in the region, from donors, from allies, one is struck by the extent to which talk is cheap – in diplomacy. There was no shortage of calls to end the conflict, to stop the atrocities, to deliver humanitarian relief. The message was: the international community *must do* something.

The use of humanitarian ideals in such diplomatic settings is important because they serve to give meaning to diplomatic meetings that may otherwise appear simply as a 'gathering of business suits' to talk, with no real solution on the horizon. The legitimacy of such diplomatic settings hinges on the existence of dialogue – an effort to talk to find a solution – even if all parties recognize that no such solution is achievable in the immediate future. The humanitarian framework – defined by international humanitarian law and advanced by its professionals as impartial, independent and neutral – allows for action that is seen as less controversial and political (Barnett 2011, Calhoun 2010). In the words of a former UN official, it offers an opportunity 'to do something when political action is not possible'.[2] The role of the UN in the Balkans, in Cambodia, and elsewhere initially started with reference to humanitarian ideals (Powers 2008).

---

2 Author's interview, former UNOCHA official. Oslo, November 2010. See also Sending 2011.

More generally, the justificatory role or meaning of dialogue is closely linked to the image of diplomacy as a progressive force. If diplomacy were seen as merely the representation and advancement of national interests, the idea that diplomacy 'succeeds' in preventing war or ending hostilities, or in negotiating new international arrangements, would not exist. The popular image of diplomacy as being about dialogue with other states and about seeking out solutions means that there is a symbolic profit to be reaped by presenting all kinds of diplomatic activities as progressive and committed to some shared understanding and the use of reason. The justificatory role of dialogue is pervasive, since what passes for diplomacy is clearly seen as being distinct from, even antithetical to, war. As Tarak Barkawi has argued, the US has since the Second World War succeeded in presenting war-making and imperial governance under the guise of 'diplomacy' (Barkawi, forthcoming). In this sense, calling something 'diplomacy' is effective as a legitimating device for governing others precisely because the public image of diplomacy is linked to some notion of dialogue. This justificatory role is linked to, but should to be distinguished from, the relationship between dialogue, diplomacy, and the position of the mediator, as discussed below.

Mediation

The role of a mediator is deeply embedded in theology, with – for example – the figure of Christ and of the bible as central vehicles for mediation between omnipotent God and powerless man. This set-up is mirrored in religious organization, with religious authorities (priest, imam etc.) mediating between God and man. The Pope and the Roman Catholic Church, claiming universal (spiritual) jurisdiction, mediated between European monarchs whose jurisdictional claim were territorial (Orford 2011: 143). James der Derian has used the concept of mediation as an analytical tool with great effect to argue that diplomacy is essentially 'mediation of estrangement' where man's estrangement from God and subsequently from one another spawns practices where by such estrangement is to be managed through different types of mediation (1987: 51–67).

There is a significant yet often unacknowledged dialogical element to this concept of mediation – and we can detect an interesting relationship between dialogue and the power of the mediator. A recent article in the *New York Times*, reporting from an Asian regional security conference in Singapore attended by US Defense Secretary Chuck Hagel, notes that as China is 'pushing and probing' at US allies in the region, the USA has moved from a position as referee to one where it is forced to 'simultaneously choose sides and try to play the role of referee' (Cooper and Perlez 2014). Regardless of whether this is an accurate description of the relationship between China and the United States, it brings out what is implied in the position as referee, or *mediator*.

The USA has since the Second World War sought a position as a mediator in various corners of the world – such a role being inherently tied to the self-defined, and recognized, position as superpower. But whereas the USA has sought to act as mediator in all regions, and over the full spectrum of political issues, various other states have sought to stake out positions as mediators in particular conflicts. These states typically claim that they have no stakes in the r conflict in question: and because they have no stakes in the conflict, they can be a trusted arbiter, adjudicating between the parties competing demands (see Thune and Nome and Saurette and Thune, both in this volume).

Being recognized as a mediator, then, confers considerable powers. Importantly, the task of mediation, and thus the power of the mediator, is intimately linked to dialogue, because a mediator is expected to listen to both parties, to understand both sides, and to offer a reasoned assessment of and adjudicate between the competing claims made by the parties to a conflict. In this sense, mediation rest fundamentally on *some* concept of dialogue as its central ingredient. In this conceptualization, dialogue becomes a significant symbolic resource for diplomatic processes writ large. By foregrounding dialogue as a distinct diplomatic tool, one can establish a position that approximates that of an arbiter by organizing and refereeing a dialogue of others.[3] Dialogue, then, can be a tool to confer power as mediator by virtue of being recognized as sufficiently competent to adjudicate competing claims by listening to and engaging with parties to a conflict. The Norwegian government has invested considerable resources in efforts aimed at peacemaking and reconciliation; and while these investments are surely geared at some level to an idea of shaping outcomes in a peaceful direction, we should also be attentive to the more self-serving aspect of such diplomatic efforts. By investing political resources in 'dialogue' and 'reconciliation' for other actors, a state can establish oneself as a focal point for political processes beyond the conflict in question (Neumann 2015).

Conclusions

Diplomacy can be seen as an institutionalized system for representation and communication between established political units. This is reflected in international law and in the system of embassies and resident representatives on the territories of other states. Such a system facilitates communication and cooperation. But diplomacy is also geared towards intervening in and seeking

---

3 Being recognized as having a 'view from nowhere'. This is Thomas Nagel's (1986) formulation. See also Bhuta 2008.

to act on and change the behaviour of others, in order to further particular interests. In this latter sense, diplomacy is linked to the exercise of power, albeit through a system that sets clear limits for *how* such power is to be exercised. In that sense, diplomatic practice is about the application of power to get what one wants – but this is couched in protocol and diplomatic language in such a way that diplomacy is made to appear as a practice that is not about power, but about communication, negotiation, and – dialogue.

Adam Watson has defined diplomacy as 'the process of dialogue and negotiation by which states in a system conduct their relations and pursue theirs purposes by means short of war' (1982: 11). Here, dialogue serves to describe diplomacy as set of practices that are not so much about power as about maintaining relations, managing frictions and mediating between different interests. States advance a similar image of diplomacy under the heading of 'public diplomacy'. In 2003, the UK government launched its public diplomacy by describing it as 'work which aims at influencing in a positive way, including through the creation of relationships and partnerships, the perceptions of individuals and organisations overseas about the UK and their engagement with the UK, in support of Her Majestys Government overseas objectives' (Select Committee on Foreign Affairs, 2014)

Diplomacy here becomes a public practice based on dialogue with a multitude of audiences. It is a strategy involving the use of power couched in the language of dialogue and public debate with societal actors. Perhaps one of the more significant aspects of the role of dialogue in diplomacy can be found precisely in its role in legitimizing and justifying a wide range of efforts that involve the use of power to shape outcomes and advance interests. Because of the widely shared view that dialogue is commendable and progressive, it is invoked in order to legitimize the exercise of power. But this is not to suggest that dialogue is solely a justificatory tool. It is also – as the contributions to this volume demonstrate – a central component of diplomatic efforts that may shape outcomes by facilitating problem-solving, by avoiding misunderstandings, and sometimes changing actors' understandings and interests.

References

Abbott, A. 1988. *The System of Professions*. Chicago, IL: University of Chicago Press.

Adler-Nissen, R. 2015. Just Greasing the Wheels? Mediating Difference and the Evasion of Power and Responsibility in Diplomacy. *Hague Journal of Diplomacy*, 10(1), 22-8.

Archibugi, D. 2004. Cosmopolitan Democracy and its Critics: A Review, *European Journal of International Relations*, 10(3), 437–73.

Avant, D., M. Finnemore and S. Sell, eds, 2010. *Who Governs the Globe?* Cambridge: Cambridge University Press.

Barnett, M. 2011. *Empire of Humanity: A History of Humanitarianism*. Ithaca, NY: Cornell University Press.

Bartelson, J. 2006. Making Sense of Global Civil Society, *European Journal of International Relations*, 12(3), 371–95.

Bhuta, N. 2008. Against State-Building, *Constellations*, 15(4), 517–42.

Bull, H. 1977. *The Anarchical Society: A Study of Order in World Politics*. London: Macmillan.

Calhoun, C. 2010. The Idea of Emergency: Humanitarian Action and Global (Dis)Order, in *Contemporary States of Emergency*, edited by D. Fassin and M. Pandolfi. New York: Zone Books, 29–58.

Constantinou, C. 1996. *On the Way to Diplomacy*. Minneapolis, MN: University of Minnesota Press.

Cooper, A.F., Hocking, B. and Maley, W. eds., 2008. *Governance and Diplomacy: Worlds Apart?* New York: Palgrave Macmillan.

Cooper, H. and Perlez, J. 2014. U.S. Sway in Asia is Imperiled as China Challenges Alliances. *New York Times* [Online, 30 May]. Available at: http://mobile.nytimes.com/2014/05/31/world/asia/us-sway-in-asia-is-imperiled-as-china-challenges-alliances.html?emc=edit_th_20140531&nl=todaysheadlines&nlid=28873465&_r=2&referrer [accessed: 13 August 2013].

Der Derian, J. 1987. *On Diplomacy: A Genealogy of Western Estrangement*. Oxford: Blackwell.

Eriksen, Stein, S. and Sending, O.J. 2013. There is No Global Public, *International Theory*, 5(2), 213–37.

Habermas, J. 1985. *The Theory of Communicative Action*. Boston, MA: Beacon Press.

Jönsson, C. 2002. Diplomacy, Bargaining and Negotiation, in *Handbook of International Relations*, edited by W. Carlsnaes, T. Risse and B. Simmons, London: Sage.

Keck, M.E. and K. Sikkink. 1998. *Activists Beyond Borders: Advocacy Networks in International Politics*. Ithaca, NY: Cornell University Press.

Kissinger, H. 1994. *Diplomacy*. New York: Simon and Schuster.

Krebs, R. and Jackson, P.T. 2007. Twisting Tongues and Twisting Arms: The Power of Political Rhetoric. *European Journal of International Relations*, 13(1), 35–66.

Mitzen, J. 2005. Reading Habermas in Anarchy: Multilateral Diplomacy and Global Public Spheres, *American Political Science Review*, 99(3), 401–17.

Mitzen, J. 2013. *Power in Concert: The 19th Century Origins of Global Governance*. Chicago, IL: University of Chicago Press.

Mitzen, J. 2015. From Representation to Governing: Diplomacy and the Constitution of International Public Power, in *Diplomacy and the Making of*

World Politics, edited by O.J. Sending, V. Pouliot and I.B. Neumann. Cambridge: Cambridge University Press.

Nagel, T. 1986. *The View from Nowhere*. New York: Oxford University Press.

Neumann, I.B. 2002. Returning Practice to the Linguistic Turn: The Case of Diplomacy. *Millennium: Journal of International Studies*, 32(3), 627–52.

Neumann, I.B. 2012. *At Home with the Diplomats*. Ithaca, NY: Cornell University Press.

Neumann, I.B. 2015. Peace and Reconciliation as Systems Maintenance in *Diplomacy and the Making of World Politics*, edited by O.J. Sending, V. Pouliot, and I.B. Neumann. Cambridge: Cambridge University Press.

Orford, A. 2011. *International Authority and the Responsibility to Protect*. Cambridge University Press.

Powers, S. 2008. *Chasing the Flame: One Man's Fight to Save the World*. New York: Penguin.

Price, R.M. 2003. Transnational Civil Society and Advocacy in World Politics, *World Politics*, 55(4), 579–606.

Rathbun, B. 2011. *Trust in International Cooperation*. Cambridge University Press.

Risse, T. 2000. Let's Argue: Communicative Action in World Politics, *International Organization*, 54(1), 1–39.

Satow, E. [1917] 2009. *Guide to Diplomatic Practice*, 6th ed. London: Longman.

Scholte, J.A. 2004. Civil Society and Democratically Accountable Global Governance, *Government and Opposition*, 39(2), 211–33.

Select Committee on Foreign Affairs, 2014. Third Report. UK Parliament [Online]. Available at: http://www.publications.parliament.uk/pa/cm200506/cmselect/cmfaff/903/90305.htm [accessed: 13 August 2014].

Sending, O.J. 2011. United by Difference: Diplomacy as Thin and Humanitarianism as Thick Culture, *Future of Diplomacy*, Special Issue, *International Journal* (Canada), 66(3)

Sending, O.J. 2015. Diplomats and Humanitarians in Crisis Governance, in *Diplomacy and the Making of World Politics*, edited by O.J. Sending, V. Pouliot, and I.B. Neumann. Cambridge: Cambridge University Press.

Sending, O.J., Pouliot, V., and Neumann I.B. (eds) 2015. *Diplomacy and the Making of World Politics*. Cambridge: Cambridge University Press.

Sharp. P. 2009. *Diplomatic Theory of International Relations*. Cambridge University Press.

Sofer, S. 1997. The Diplomat as Stranger, *Diplomacy and Statecraft*, 8(3), 179–86.

Store, J.G. 2011. Why We Must Talk, *New York Review of Books* [Online, 7 April]. Available at: www.nybooks.com/articles/archives/2011/apr/07/why-we-must-talk [accessed: 13 August 2014].

Watson, A. 1982. *Diplomacy: The Dialogue Between States*. London: Routledge.

Chapter 3

The Dysfunctions of Non-party Conflict Diplomacy

Henrik Thune and Frida Nome

Introduction

The study of conflict management and third-party mediation is fraught with empirical ambiguities and conceptual imprecisions. These problems stem in part from the subject matter itself: conflicts are, after all, 'a pervasive social process of a multidimensional character', as Jacob Bercovitch et al. (1991: 7) observed in one of the first studies of international mediation written in the post-Cold War era. Conflicts are present at all levels of social systems – from the noisy, physical quarrels between kids fighting over a piece of Lego, to large-scale, impersonal conflicts like the 'war on terrorism' after 11 September 2001, with all its terror groups, civil wars, polarized identities, sectarianism and geopolitical rivalries. Attempting to understand third-party mediation of armed conflicts is therefore an inherently multidisciplinary enterprise that involves a wide range of fields, from psychology, sociobiology, semiotics and economics to international law, international relations, anthropology and political science. It is also an academic enterprise firmly placed at the intersection between theory and practice (Miall 2011, Burton 1987, Galtung 1996, Boulding 1975). As Hugh Miall, Oliver Ramsbotham and Tom Woodhouse (2011: 42–8) have pointed out, the field expanded its remit during the 'foundational period' in the 1950s and 1960s, with the keen interest in preventing a global nuclear war during the bipolarity of the Cold War; and entailed an uneasy balance between scholarly research and problem-solving policy strategies.

Likewise with the current academic debate about the role of dialogue, mediation and reconciliation processes in international politics: much of this scholarship brings with it the often explicit goal of moving from academic research to becoming a useful tool for diplomacy and real-world peacemaking (Reimann 2004: 44, Kleiboer 1996: 360, Galtung 1996, Galtung and Jacobsen 2000, Burton 1987, Ury 1999). Thus, it is hardly surprising that many of the articles and books published have been inspired by a mode of instrumental rationality (Habermas 1987), exploring alternative techniques of formal and civic diplomatic interventions in international conflicts and civil wars in the form of 'Track I', 'Track II' and 'Track III' mediation strategies. The central aim of much of this work has been to identify criteria of success – often using the *contingency approach,* where the outcome of mediation efforts (success/no success) is seen as contingent on a number of 'contextual' and 'process' variables (Reimann 2004, Bercovitch et al. 1991, United Nations 2012).

Starting from a similar interest in real-world diplomacy and problem-solving, this chapter presents a twofold argument. Firstly, we hold that the current conceptual underpinning of much recent research does not live up to its own ambition of real-world correspondence and relevance. Having different, identifiable, 'tracks' of mediation may provide easy labels for various forms of dialogue and mediation strategies – but they fit poorly with how peaceful attempts to ease and solve conflict are actually conducted. Today's conflicts have become arenas for 'swarms' of third-party actors and a multitude of integrated mediation efforts and channels that fall outside current terminology and are better described as a new (global) *peacemaking apparatus.* Secondly, in order to understand the achievements and failures of third-party mediation, it is necessary to study the structure and modus operandi of this apparatus. Many of the defining conflicts of recent years – such as the wars in Afghanistan, Libya, Iraq and Syria – have been subjected to concerted attempts at resolution by the peacemaking apparatus. As of yet, these integrated international mediation efforts have not been properly included and analysed in scholarly work.

This chapter addresses the conceptual deficiency in academic attempts to understand (and improve) the world of third-party conflict mediation, starting with a brief discussion of the established terminology and theoretical approaches. Thereafter, we begin to draw the empirical contours of the peacemaking apparatus. The chapter concludes with a discussion on some of the dysfunctions of this global architecture, and the extent to which these represent shortcomings for the productivity (or success) of third-party conflict diplomacy.

Waiting at the Wrong 'Track'

In a recent meta-analysis, Cordula Reimann (2004) makes the point that the academic literature on international third-party mediation is marked by an inflation of competing and often overlapping concepts referring to the same strategies. 'In most of the academic literature, the terms "conflict management", "conflict resolution" and "conflict transformation" are often used loosely and interchangeably, in many cases referring to the same strategies. Similarly, one may also come across the term mediation to cover all different forms of third-party intervention' (Reimann 2004: 46).

In the following we deliberately avoid these general and all-embracing tags. What we propose is a much more restrictive and, we believe, workable definition of international dialogue and mediation policies – *non-party conflict diplomacy*. By this we mean the attempts of a third-party actor – a state, international organization, NGO or individual – to engage one or more contending parties in dialogue in search of a peaceful solution to an armed conflict, without using coercion and with no direct interest in a specific outcome.

This definition involves several important limitations. Most importantly it excludes the type of interventions whereby a third party applies force or the explicit threat of use of force in the form of military actions or sanctions to resolve or reduce a conflict. Examples could be NATO's aerial war over Kosovo in 1999, forcing Serbian military out of Kosovo; or the attempt by the EU and the US administration to prevent a Russian intervention of eastern Ukraine in March 2014, using targeted economic sanctions. Our definition also excludes the type of instrumental mediation effort that has been initiated by international powers such as attempts to ease tensions between North and South Korea, as well as US Secretary of State John Kerry's ambitions of re-launching a peace process in the Middle East after 2013 (Crowley 2014). Both these external involvements are relevant examples of conflict management. However, as the external parties involved had direct and tangible interests in a particular outcome to the conflict, they are examples of collective or unilateral power politics rather than third-party conflict resolution. If an external party has clearly defined strategic vested interests in a certain outcome of its involvement, this can hardly be defined as third-party mediation, but should instead be understood as a typical foreign policy strategy aimed at serving national interests. We hold that a proper definition of dialogue and third-party mediation as a foreign policy strategy must exclude any deliberate self-interests of the third party, and also the use of force to bring about a settlement or initiate a peace process.

How does this way of defining (and limiting) the concept of third-party conflict diplomacy fit with the existing literature? Let us jump back in time, to the aptly titled article, 'Foreign Policy According to Freud', published in *Foreign Policy* in 1981, by the US diplomat Joseph Montville and the psychiatrist William D. Davidson. The primary aim of the article, written in the midst of the 'second cold war', was to underscore the significance of psychology in the conduct of foreign policy. As the authors argued, 'psychological factors also contribute to escalation … of conflict by creating barriers to the occurrence and perception of change' (Davidson and Montville 1981: 150). In their discussion of a possible (and at that time highly hypothetical) peace settlement between Israel and the Palestinians, the authors coined the term 'Track II diplomacy' to refer to a type of diplomacy that 'is unofficial, non-structured interaction. It is always open minded, often altruistic … and strategically optimistic based on the best case analysis. Its underlying assumption is that actual or potential conflict can be resolved or eased by appealing to common human capabilities to respond to good will and reasonableness' (ibid: 155). Further, they suggested that scientific and cultural exchanges could be seen as examples of this kind of diplomatic activity. Montville and Davidson also point out how this kind of third-party conflict resolution differs from traditional Track I diplomacy, which includes 'traditional policy statements by the president and secretary of state, for example, or official visits or meetings' in which government would draft official positions and present statements (ibid.: 154).

Hardly ever with reference to its original Freudian roots, the concept formulated by Montville and Davidson has become the standard textbook definition of what conflict mediation and third-party peace processes are all about. 'Track I', 'Track II' and even 'Track III' comprise a typology widely used to distinguish between different types of third-party mediation strategies (see Agha et al. 2003, Chataway 1999, Diamond and 1996, Dixon 1996, Frazier and Dixon 2006, Gleditsch and Beardsley 2004, Lieberfeld 2002, Nan and Strimling 2004). The common description of what these different strategies entail is fairly straightforward, and focuses on two different aspects of third-party involvement: On the one hand, what type of actors are involved; on the other, the means and measures used by these actors to transform an ongoing conflict. 'Track I' entails mediation strategies that are official, and are conducted by governmental diplomatic actors. It includes activities that range from the non-coercive – such as fact-finding missions, facilitation of negotiations, peacekeeping operations, and economic assistance to uphold cease fires – to coercive measures like the use or threat of sanctions, military enforcement of peace agreements or direct military pressure in case of noncompliance (Fisher 2011, Hansen, Ramsbotham and Woodhouse 2004, Reimann 2004, Mapendere 2005). The British strategy for ending the conflict in Northern Ireland is sometimes cited to illustrate this kind of mediation approach. It was an integrated approach of simultaneously applying force and offering concessions to bring about a peace process (Bloomfield 1997).

Track II diplomacy, on the other hand, is understood as the informal and unofficial version of conflict mediation (Nan and Strimling 2004, Montville 1991, Lieberfeld 2002). The concept usually includes activities conducted by individuals, NGOs, academic institutions, civil mediators and/or religious organizations. The conflicting parties involved are represented by non-official actors, and the measures are typically non-coercive and soft, as Montville and Davidson also pointed out. Such measures may consist of everything from workshops, to cultural exchanges aimed at creating a secluded environment where conflicting parties can meet, sort out differences, and agree on roadmaps or simply test out ideas or future peace plans. The Oslo Process leading up to the Oslo Accords in 1993 is widely seen as an example of this type of approach (Ledetach 1997: 32–4): it was initiated and led by individuals outside official diplomatic circles in Oslo, at a research institution (FAFO). A more appropriate description of the process, however, would probably consider it an illustration of what has become known as the Norwegian model for peace and reconciliation, whereby unofficial initiatives are usually funded by or hedged at the Ministry of Foreign Affairs, and where official and unofficial 'tracks' are closely coordinated (Waage 2005). All the secret talks leading up to the final agreement included a mix of unofficial individuals and formal diplomats from the Norwegian side.

Track III is often defined even more loosely, as 'all process and structure oriented initiatives undertaken by actors involved in grassroots training, capacity building and empowerment, trauma work, human rights and development work and humanitarian assistance' (Reimann 2004: 5). In other words, Track III is understood as bottom-up approaches to peace-building, rarely directly linked to actual peace process, but to long-term engagement for reconciliation, capacity-building on the societal level and network-building for future dialogue openings.

Taking these established categories as a point of departure (see table 1 at page 4 in the introduction), our argument is the following: The distinction between different 'tracks' that international actors can pursue in their involvement in conflict resolution offers an ordering typological device and offers a language that can simplify communication about mediation processes. However, there are three important shortcomings. *First*, the distinctions are certainly not 'ideal types' in the normal Weberian sense: they are not 'analytical constructs' but are simply popular, easily recognizable linguistic markers. *Second*, the notion of 'tracks' gives a sense of clearly distinguishable tools or strategies that actors can choose between, with different aims or measures. Empirically, however, Track I and Track II are very often indistinguishable as approaches. Moreover, the essential thinking behind much of the recent peace and reconciliation engagement, for instance by states like Norway or Switzerland, is the exact opposite. There, Track I and II and even long-term peace-building activities are part of integrated approaches that are launched, funded and coordinated by the state, and outsourced to various national and international actors (Egeland 1988).

Third, and more importantly: Since the popular Track I, II and III typology is not analytically generated, its value and relevance will necessarily depend on its empirical correspondence. However, the idea of different 'tracks' does not fit easily with how mediation efforts are actually conducted in today's conflicts. Most non-party conflict diplomacy falls somewhere in-between. [1] To put it simply, most mediation efforts are Track I and Track II at the same time; they are not separate initiatives or processes – one official and the other unofficial – but are often deliberately combined. Moreover, many of the 'informal actors' –

---

1 See further discussion of the Consequential Conflict Transformation Model in Mapendere 2000.

like private NGOs that facilitate peace processes or former diplomats who often rush into a conflict situation in order to seek a role to play – are not really unofficial: they should be recognized as official subcontractors. Take, for example, the lengthy conflict in Iraq in the ten-year period after the US-led invasion in March 2003. Hordes of actors – ranging from civic peacemaking groups, to former diplomats, NGOs, and academics – have been working on the difficult Arab-Kurdish issue and on trying to bring violent elements of the Sunni community back into the political fold in Baghdad, all of which seem like Track II initiatives. On closer inspection, however, most of this activity emerges as either part of state-run strategic initiatives or linked to official diplomatic involvement that has been initiated by state actors. Unofficial and non-governmental actors working in this field are frequently part of a state diversification strategy, not independent actors.

Another example: the attempt at peaceful resolution of the conflict in Libya during NATO's bombardment after UN Security Council Resolution 1973 established a no-fly zone in March 2011. During a period of five months, from the beginning of the military campaign until opposition forces broke through Gaddafi's inner defence lines in Tripoli and the regime lost control, at least six different states were involved in various types of conflict diplomacy seeking to end the violence. Some of these were states and actors that traditionally had close relations to the Gaddafi regime – among them, South African President Jacob Zuma, the African Union (AU), the United Arab Emirates and the Organization of Islamic Cooperation (OIC). Others were states like Turkey that supported the Transitional National Council (TNC) and the uprising in Benghazi. Some of these initiatives were conducted as typical Track I activities, with meetings between official diplomats and envoys; some were also highly self-interested and can hardly be regarded as non-party conflict diplomacy. Nonetheless, parallel to this and instigated by various states, there was a whole micro-cosmos of other actors also actively engaged in seeking openings for negotiations, establishing contacts, and testing the ground for separate ceasefire agreements. These were business community representatives, NGOs, individual politicians, older statesmen and humanitarian organizations, communicating closely with diplomats and UN representatives. There were also examples of classic Track II, but most activity was conducted by an inter-related network in a Track 1 + II fashion, meaning that the process was funded and closely coordinated by official state actors.

Much of the same also characterized the first period of the international attempts to resolve the conflict in Syria after the outbreak of civil war in 2011. Track I-type initiatives, in the form of state-to-state diplomacy and negotiations between Damascus and some of the opposition, was certainly part of the work aimed at minimizing the intensity and length of the conflict, the best-known being the Geneva process. But there was also intense activity on many other levels, conducted by a multitude of actors. One such initiative – the Harvard–NUPI–Trinity project, in which the authors of this chapter also participated – was symptomatic (Lesch et al. 2013). The project included a handful of individuals, including a prominent US Syria scholar with good contacts with the leadership in Damascus, a Syrian businessman, and several former diplomats and scholars with many years of experience from studying and being involved in mediation processes and conflict resolution. The aim of the project was to conduct interviews with major international actors, regime and opposition, to enable a more comprehensive understanding of the conflict and identify possible overlapping views. The work included travels to Moscow, Damascus, and meetings with the leaders of the opposition as well as with regime representatives, and the ambition was to produce knowledge that could be of use in a potential negotiation situation. The project was funded by several European states and coordinated with diplomats and a range of actors who attempted to help get the Syrian parties to the negotiation table. Many of these activities, which may look like typical non-official Track II diplomatic processes, were rather hybrid, neither Track I nor Track II.

The central points are twofold: On the one hand, the typical description of international mediation as being conducted along different tracks, so dominant in the academic discourse on third-party conflict diplomacy, refers not to analytical categories but empirical ones, and must be judged and assessed as such. On the other hand, as empirical categories the dichotomies of current scholarship do not properly represent the empirical universe. Placing activities into a rigid Track I/Track II scheme exaggerates the sense that there are separate strategies and measures for activities at different levels, and fails to grasp the occurrence of non-party conflict diplomacy that crosses the barriers of the scheme. Track I is indeed a simple matter of fact, but Track II is less so. And much of what should be studied falls outside both categories. Thus, the value of the established categories is disputable.

The Global Peacemaking Apparatus

Leaving aside the formal argument, in the following we draw up the empirical contours of the new global *peacemaking apparatus*. We begin defining the global peacemaking apparatus in line with Mill's (1970: 406) seminal work on social institutions, as a setting of multiple third-party actors that, dependent and/or independent of formal state actors, are involved in concurrent attempts at resolving the same armed conflict. However, this definition does not specify whether the resolution attempt may involve coercive measures, or be the result of direct third-party interests in the conflict – as discussed above. By including these two factors in Mill's definition, we can delimit the peacemaking apparatus as *a setting of multiple non-party actors that, dependent or independent of formal state actors, are involved in concurrent dialogue attempts at resolving the same armed conflict.*

Dialogue is both a core tool and a central aim for the peacemaking apparatus. It can broadly be understood as the meaningful exchange of ideas and worldviews related to a conflict, between a non-party actor and a party to the conflict, or between representatives of two or more contending parties. Dialogue is present at all stages of third-party involvement; it includes network- and confidence-building, informal dialogue seminars and capacity-building, shuttle diplomacy, as well as formal negotiations. As discussed above, these steps are often meshed together in an integrated and intricate back-and-forth movement, aimed at getting contending parties to accept the idea of peaceful resolution and to speak with each other, to make possible the outcome aim of solving or easing a conflict.

The Architecture

What is this peacemaking apparatus made up of? In order to identify the types of actors involved in peaceful non-party conflict diplomacy, let us begin with a brief visit to the Oslo Forum – an annual event for 'senior conflict mediators, high level decision makers, key peace process actors, analysts and experts from a variety of institutional backgrounds…' (OsloForum 2013/2014a). The Forum is co-hosted by the Geneva-headquartered Centre for Humanitarian Dialogue (CHD) and the Norwegian Ministry of Foreign Affairs, and is, according to the organizers, 'widely regarded as the leading international network of armed conflict mediation practitioners' (OsloForum 2013/2014a). With its interesting blend of people who get together to discuss tools, approaches and opportunities for dealing with the world's armed conflicts, the event comes close to being a miniature version of what we seek to describe in this chapter. The lists of participants, from the first Oslo Forum in 2003 and through the ten succeeding years, can serve as a stepping stone for identifying categories of actors involved in peaceful non-party conflict mediation.[2] As it is up to the organizers to invite the participants to this annual event, the list might give an imbalanced image of the figures actually involved in peacemaking. The forum is tilted towards elite actors, as well as reflecting who counts and who doesn't from the Norwegian and Swiss points of view. Nevertheless, we believe the Oslo Forum captures well the *types* of actors involved in what we define as the peacemaking apparatus, even if the Forum may not be fully representative as regards the geographical or social distribution of relevant people in the field.

---

2 The official list numbered 361 individuals altogether in 2013 – many of whom have participated several times (OsloForum 2013/2014b).

From the list, and recalling the limitations set in our definition above, we can identify the following categories:

i. *Representatives of international organizations*
ii. *Diplomats and representatives of states*
iii. *NGOs or academic institutions specializing in various forms of mediation and mediation research*
iv. *Individual entrepreneurs and groups created around specific mediation initiatives and processes.*

The Oslo Forum also brings in representatives of conflicting parties that are involved in mediation initiatives, official negotiation delegates, or that play roles in instigating dialogue initiatives in their own communities. These may be state representatives, activists or members of oppositional groups, and are often partners or otherwise closely linked to the work of the peacemaking apparatus. They nevertheless remain outside our definition of the 'peacemaking apparatus' due to their explicit partiality.

Although clearly diverging in terms of their institutions' primary objectives and activities, these four categories of actors together form the pillars of the peacemaking apparatus. They meet in the Oslo Forum as well as in the world of conflicts: as mediators between warring parties, as funders for peacemaking activities, as facilitators for dialogue initiatives, as experts on particular conflicts, and as grassroots activists. As the following examples will show, the tasks and activities here are rarely neatly split between formal and informal actors, but are spread *across* the apparatus.

Activities

How can these diverse actors work and interact? What makes them all part of the same endeavour? By presenting the workings and self-presentations of some leading actors within each actor category, we aim to show the range of activities and interconnections of the various actor types within the peacemaking apparatus.[3]

The first category – international and regional organizations – is populated by actors such as the UN, the EU, the AU and the OIC. To take the latter as an example, the OIC has been involved in mediation work from its very inception. As fostering cooperation and Islamic solidarity is the organization's *raison d'être*,

---

3 The examples build on the authors' personal experience as practitioners working between 2006 and 2013 in processes in the Middle East. They are not meant as exhaustive case explorations of actors and activities related to this region, but as illustrations that invite broader empirical research. Here we draw primarily on the web-pages of the selected organizations and institutions, focusing on self-presentation, collaboration with others as well as funding policies.

resolving conflicts between member states has become a key function (Al-Ahsan 2004: 137). Moreover, the OIC is actively involved in conflicts that occur within member states, and has mediation experience from countries as diverse as Iraq, the Philippines, Somalia and Thailand (Sharqieh 2012). It has sent fact-finding missions to conflict areas, engaged in talks with conflicting parties, sought help from religious leaders and led formal negotiations (ibid.: 162–73). The OIC has worked actively to strengthen its role as a mediator, following a ten-year plan launched in 2005 (OIC 2005), which led to the establishment of a special Peace, Security, and Mediation Unit (PSMU) in 2013 (Worldfolio 2013). The OIC has also been involved in mediation attempts between the parties in Libya, along with *inter alia* the AU and the Arab League, and is said to have been the only regional organization able to keep the channels open to both the regime and the rebels (Sharqieh 2012: 172). OIC's outreach and legitimacy in conflicts involving Muslim communities make it attractive as a partner to the UN; the OIC is also itself seeking cooperation with a view to more effective conflict resolution (OIC 2013). Although coordination with the UN and top-level negotiations might be expected priorities for a large regional organization, the OIC is also a visible actor on the humanitarian arena, which it sees as a grassroots entry to playing a role in conflict resolution.

In the *second category* we find state actors such as Norway, Qatar, Switzerland and Turkey, all of which have conflict mediation as important parts of their foreign policies. Norway, for example, allocates almost USD 150 million annually to conflict resolution, reconciliation and peacebuilding measures; and activities are led by a specialized unit of up to 20 diplomats in the Ministry of Foreign Affairs (MFA).

Other states have followed suit, promoting peacemaking as a prioritized area of their foreign policies. Here we could add Finland, Sweden, South Africa and Turkey, along with some of the 36 nations that signed the joint Finnish-Turkish initiative to establish the Group of Friends of Mediation in the UN in 2010 (UN peacemaker 2014). However, there are important differences in their official strategies, or at least in terminology and rhetoric. Whereas Norway highlights its role as a 'facilitator' and as being willing to long-term commitment (Norwegian MFA 2014a), Qatar accentuates its 'contributions to settlement of armed conflicts' (State of Qatar MFA 2014). Turkey emphasizes 'preventive diplomacy'(Republic of Turkey Ministry of Foreign Affairs), while Switzerland, like Norway, operates according to a broad and varied commitment to peace policy, often emphasizing its partnership with experts, NGOs and international peacemaking partners (Swiss Federal Department of Foreign Affairs 2014).

Among these countries, only Switzerland has chosen to front its peace efforts as collaborative and dependent on others, presenting its cooperation policies to an international audience through the official English websites. However, it is common knowledge among practitioners that also Norway, Qatar and Turkey seek collaboration with other actors in the peacemaking apparatus. Norway has several strategic partnerships and collaborative projects with organizations and individuals, drawing from all four categories of actors listed above. Norway is also a major financial supporter of conflict resolution initiatives. Towards its home audience, the MFA underlines the importance of Norwegian NGOs for the country's peace work, explaining (in the Norwegian-language webpages) that these frequently function as entry-points to peace and reconciliation processes because of their broad networks, providing 'access also in places where the official Norway has had little or no presence' (Norwegian MFA 2014b). This is just one example of how the actors of the peacemaking apparatus fill in for each other and complement each other's work.

The *third category* in the peacemaking apparatus is that of the specialized 'peacemaking' organizations and centres. These are usually fully or partly funded by one or several states, and typically employ former diplomats and international civil servants. This group has expanded significantly over the past decade. Some of the organizations do their work independently of states, but many cooperate closely with government representatives in coordinating initiatives, drawing on each other's networks, and sometimes handling political issues that are in the interest of governments but too sensitive for them to deal with directly. One example is the Centre for Humanitarian Dialogue (CHD) in Geneva. The organization presents itself as a leading organization in the field of conflict mediation, seeking to 'help prevent, mitigate, and resolve armed conflict through dialogue and mediation', using the tools of what it refers to as private diplomacy: 'We open channels of communication and mediate between parties in conflict, facilitate dialogue, provide support to the broader mediation and peacebuilding community, carry out capacity building work, and conduct research on mediation issues' (Center for Humanitarian Dialogue 2014). CHD initiatives are generally funded by governments. This cooperation is useful for CHD as well as its supporters: if successful, it enhances not only the organization's own status within the peacemaking apparatus, but also that of its supporters, who may take credit for the achievement.

Two smaller organizations within the same category of specialized organizations for mediation are Forward Thinking (FT) and Inter-Mediate. Both are based on the work of a handful of engaged individuals whose networks and diplomatic skills are among their key assets. FT presents itself as 'a pro-active, demand-driven, facilitative organization' (Forward Thinking 2014), working primarily with intercultural dialogue. It receives funding from states and private donations, and collaborates widely with grassroots organizations in order to obtain expertise on local conditions, legitimacy in conflict areas and expanded network (ibid). Inter-Mediate is more narrowly oriented towards the act of mediation in actual war zones, describing itself as a 'charity for negotiation and mediation' that has found its niche in focusing on 'the most difficult, complex and dangerous conflicts where other organisations are unable to operate' (Intermediate 2014). According to the organization's self-presentation, it brings together 'some of the world's leading experts on dialogue and negotiation, who operate as a small and flexible team that fills a vital gap in the conflict resolution landscape' (ibid.).

Although the image of some organization within this category may seem closer to vanguard forces than to collective-oriented peacebuilding groups, they all meet on the arena of peacemaking – if not in cooperation, then even in outright competition. All in all, these organizations are examples of the interwoven arena that peacemaking has become, integrating a wide range of activities and actor types within one organization.

In the *fourth category* we find individual entrepreneurs, former politicians and diplomats, as well as academics and NGOs working on specific conflicts but with their core agendas elsewhere. What the members of this diverse group have in common is primarily their knowledge and networks, in conflict areas or at the elite level of world politics, as a result of earlier careers or involvements. They are either invited into the peacemaking apparatus, or are looking for ways to use their skills and engagement to resolve conflicts. They may work singlehandedly, or with organizations and as part of smaller private initiatives. While maintaining institutional independence from the state, they are, as much as the other categories that make up the peacemaking apparatus, economically and operationally integrated into official foreign policy, often as strategic tools to support and strengthen the state's policies and activities. Finland's Martti Ahtisaari is one such example. Building on his experience and authority as president, he established an organization for peace diplomacy, the Crisis Management Initiative. The main funder is, unsurprisingly, the government of Finland, with a share of 66 per cent (Martti Ahtisaari Centre 2014). Another example is a former prime minister of Norway, Kjell Magne Bondevik. The networks he built up while in office were given as a *raison d'être* for establishing the Oslo Centre for Peace and Human Rights (Johnsen 2006).

Defining the Success of Non-party Conflict Diplomacy

The names and organizations listed above represent but a small portion of the entire global apparatus that at any given time is involved in processes of mediation around the planet. Again, our aim here is not to present detailed components or workings of this entire apparatus. Instead we simply maintain that the architecture described above should be taken as an indication of institutional and social facts of international politics that other typologies tend to overlook. From the civil wars in Iraq between 2004 and 2009, to the conflicts in Afghanistan, in Libya in 2011 and in Syria today, international efforts to reduce the violence and halt the fighting should be viewed according to such an integrative institutional approach – the mixture of state and non-diplomacy, and of civil and official actors, linked through economic dependency, social relations, common identity and integrated strategies.

How is this relevant for our general understanding of peaceful non-party conflict mediation? There is a growing international literature that seeks to explain the reasons for success and lack of success of international mediation efforts and reconciliation processes (Lieberfeld 2002, Agha et al. 2003, Bercovitch 1997, Reimann 2004, Kleiboer 1996). As we see it, describing the functioning of the peacemaking apparatus is directly relevant to this academic endeavour. However, this is not yet well understood and constitutes a double blindspot in the current literature. Firstly, we believe that the concept of the peacemaking apparatus enables more precise empirical descriptions of third-party diplomatic involvement in the world's conflicts. Secondly, and related to our interest in real-world diplomacy and actual problem-solving, understanding the architecture and operation of the peacemaking apparatus is important also for the real-world conduct and effectiveness of such international involvement. Let us briefly try to substantiate these two claims.

The starting point for much scholarship is to explain why some attempts at mediation are successful and others are not. But what is the dependent variable here? What constitutes a success? Is it the quality of a peace process as such or is it the outcome of the process which should be deemed successful or unsuccessful? Moreover, is a successful mediation effort 'a situation in which both parties of the conflict … accept a mediator' and thereby show an interest for a process (Frei 1976: 69). Or is a process successful only when external third-party involvement leads to 'producing a cease fire, a partial settlement or a full settlement' (Bercovitch et al. 1991: 8)? Further: is success solely a question of formal or informal agreements between parties – or can it also be understood and measured as the effect a mediation process may have on the intensity of a conflict even when the conflict is ultimately not resolved through mediation? One possible illustration could be Norway's efforts to facilitate an agreement between the Sri Lankan government and the Tamil Tigers (LTTE) between 1997 and 2009. The success of the process has been sharply questioned by observers (Sørbo et al. 2011); some have even indicated that Norway's involvement may have prolonged the conflict and that lives would have been saved without a process because this could have led to an early military victory for the government (Roberts 2013). All the same, it may still be argued that the process was a success because it reduced the intensity of the fighting through several ceasefires, thereby saving human lives. Thus, a proper definition of success may be based on the counterfactual hypothesis as to what the overall consequence of a conflict would have been without external third-party involvement: this is not irrelevant, but it is certainly a definition that gives rise to several difficult methodological challenges (Ferguson 1999).

Furthermore, there is always the risk that what at one point has been seen as successful mediation loses its status as details of the process become known. The Oslo Process might be one example. When agreement between Israel and the PLO was brokered in 1993 the world was in awe. Later, however, as the process became derailed, the Norwegian mediators were criticized for having treated the Palestinians unfairly in their attempts to 'protect their role in the process' (Waage 2005: 19), with a long-term negative impact on the balance of power between the parties. What was widely proclaimed as a successful mediation with a successful outcome was thus later questioned for both its process *and* its results.

In other words, and as Kleiboer (1996) made clear almost twenty years ago, there is no agreed-upon Archimedean point for evaluating the success of third-party conflict mediations. It is simply a question of definition and measurability. And the criteria also depend on the context and the nature of the conflict. To get the parties in the Syrian civil war to sit around the same table, and to keep them there, would certainly have been a great success in 2013. However, in the peace process between the FARC guerrilla and the Colombian government the same year, as with the international mediation over Iran's nuclear industry, the table and the process were already in place, and success had to be judged on the base of a real and lasting settlement. To be sure, since peace mediation and reconciliation processes always occur through an intersubjective process, any sound and durable definition of success will hinge on when in that process the third-party actors become involved.

Instead of searching for answers to the dichotomous question of success or failure of mediation outcomes, we here propose an approach that focuses more on the architecture and functioning of third-party mediation. The point is not to question the need for a peacemaking apparatus. What we do question, however, is how some of the work is organized and conducted. What are the structural dysfunctions of third-party conflict mediation as it is practised today? How can peacemaking become more effective?

The scholarly community is divided about how to measure mediation success, but there is significantly more consensus concerning the key independent variables that affect a mediation outcome. As noted in the introduction to this book, the seminal 'contingency approach' sees the outcome of mediation efforts (i.e. the definition of success) as contingent on several *contextual* and *process* variables. The contextual variables are typically variables that characterize the conflict – like the intensity of fighting, the parties involved and the surrounding international context, sometimes specified as 'the nature of parties', 'the nature of dispute', 'the international context', and 'the nature of the mediators' (Kleiboer 1996: 368, Bercovitch 1991: 10–15).

By contrast, the process variables describe the effect of the third party itself. This refers to the relationship between the behaviour of the mediator and the outcome – for instance, the diplomatic approach, the strategies, the choice of settings, and the experience of the facilitator or mediator. During the actual conduct of a process, these kinds of practical considerations may often require considerable time and resources. How actively involved should a third party be? How much emphasis should be put on actual mediation, and how much on trust-building measures? Should formal diplomats run the show, or should the process be 'outsourced' to informal actors? Should political leaders be involved? And is the role that of a facilitator, as was the case with Norway during the meetings between PLO and Israel throughout the Oslo Process, or a more active and forward-leaning one, as when Martti Ahtisaari helped to resolve the conflict in Aceh in 2005? And what is the right setting – should parties be placed around the same table? Should the table be rectangular or circular? or should they sit in different rooms? These seemingly minor factors are crucial issues in any serious mediation process, and they take up much of the time.

Conclusions: Five Shortcomings of the Peacemaking Apparatus

How does the existence of the peacemaking apparatus fit in with this analytical framework of contextual and process variables? The short answer is that is does not. The existence and possible effect of what we defined above as a setting with multiple non-party actors that dependently and/or independently of formal state actors are involved in concurrent attempts at peaceful resolution of the same armed conflict must be said to fall outside the scope of the core of the scholarly debate. The peacemaking apparatus is neither a contextual variable nor a process variable, but contains elements of both. However, its operations are important for fully describing and understanding the success or lack of success of international third-party intervention, a central topic in much of the ongoing scholarly research.

Below are five factors that we see as important dysfunctions of the peacemaking apparatus.

1. The Swarming Factor

The first and most straightforward shortcoming of the peacemaking apparatus is the inflation of the number of actors involved at any given time in resolving ongoing conflicts. This is the 'swarming factor' whereby many different states fund hundreds of different actors and initiatives along different tracks in an often uncoordinated and chaotic fashion. The intention might be to let the thousand flowers bloom, but the real-world consequence may be confusion –

among the parties as well as among the various third-party actors themselves, who may get in the way of each other, or unintentionally (or perhaps even deliberately) seek to foil others' initiatives in order to foster their own success. For a recent example of such a dysfunctional setting take the unsuccessful attempts to resolve the conflict in Libya during NATO's aerial campaign in 2011, mentioned above. At least six states initiated different processes, several of them mobilizing and funding scores of non-state actors and organizations, in addition to various other informal diplomats and individuals.[4] The result was not only an overload of competing initiatives and conflicting ideas of various ceasefire agreements, but also, as a central actor on Libyan side later put it, 'confusing signals and contradictory analyses and plans that made it difficult for us to know what to think'.[5]

2. The Internal Competition Factor

A second possible shortcoming is the intrinsic relationship between third-party actors themselves. The swarm of actors and parallel initiatives that often are set in motion tend to produce internal competition among third-party actors. Playing a role can become an aim in itself, even more important than the actual outcome. Instead of unified international initiatives and policies, outside actors tend to develop their own competing processes. As a result the overall international effort risks becoming too multifaceted, with no common strategy and policy solutions, often undermining the ability of the international community to put joint pressure on the parties. Competition among third-party actors may also lead to a 'lip-service' syndrome, with actors eager to please the parties in order to gain a role. This might lead them to give an untruthful analysis of the situation to the parties, and to play along with the hardliners that often surround the leadership of warring parties. (An instance of this occurred during the first phase of the civil war in Syria, when several non-state actors and states sought to gain a footing with the parties either with formal envoys or through unofficial mediation organizations and individuals.)

3. The Process-dependency Factor

For many third-party actors, involvement in ongoing attempts at conflict resolution is existential. A large portion of the global peacemaking apparatus is highly dependent on funding from state donors – and much of this funding depends on keeping processes and initiatives going. The same goes for individual

---

4 See speech by Mahmoud Jibril, Chairman of TNC, September 2011, Paris and interview with Guma El-Gamaty, *The Foreigner*, 24 June 2011.

5 Interview with former diplomat, Cairo, February 2012.

operators and even professional diplomats who have developed a career based on their role in specific conflicts. In this way, individuals and organizations may become financially or socially wedded to a process. This may have two negative side-effects. First, there is the tendency for states, diplomats and mediation organizations to let a process go on for too long, instead of searching for alternative strategies and solutions, or letting an initiative undergo a process of constructive breakdown. Second, over-eagerness to save third-party initiatives may prevent the international community from seriously considering what Luttwak (1999) called the 'give war a chance'-argument. According to this argument, which has been discussed in relation to Norway's involvement in the process on Sri Lanka (Sorbo et al. 2011), the continuation of a peace process may at times lead to prolonged war – preventing a conflict from running its natural course either by burning out when all belligerents become exhausted, or by a decisive victory by one of the parties.

4. The Visibility Factor

A further complicating factor of parallel involvement of multiple states and non-state actors is the gap between the need for patience and long-term involvement and the third party's interest in rapid success and short-term political gains. This might lead some actors to be too open about the processes they are involved in (in order to show that they have impact, to get funding, or to get attention); or states may utilize their role for political purposes, for instance in relation to domestic constituency and public opinion. Again the attempts to resolve the conflict in Libya in 2011 offer an example. Turkey was one of the states that sought to bridge the gap between the Gaddafi regime and the leadership of the opposition, TNC. However, Turkey also had a keen self-interest – regionally as well as domestically – in presenting itself as a supporter of the Arab Spring, and thus publically announcing the country's role. In consequence, trust in any confidential process within the Gaddafi regime was severely hampered, and attempts by other actors to seek a ceasefire were probably undermined (Black 2011).

5. The (Mis)information Factor

Finally, there is the importance of correct information and unambiguous signals from the international community. Multiple actors, multiple processes and numerous parallel channels of communication between the international community and parties in an ongoing conflict may produce misinformation and galvanize opposing worldviews among parties. As noted, in the midst of a conflict, warring parties will often be surrounded by hardliners with a keen interest in continued fighting, playing down any prospect for a negotiated solution. Given such a setting, with various third-party actors keen to play a central role, as well as multiple ongoing processes and channels, hardliners will often get the chance to prioritize information (and invite parties) that fit with their own views. Impartial readings of the situation may be weakened, with the possible consequence that established hardliner worldviews may be further toughened.

These five factors are shortcomings of the collective efforts of non-party diplomacy. From the perspective of policymaking and real-world diplomacy they can be viewed as warning signs that states, diplomats and other international actors should look out for when they design, fund and conduct third-party involvement in concrete conflicts. However, they are also contextual and process variables that affect mediation outcomes. And that means they are attributes that should be included in scholarly attempts to explain the failure or success of international mediation.

References

Hussein, A., Feldman, S. and Schiff, Z. 2003. *Track-II Diplomacy: Lessons from the Middle East.* Cambridge, MA: MIT Press.

Al-Ahsan, A. 2004. Conflict among Muslim Nations: Role of the OIC in Conflict Resolution, *Intellectual Discourse*, 12(2), 137–57.

Bercovitch, J. 1997. Mediation in International Conflict: An Overview of Theory, A Review of Practice, *in Peacemaking in International Conflict: Methods and Techniques,* edited by W. Zartman and J.L. Rasmussen. Washington DC: United States Institute of Peace Press, 125–54.

Bercovitch, J. and Houston, A. 2000. Why do they do it like this? An Analysis of the Factors Influencing Mediation Behavior in International Conflicts, *Journal of Conflict Resolution*, 44(2), 170–202.

Bercovitch, J., Wille, D.L. and Anagnoson, J.T. 1991. Some Conceptual Issues and Empirical Trends in the Study of Successful Mediation in International Relations, *Journal of Peace Research*, 28(1), 7–17.

Bloomfield, D. 1997. *Peacemaking Strategies in Northern Ireland: Building Complementarity in Conflict Management Theory.* Basingstoke: Macmillan.

Black, I. 2011. Turkey Asks Libya Summit to Back Peace Negotiation, *The Guardian* [Online, July 2014]. Available at: http://www.theguardian.com/world/2011/jul/14/libya-turkey-peace-negotiations-roadma [Accessed: 2 July 2014].

Boulding, K. 1975. *International Systems: Peace, Conflict Resolution, and Politics,* Boulder, CO: Colorado Associated University Press.

Burton, J. 1987. *Resolving Deep-rooted Conflict: A Handbook.* Lanham, MD: University Press of America.

Center for Humanitarian Dialogue. 2014. *Who We Are* [Online]. Available at: http://www.hdcentre.org/en/about-us/who-we-are [Accessed: 1 April 2014].

Chataway, C.J. 1998. Track II Diplomacy: From a Track I Perspective, *Negotiation Journal*, 14(3), 269–87.

Chataway, C.J. 1999. The Evolution of Diplomacy: Coordinating Tracks I and II, in *World Order for a New Millennium: Political, Cultural and Spiritual Approaches to Building Peace*, edited by A.W. Dorn New York: St. Martin's, 139–46.

Crowley, M. 2014. The Big Questions Behind John Kerry's Latest Push for Middle East Peace, *Time Magazine* [Online , 6 January]. Available at: http://swampland.time.com/2014/01/06/the-big-questions-behind-john-kerrys-latest-push-for-middle-east-peace [Accessed: 1 April 2014].

Davidson, W.D. and Montville, J.V. 1981. Foreign Policy According to Freud, *Foreign Policy*, 45, Winter, 145–57.

Derrick, F. and Dixon, W. 2006. Third-party Intermediaries and Negotiated Settlements, 1946–2000, *International Interactions*, 32(4), 385–408.

Diamond, L. and McDonald, J.W. 1996. *Multi-Track Diplomacy: A Systems Approach to Peace*. Sterling, VA: Kumarian Press.

Dixon, W.J. 1996. Third-party Techniques for Preventing Conflict Escalation and Promoting Peaceful Settlement. *International Organization*, 50(4), 653–81.

Egeland, J. 1998. *Impotent Superpower - Potent Small State: Potentials and Limitations of Human Right Objectives in the Foreign Policies of the United States and Norway*. Oslo: University of Oslo Press

Ferguson, N. 1999. *Virtual History: Alternatives and Counterfactuals*. New York: Basic Books.

Fisher, R. 2011. Methods of Third-Party Intervention, in *Advancing Conflict Transformation: The Berghof Handbook II*, edited by B. Austin, M. Fischer and H.J. Giessmann. Opladen/Framington Hills: Barbara Budrich Publishers, 158–82 [Online]. Available at: www.berghof-handbook.net [Accessed: 22 July 2014].

Forward Thinking. 2014. *What We Do* [Online]. Available at: http://www.forwardthinking.org/?page_id=75 [Accessed: 1 April 2014].

Frei, D. 1976. Conditions Affecting the Effectiveness of International Mediation, *Peace Science Society (International) Papers*, 26, 67–84.

Galtung, J.1996. *Peace by Peaceful Means*. London: Sage.

Galting, J. and Jacobsen, C.G. 2000. *Searching for Peace*, London: Pluto.

Gleditsch, K.S. and Beardsley, K. 2004. Nosy Neighbours: Third-party Actors in Central American Conflicts, *Journal of Conflict Resolution*, 48(3), 379–402.

Habermas, J. 1987. *Knowledge & Human Interest*. London: Polity Press.

Inter-mediate. 2014. *About us* [Online]. Available at: http://www.inter-mediate.org/about_us.html [Accessed: 1 April 2014].

Johnsen, J.L.N. 2006. *Ga seg selv drømmejobben.* Dagsavisen [Online]. Available at: http://www.dagsavisen.no/samfunn/ga-seg-selv-drommejobben [Accessed: 2 May 2014].

Kaye, D. 2001. Track Two Diplomacy and Regional Security in the Middle East, *International Negotiation,* 6(1), 49–77.

Kleiboer, M. 1996. Understanding Success and Failure of International Mediation, *Journal of Conflict Resolution,* 40(2), 360–89.

Lederach, J.P. 1997. *Building Peace: Sustainable Reconciliation in Divided Societies,* Washington DC: United States Institute of Peace Press.

Lesch, D.W., Nome, F., Saghir, G., Ury, W., and Waldman, M. 2013. *Obstacles to a Resolution of the Syrian Conflict,* Harvard–NUPI–Trinity Syria Research Project, Oslo: NUPI.

Lieberfeld, D. 2002. Evaluating the Contributions of Track-Two Diplomacy to Conflict Termination in South Africa, 1984–1990, *Journal of Peace Research,* 39(3), 355–72.

Luttwak, E.N. 1999. Give War a Chance, *Foreign Affairs,* July/August, 36–44.

Mapendere, J. 2000. *Consequential Conflict Transformation Model, and the Complementarity of Track One, Track One and a Half, and Track Two Diplomacy.* (Available from The Carter Center, Conflict Resolution Program, 453 Freedom Parkway, Atlanta, GA 30307).

Martti Ahtisaari Centre. 2014. Funding [Online]. Available at: http://www.cmi.fi/about-us/funding [Accessed: 1 April 2014].

Mapendere, J. 2005. Track One and a Half Diplomacy and the Complementarity of Tracks, *Culture of Peace Online Journal,* 2(1), 66–81.

Miall, H., Ramsbotham, O. and Woodhouse, T. 2011. *Contemporary Conflict Resolution: The Prevention, Management and Transformation of Deadly Conflicts.* Cambridge: Polity Press.

Mills, C.W. 1970. The Cultural Apparatus, in *Power, Politics, and People: The Collected Essays of C. Wright Mills,* edited by I.L. Horowitz Oxford: Oxford University Press.

Montville, J.V. 1991. Track Two Diplomacy: The Arrow and the Olive Branch: A Case for Track Two Diplomacy in *The Psychodynamics of International Relations: Vol. 2, Unofficial Diplomacy at Work,* edited by V.D. Volkan, J.P. Montville and A.J. Demetrios. Lanham, MD: Lexington, 161–75.

Nan, S.A. and Strimling, A., 2004. Track I–Track II Cooperation, in *Beyond Intractability,* edited by G. Burgess and H. Burgess. Boulder, CO: Conflict Research Consortium, University of Colorado.

Norwegian MFA. 2014b. Peace and Reconciliation Efforts: The Norwegian model [Online]. Available at: http://www.regjeringen.no/en/dep/ud/selected-topics/peace-and-reconciliation-efforts.html?id=1158 [Accessed: 1 April 2014].

Organisation of Islamic Cooperation (OIC) Secretary General. 2013. Security Council Meeting on UN-OIC Cooperation [Online]. Available at: http://www.oicun.org/oic_at_un/79/20131104041141564.html [Accessed: 1 April 2014].

Organisation of Islamic Cooperation (OIC) 2005. OIC Ten Year Program of Action [Online]. Available at: http://www.oic-oci.org/oicv2/page/?p_id=228&p_ref=73&lan=en [accessed: 5 May 2014].

OsloForum. 2013/2014a. Osloforum about [Online]. Available at: https://www.osloforum.org/content/about [Accessed: 5 May 2014].

OsloForum. 2013/2014b. Osloforum Participants [Online]. Available at: https://www.osloforum.org/content/participants [Accessed: 5 May 2014].

Reimann, C. 2004. Assessing the State-of-the-Art in Conflict Transformation, in *Transforming Ethnopolitical Conflicts*, edited by F. Austin, M. Fischer and N. Ropers. The Berghof Handbook for Conflict Transformation, 41–66.

Republic of Turkey MFA. 2014. *Resolution of Conflicts and Mediation* [Online]. Available at: http://www.mfa.gov.tr/resolution-of-conflicts-and-mediation.en.mfa [Accessed: 1 April 2014].

Roberts, A. 2013. Introduction on Norway and the Peace Process in Sri Lanka, Noref Seminar, Nobel Institute Oslo, November 2013.

Sharqieh, I. 2012. Can the OIC Resolve Conflicts?, *Peace and Conflict Studies*, 19(2), edited by R. Cooper (Brookings Institution) [Online]. Available at: http://www.brookings.edu/~/media/Research/Files/Articles/2012/11/oic%20conflict%20resolution/Sharqieh%20November%202012%20OIC.pdf [accessed: 22 July 2014].

State of Qatar MFA. 2014. *Deliverables in the International Cooperation Domain* [Online]. Available at: http://www.mofa.gov.qa/en/InternationalCooperation/Pages/Achievements.aspx [accessed: 1 April 2014].

Swiss Federal Department of Foreign Affairs. 2014. *Peace* [Online]. Available at: http://www.eda.admin.ch/eda/en/home/topics/peasec/peac.html [accessed: 1 April 2014].

Sorbo, G., Goodhand, J., Klem, B., Nissen, A.E. and Selbervik, H. 2011. *Pawns of Peace: Evaluation of Norwegian Peace Efforts in Sri Lanka, 1997–2009*, Chr. Michelsen Institute/School of Oriental and African Studies/University of London, September.

United Nations Peacemaker. 2014. *Group of Friends of Mediation* [Online]. Available at: http://peacemaker.un.org/friendsofmediation [accessed: 1 April 2014].

United Nations 2012. *Strengthening the Role of Mediation in the Peaceful Settlement of Disputes, Conflict Prevention and Resolution*, Report to the Secretary-General, A/66/811.

Ury, W. 1999. *Getting to Peace: Transforming Conflict at Home, at Work, and in the World*. New York: Viking.

Wibke, H., Ramsbotham, O. and Woodhouse, T. 2004. Hawks and Doves: Peacekeeping and Conflict Resolution, in *Transforming Ethnopolitical Conflicts*, edited by A. Austin, M.A. Fischer and N. Ropers. The Berghof Handbook, 2–21.

Wilkenfeld, J., Young, K., Asal, V. and Quinn, D. 2005. *Mediating International Crises*. New York: Routledge.

Worldfolio 2013. A Leader in International Mediation, *AFA Press, OIC* [Online]. Available at: http://www.worldfolio.co.uk/reports/oic/muslim-countries-oic-n2371 [Accessed 5 May 2014].

Waage, H.H. 2005. Norway's Role in the Middle East Peace Talks: Between a Strong State and a Weak Belligerent. *Journal of Palestine Studies*, 34(4), 6–24.

Chapter 4
Dialogue in a World of Emotional Politics[1]

Paul Saurette and Henrik Thune

Introduction

For much of its post-WWII history, the study and practice of international politics has dismissed the idea that emotional elements might play an important role in international conflicts. On one hand, realists have represented international politics as the ultimate Hobbesian state of nature: an arena where rationality, strategy, state interest and cold calculations trump all other human considerations – including the feelings of sympathy, generosity, fear, empathy and solidarity that are often seen as crucial in the sphere of domestic politics. Idealists, on the other hand, have often suggested that logic clearly demonstrates that states should and must use global norms, international institutions and practices of cooperation to avoid slipping into emotional misunderstandings and responses that only exacerbate the challenges of global politics.

Perhaps unsurprisingly, many policymakers and observers have voiced similar views about the role that that dialogue can, should and should not play in foreign policy. Dialogue sceptics (of which there are many today) often argue that dialogue can never resolve any international tension and conflict of real importance, and routinely dismiss policies of dialogue as procrastination at best and 'appeasement' at worst. In turn, dialogue instrumentalists (who are closely related to, but distinct from, dialogue sceptics) hold that although diplomatic dialogue might sometimes be useful, it is a purely strategic and instrumental state-to-state communication whose main purpose is to clarify the material consequences of certain potential actions. Even many dialogue idealists (who argue that dialogue is an essential diplomatic practice) forward narrow conceptions of dialogue – frequently assuming that the problem in most conflicts is a lack of information or preventable misinterpretations, and

---

1 Some of the material in a few parts of this chapter has been previously published in Saurette, P. 2006. You Dissin' Me? Humiliation and Post 9/11 Global Politics, *Review of International Studies*, 32, 495–522.

that the solution is simply to dialogue more, and/or more effectively, about the core interests of the various parties.

The problem is that all of these perspectives misrepresent the role and nature of emotion in international politics – something that substantially weakens their analytic accuracy and prescriptive utility. Both emotion and dialogue are complex and inter-related phenomena that play key, but complicated, roles even at the highest levels of international politics. The nature and length of NATO's air campaign in Libya, for example, was apparently at least in part determined by highly emotional factors. Members of the Libyan delegation to France reported that while discussing a possible halt to the bombardment (which was then taking place), French president Nicolas Sarkozy rose from his chair and started to shout at the Libyans, claiming that they had wounded his personal feelings as well as French economic interests when they had earlier refused to purchase French nuclear reactors, and declaring that he would therefore reject any form of negotiated settlement to end NATO's air campaign in Libya.[2]

The idea that emotion and dialogue are crucial elements in international politics is certainly not a new insight. Nearly a century ago, John Maynard Keynes noted their importance in his celebrated critique of the outcome of the Versailles peace, in *The Economic Consequences of the Peace* (1921) (Keynes 1919). Arguing that a stable national emotional climate in Germany would be essential to the long-term durability of the peace settlement, Keynes harshly criticized the terms of the treaty (particularly the undertones of blame and the compensation payment required of Germany) and argued that it would become an emotional spark for yet another European war: 'the policy of reducing Germany to servitude for a generation, of degrading the lives of millions of human beings, and of depriving a whole nation of happiness ... will sow the decay of the whole civilised life of Europe'. However, most students and practitioners of international politics have forgotten these insights. Although some scholars have begun to study this complex role of emotions in international politics more explicitly over the last decade, this area remains little understood (Moisi 2010, Coleman 2011). Moreover, the question of what a proper understanding of emotions might mean for how we think about the practice of dialogue in international politics has gone virtually unasked.

Given this context, our aim in this chapter is to outline the central role that emotions play in international politics, and explore the implications this holds for how we understand the potential and the limits of the practice of dialogue in a world of emotionally charged international politics. We begin by examining how scholars and practitioners of international politics have traditionally understood the role that emotions play (or do not play) in their world. In section 2, we critically evaluate this traditional understanding and draw on scholars from

---

2 Interview with former Libyan representatives, February 2012.

a range of disciplines to illustrate the key role that emotions actually play in international politics. In sections 3 and 4 we apply these insights to the question of dialogue by analysing several case studies. Finally, in the concluding section 5, we focus on some of the implications of these case studies for understanding the role that emotions and dialogue play in international politics.

Traditional Perspectives on Emotions and International Politics

Traditionally, international relations theory (IRT) has held an ambivalent view of the importance and place of emotions and emotional dynamics in global politics – one in which emotions are sometimes implicitly recognized as important, but are rarely explicitly theorized and acknowledged.

Close readings of many of the 'founding theorists' of IRT, for example, show that many of these authors held sophisticated and nuanced views about emotions. Thucydides, for example, clearly believed that a variety of emotions (such as a sense of honour) were crucial for understanding inter-state politics. Similarly, although Hobbes is sometimes reduced to a caricature in IRT, a careful reading of his work reveals that his theory of politics is actually founded on a remarkably broad conception of the 'passions' and a wide-ranging physiological theory about the interplay between instrumental reason and the emotions (Flathman 1993, Frost 1993). Other analyses have also shown that assumptions about the role and nature of emotions are both crucial to, but deeply under-theorized by, a wide range of modern scholars of international politics. Neta Crawford, for example, has shown that implicit assumptions about the role of emotions have heavily influenced (and continue to) a variety of seminal IR studies of the causes of war, patriotism, militarism, nationalism, and international cooperation (Crawford 2000). Other works also support this contention historically by showing that the rich psychological theories of Freud and Spengler (which challenged the optimism of *belle époque* rationalism and highlighted the role of darker drives and emotions in the human psyche) not only influenced general European attitudes about war and the shape of modern wars, but also deeply impacted the thought of many of the founders of the modern discipline of IR theory, such as E.H. Carr, Reinhold Niebuhr, Hans Morgenthau, and John Herz (Coker 1994, Ross 2005).

As such, it is clear that many foundational observers of international politics have explicitly or implicitly believed that, despite the methodological challenges of defining, investigating, and measuring the role of emotions, IRT must study the role and impact of emotions in international politics.

Overall, however, most post-World War II IRT has downplayed the role of emotions and badly under-examined their impact on global politics. Consider how Morgenthau deals with emotions. On one hand, as Crawford shows, emotions and desire are key elements of his writings (Crawford 2000). However, even Morgenthau's examination of emotions tends to subsume them into a framework that treats emotions through a lens of 'rationality' and 'irrationality', and focuses on only a strictly limited list of desires and instincts that are re-cast as 'rational' (e.g. desire for security and power – or in Thucydides' terms, 'fear' and 'interest'). Thus even in Morgenthau, virtually all other types of emotionally-tinged commitments and beliefs – for instance, ideological extremism, honour, respect – are dismissed as irrational and largely irrelevant to the study and practice of international politics.

This normative disavowal and analytic over-simplification of emotions can be found in the views of much of US post-World War II international policymaking community as well. It is well known that Edward Said's analysis of Henry Kissinger's writings on foreign policy reveals profoundly Orientalist tendencies at the core of Kissinger's approach (Said 1979: 47–50). What is less obvious, however, is that Said's analysis also inadvertently highlights the degree to which Kissinger's conceptual framework paralleled the classical realist strategy of simultaneously relying on a theory of emotions while also dismissing them as irrational and irrelevant for US policy. Kissinger saw the Cold War world as characterized by two distinct types of foreign policy. On one hand, he presented the developed, industrialized Western world as being deeply committed to rationalist, objectivist types of data recording and interpretation. This, Kissinger argued, leads to a rational, 'political' style of foreign policy in which diplomatic and strategic messages are easily sent and interpreted since everyone understands how to calculate the rational interests behind the posturing. In contrast, Kissinger identified a very different model of conducting foreign policy – something he termed the 'prophetic' model – which he mapped primarily onto the developing world. On Kissinger's telling, in this model, foreign policy is not conducted according to objective rational interests. Instead, it is influenced by opaque, internal, and irrational cultural desires and emotions. Tellingly, the key example used to highlight the difference between the two styles is Kissinger's assertion that it is utterly alien to the Western 'political' model to base any foreign policy decisions on the irrational desires for 'honour' and concerns about 'shame' or humiliation (which was precisely what he saw as characterizing 'Arab' foreign policy). In this context, if concerns about honour, shame, humiliation and respect were to be accepted as legitimate, they would have to be translated into the neutral language of 'credibility'.

This practical disavowal of the relevance of emotion to international politics has hardly been limited to realist hawks, however. In many ways, the core logic of diplomacy and diplomatic culture is the idea that the international community can (and should) eliminate the cultural differences and emotional elements from international politics. One main goal of the almost ritualistic repetition of very precise diplomatic protocols and norms is to minimize and control the misunderstandings and heightened emotional reactions that often emerge from less-structured interactions between actors with very different cultural expectations, norms and triggers. Meetings, peace negotiations and conferences are often held at the same hotels. Communiqués are issued using very similar words and formulations. All this creates the appearance of a level field of engagement, with a globally set of shared norms, meanings, modes of communication. And that, in turn, encourages practitioners and observers to assume that emotional and cultural elements are largely irrelevant to diplomacy and conflict mediation.

It was the behaviouralist turn in the social sciences, however, that cemented the academic belief that we should ignore the role of emotions in international politics. The behaviouralist perspective not only intensified the classical realist tendency to reject the legitimacy of 'emotions' other than fear/security and interest/power. It also shut out the study of emotions by dramatically narrowing the forms of authorized scholarly investigation and methodological approaches to perspectives that had no room or tools for examining emotion – a variable deemed too fuzzy and unmeasurable for behaviouralist orientations (Cox 1990, Ashley 1990). This in turn meant that even those few IR scholars (such as Robert Jervis and Irving Janis) who sought to examine the impact of emotion tended to conceptualize emotions as anomalous limiting conditions that could explain otherwise irrational exceptions to the norm. Many of the key studies of conflict resolution reproduce this tendency to minimize the importance of emotions. In *Getting to Yes*, for example, seminal negotiation scholars Fisher and Ury assume that in interactions between states and individuals, actors are able 'to separate the people from the problem' and find constructive outcomes by focusing on interests, not positions (Fisher and Ury 1991: 17–40). Not only does such a position assume that emotions themselves are not central factors in conflicts. It also assumes that if any emotional elements are ever at play, actors can easily and quickly rid themselves of such epiphenomenal elements and focus on the real interests at stake. This tendency is not unique to Fisher and Ury, moreover. Similar tendencies can be seen in much of the other seminal literature on conflict resolution and international mediation discussed in the introductory chapter of this book.

One consequence of this broad tendency to downplay and ignore the role of emotions is that most scholars and practitioners of international politics refuse to raise the question of emotions in conflicts, even in cases where the potential impact of emotions would seem almost impossible to deny. Take, for example, the case of the role of the emotion of humiliation – something that would seem to have been particularly relevant to the post-9/11 global politics of the 21st century thus far. When we previously examined the role of humiliation in post-9/11 politics (Saurette 2006), we found only a few studies that examined the impact that humiliation has played in historical political events;[3] even fewer studies that attempted to examine the role of humiliation in relation to the United States;[4] and virtually no scholarly attempts at systematically and critically examining the influence of humiliation in post-9/11 global politics. Today, there are still fewer than a handful of studies that have pursued this theme further, despite its obvious and widespread potential relevance to contemporary conflicts in global politics.

Emotions and International Conflicts – New Perspectives

Recently, however, there has been a resurgence of interest in the role of emotions. Scholars in a wide variety of disciplines have again taken up the study of emotions in ways that appreciate both the many cross-cultural similarities and the historically and culturally specific dimensions of virtually all types of emotions that have been studied (Ahmed 2004, Barbalet 2003, 2001, Turner and Spets 2005). An increasing, and increasingly diverse, number of scholars interested in the study of politics have also begun to examine the intersection of emotion and politics. Since the late 1990s, political theorist William Connolly has critically engaged the work of a range of cutting-edge neuroscientists (including Antonio Damasio, Joseph LeDoux, V.S. Ramachandran and Francisco Varela) in an effort to help political scientists understand the central role of affect and emotion in politics, especially various forms of identity politics (Connolly 2005, 2002, 1999). The work of Drew Westen – a professor of psychology who has increasingly examined political psychology – has added important empirical studies of how emotion impacts elections and other political phenomena as well as theoretical reflections that further highlight its place in politics (Westen 2007). In fact, Nobel Prize winner in economics Daniel Kahneman's 2011 *Thinking Fast, Thinking Slow* (a book that summarizes the ways that emotional and other 'non-rational' components essential to thinking play a significant role in human decision-making and profoundly affect an array of social, economic and political phenomena) even became a *New York Times* bestseller.

---

3 There are some sociological and psychological studies which examine and catalogue the specific impact of humiliation in certain conflicts – but none outline a robust theory of humiliation nor offer a broader consideration of its role in international politics. Within IR theory, some articles have touched on questions of humiliation, but without offering a robust theory of humiliation or applying it to broader issues of IR theory (Callahan 2004, Harkavy 2000).

4 The fascinating work of Blema Steinberg is one of the few sustained examinations of themes of shame and humiliation in foreign policy decisionmaking. See Steinberg 1991a, 1991b; Renshon 1997.

It is thus perhaps not surprising that some of these insights have begun to seep into the practice and study of international relations as well. For example, the clear consensus about the rationalist grounds of 'normal' foreign policy no longer seems quite clear-cut – even from a realist perspective. The end of the Cold War and the emergence of fears about renewed wars of nationalism have made it less easy to remain so confident that the boxes of 'interest' or 'fear' were sufficient for conducting and understanding global politics. Public intellectuals and academics have also begun to offer more nuanced theories that reflect a similar interest. Perhaps most notably in the post-9/11 context, scholars such as Bernard Lewis and Samuel Huntington have outlined a realist view of politics that takes seriously the importance of honour and humiliation in contemporary conflicts in international politics (although they too reproduced Kissinger's orientalized perspective by highlighting honour and humiliation as irrational preoccupations found primarily in 'Arabic' or 'Islamic' cultures) (Lewis 1990, Huntington 1993, Said 1998)

A wide range of scholars who operate with very different methodological, political and ethical commitments (ones often deeply opposed to those of Lewis and Huntington) have also begun to argue that a wider swathe of emotional concerns than simply fear and interest might be crucial to the formation of Western foreign policy. There are, in fact, several broad traditions whose methodological bases offer more room for an analysis of the role of emotions in international politics. Since the 1980s, for example, the work of a variety of critical feminists has produced a diverse set of stimulating, provocative and valuable insights about the types of concrete impacts that gendered emotional and identity-based commitments and performances can have on global politics (Cohn 1987; Cooke and Woollacott 1993; Enloe,1989,1993, Weber 1994, 1999, Goldstein 2001) These and other studies call attention to a range of what are seen as masculine emotional investments and demands (for macho respect, for self-sufficient sovereignty, for domestic and personal relations of control, for national credibility, etc.), chronicling their role in the specific practices of statecraft. Various 'critical IRT' approaches – perspectives that study the precise mechanisms and symbols of identity construction and the impact this has on global politics – offer the possibility of taking seriously the ways in which multiple layers of emotion are essential to global identities and politics (Campbell 1998a, 1998b, Neumann 1998, Doty 1996). Constructivism, with its attempt to provide a more nuanced account of the constructed and constructive role of beliefs and emotions, should in theory also be more open to these questions. There is also a small but growing number of IR theorists willing to explore questions of emotion in detail (Edkins 2002, 2003, Lifton 2005). That said, surprisingly few critical IR theorists[5] and constructivist[6] scholars have taken up the challenge of studying the role of emotions. With the notable exception of Andrew Ross, there has been relatively little systematic theorization and exploration of the role of emotions in international politics (Ross 2006, Mercer 2005). Further exploration of the role of emotions in global politics therefore remains a pressing task.

A Hard Case: The Cuban Missile Crisis

But what does understanding the role of emotions mean, concretely, for the study of international conflicts? And what does all this have to do with the role that dialogue plays in resolving conflicts? Since the discussions in the sections above have been largely theoretical, it might be useful to turn now to several case studies to shed light on the role that emotions can play in international politics – and the possible implications for our evaluation of the potential and limits of dialogue as a practice in international politics.

As noted in the introduction to this chapter, sceptics often charge that dialogue is a hopelessly idealistic strategy – one that assumes we live in a utopian world of good intentions. Such a strategy, they argue, does little more than allow ruthless actors to manipulate things for their own benefit. But is this true across the board? Hardly. If we examine the examples of history, we can see how mistaken a generalized scepticism to dialogue is.

So as not to be accused of ignoring the 'hard cases' of history, we begin with one of the most potentially disastrous and seemingly intractable strategic crises of the post-World War II era: the 1962 Cuban Missile Crisis. In many ways, it presents an ideal case for dialogue sceptics. Here was a classic example of what is often called a Track I negotiation setting (see the introduction for a more detailed discussion of Track I, II and III negotiation). It started as a conflict in which all main actors believed that their basic existential security was at stake. It evolved into a crisis where the main actors eventually believed that military conflict was almost inevitable and that there was virtually no chance of a negotiated solution. To dialogue sceptics, this seems to be a perfect example

---

5 As we have argued elsewhere, while a few critical IR theorists of identity have attempted to consider the role of emotion, much of this literature has focused on the symbolic and discursive techniques and tactics of identity creation rather than embracing the Deleuzian challenge of creating a critical ethology that would trace the emotional dimensions of the key social assemblages and structures of global politics (Saurette 2000).

6 Constructivism has largely ignored this area by under-playing the visceral nature of emotions and too quickly reducing emotional elements to 'beliefs' as opposed to affective forces (Mercer 2005, Ross 2006).

of a rational-actor crisis situation that was to be solved only through strong military action (naval blockade) with threats of further armed intervention.

But this interpretation leaves out many key dimensions of the story. In particular, it overlooks the central role that emotion and dialogue played in one of the most high-stakes international crises of negotiation and armed confrontation in the post-WWII era of international politics and negotiation. Most historical analyses of the crisis have highlighted (without always explicitly naming it as such) that some of the key factors in creating the conditions that allowed the crisis to emerge initially were (i) the gut feeling in the Soviet leadership that J.F. Kennedy was emotionally weak and indecisive and (ii) deep-seated, viscerally powerful emotional dislike and distrust between key decisionmakers in the USA and USSR. Moreover, this animosity and distrust became even more emotionally charged and influential amongst US decisionmakers when it became clear that the Soviets had openly deceived the USA at various points in the lead-up to the crisis.

If the Cuban Missile Crisis highlights the impact of emotional factors, it also underscores the relevance of dialogue even in situations that seem inextricable. For although many claim that the crisis was resolved solely through the US naval blockade and the threat of the use of further force (and these were important factors), it is also undeniable that dialogue at various levels – between embassies, between third-party countries and institutions like the UN, and between Kennedy and Khrushchev directly – was crucial for finding a solution that averted war. These dialogue processes allowed the parties to slowly counteract and shift the emotional animosity that had been building up – and, interestingly, these processes were far from straightforward and easy. The letters between Khrushchev and Kennedy are particularly striking, showing the back-and-forth, start-and-stop, sometimes tough sometimes conciliatory, nature of dialogue in international politics. They also reveal the degree to which the solution that ultimately allowed the defusing of the crisis was not evident *before* dialogue. With no dialogue, the crisis seemed irreconcilable and destined for military confrontation. With dialogue, Kennedy and Khrushchev discovered a way to avoid armed conflict.

Dialogue did not solve all the strategic issues at stake, of course. It did not resolve all the mistrust, animosity and competition between the countries. Nor was it dialogue alone that solved the crisis. However, it was an essential element. Moreover, we have a fairly good idea of what probably would have happened if dialogue rejectionism had prevailed in October 1962 – and that is sobering. Although the US leadership did not know it then, there were already 162 nuclear warheads in Cuba at the time of the crisis. Moreover, Fidel Castro later confirmed not only that he *would have* recommended that the USSR use them if Cuba had been invaded, but that he in fact *had* recommended to Khrushchev that they be used in the event of an attack. Dialogue may not have ended the Cold War in October 1962. But it probably achieved something far more important: avoiding nuclear war.

In the striking 2003 documentary *The Fog of War*, Robert McNamara (US Secretary of Defense at the time of the crisis) draws up various lessons from the Cuban Missile Crisis and his other experiences as Defense Secretary in the 1960s (*The Fog of War*, 2003). It is striking that the two first lessons he mentions are that 'rationality will not save us' in international politics, *and* that the key tactic for dealing with this situation is to 'empathize with your enemy'. What he means by this is not that we simply need to be more altruistic. Rather, he is saying that decision makers must try to understand both the logical *and* emotional motivations of their opponents – in McNamara's words: 'try to put ourselves inside [our opponent's] skin and try to look at us through their eyes, just to understand the thoughts that lie behind their decisions and their actions'. Decision makers must put an enormous amount of energy into this task, he says, because humans not only possess incomplete information, but also are deeply 'feeling' beings whose emotional reactions often influence them in ways they cannot easily understand. Even elite decision makers are deeply susceptible to misinterpreting the meaning of events, to 'seeing what they want to believe', and to allowing their feelings guide their behaviour in ways that are often far from rational.

According to McNamara, key to the resolution of the Cuban Missile Crisis was that some US decision makers were eventually able to empathize with Khrushchev. How was this possible? Notably for the argument in this chapter, that ability to empathize was partially a result of the various processes of dialogue that took place throughout the crisis. It was also due to the fact that Kennedy was able to rely on a key advisor (Llewellyn E. 'Tommy' Thompson) to interpret correctly the contradictory messages that had been sent by the Soviets and champion a solution that both Kennedy and Khrushchev could accept.

Why was Thompson able to do this? An important part of the explanation is that Thompson, the US Ambassador to the Soviet Union both before (1957–February 1962) and after (1967–1969) the crisis, had actually lived with Khrushchev for a period of time and had dialogued with Khrushchev in many contexts (some Track I, some Track II), on many different topics, over the years. On one level, those experiences of dialogue were crucial, probably creating a deep level of understanding that allowed Thompson to read between the lines, understand some of the less obvious (human) contexts driving the dynamics in the Politburo, and craft a solution that would allow both the USSR and the USA save face. Thompson was able to achieve this because he was capable of being emotionally open to empathizing with the Soviet leadership. And why was he capable of this type of empathy? Most likely this was because his prior experiences of sustained dialogue had cultivated in Thompson a certain emotional sympathy for Khrushchev that helped insulate him from the intensely emotional distrust and animosity that had built up in the Kennedy Cabinet during the intensely pressurized crisis.

Nothing, of course, can guarantee that decision makers will fully empathize with an adversary and creatively problem-solve and negotiate. However, the case of the Cuban Missile Crisis shows how both immediate and long-term Track I (and Track II) dialogue processes can be crucial in creating not only the knowledge necessary to resolve international issues, but also the emotional resources (empathy, patience, openness, etc.) that can be key factors in breaking through the distrust, animosity and group-think tunnel vision often created by highly intense and emotional confrontations. It suggests, therefore, that investing in dialogue through negotiations or personal contact between decision makers at various levels and over sustained periods of time certainly improves the ability to interpret events correctly and navigate the emotional politics that are often at the core of global politics. In *The Fog of War*, McNamara suggests that the presence or absence of this type of emotional empathy is what differentiated the USA's successful resolution of the Cuban Missile Crisis from the disastrous decision to deepen its involvement in Vietnam. According to McNamara, the fact that USA had invested so little in any real dialogue with the North Vietnamese meant that it badly overestimated the strategic threat to the USA, underestimated the determination and will of the North Vietnamese to fight until the very end, and was unable to step back from its own emotional investment because of the conviction that, as the dominant superpower, the USA could not could not retreat under any circumstances.

The Emotional Formation of Conflicts: Humiliation and Post-9/11 Foreign Policy

Many analogies can be drawn between McNamara's historical analysis of the emotional aspects of the US–Soviet negotiations during the Cuban Missile Crisis and important aspects of the conflicts in the world after the events of 9/11. McNamara himself argued that the US invasion of Iraq in 2003 repeated many of the same errors that had been made in Vietnam, most importantly the 'failure to appreciate the complexities of Iraqi culture'. We could go even farther, however, and suggest that the emotional context of 9/11 – in particular, strong feelings of humiliation – not only played a key role in motivating the US decision to reject continued diplomatic efforts and instead invade Iraq, but also inhibited its key decisionmakers from properly empathizing with/planning for the reactions of various Iraqi actors to a US intervention (Saurette 2006). In this sense, then, the 2003 invasion of Iraq illustrates how ignorance of the emotional dimension and unwillingness to engage in practices of dialogue can undermine attempts at conflict resolution and dramatically erode the success of military interventions.

Let us begin with the way emotions like humiliation can motivate foreign policy. The feeling of humiliation is a complex emotion that emerges when deeply held beliefs about oneself (beliefs that act as the basis of one's self-respect and dignity) are forcibly and publicly stripped away and revealed as false. Might this emotion have been at play with George W. Bush and his senior advisors? One way to answer this (without delving into the personal biographies of these actors) is to examine the characteristics that were central to the public roles these key decision makers held. What, for example, were some of the key foundations of Bush's self-respect as the President of the United States of America?

We begin with the fact that Bush occupies the Office of the Chief Executive. What are some of the characteristics that a self-respecting president must display? And what are some of the elements that the US public commonly assumes are required for the president to retain his dignity and self-respect? While the precise bases of different presidents' self-respect vary (Kennedy's bases were certainly very different than Reagan's, as Obama's are from those of Bush), common to virtually all occupants of the office is the appearance of strength, resoluteness, determination, invulnerability and power – in sum, conventional masculinity. In *The Wimp Factor: Gender Gaps, Holy Wars, and the Politics of Anxious Masculinity*, for example, psychologist John Ducat convincingly shows not only that the bases of much masculine self-respect build on a deep phobia and disavowal of the feminine – but more specifically that modern US presidential politics have become fundamentally premised on the ability of office-holders to prove that they are not wimps, wussies, mama's boys or sissies (Ducat 2004).

If the public common sense standards that define recent US presidential politics push the office-holder to see the bases of self and public respect as heavily influenced by traditional standards of masculinity, this seems particularly true of George W. Bush. His electoral persona and character (central to both his presidential victories) were fundamentally premised on his image as a particularly down-home, good ole boy. In contrast to his more patrician father (who was once mercilessly ridiculed after asking for a 'splash' of coffee), Bush Jr. succeeded because his persona presented him as a down-home, cuppa joe Texas kind of guy. Unsurprisingly, this also became the fundamental basis for his post-9/11 Commander-in-Chief persona. Consider the metaphors Bush used early and often in the war on terror. It was the USA against 'the thugs' and 'the outlaws', and the USA was 'gonna get Saddam – dead or alive'. The world would learn not to mess with Texas because Bush was 'gonna smoke 'em out from their caves'. It is not surprising that this down-home, commonsense, man-of-the-people persona easily led into the language of good and evil, black and white. Real men don't worry about the analytic details, they decide with their gut feelings. They don't worry about rules, they get stuff done. They don't take guff – and they don't make nice.

The point is not that George W. Bush himself was a cowboy. The point is that, given the office Bush held and the public persona he employed to get elected, his external perception and self-respect – as well as the perceptions and respect for him from significant portions of the broader public – were based on expectations about resoluteness, determination, strength in the face of adversity, and unwillingness to turn the other cheek. In such a position, it would be hard not to be obsessed with questions of proper respect, credibility and the threat of humiliation. It would be hard not to experience the 9/11 attacks as a profound humiliation – revealing, as it did, the hollowness of the image of the US President as the virile Commander-in-Chief of the world, able to stand up with strength, determination, invulnerability and power without fear of reprisal or personal vulnerability. The events of 9/11 either proved this faith to be radically naïve – or, even worse, threatened to show that Bush and the Republicans had not been 'man enough' to deter and scare evil-doers. From this perspective, then, it would be almost impossible for Bush to avoid interpreting the attacks of 9/11 as not only a threat, but also a very deep humiliation.

Moreover, there is evidence to suggest that this feeling of humiliation was probably intensely operative not only for the President, but also for other key senior political decision makers as well as the strategic community (Saurette 2006). Take, for example, a policy paper titled 'National Humiliation' by Robert Kagan and William Kristol, published five months before 9/11 in the neo-conservative *Weekly Standard* and reprinted widely (for example, by the Carnegie Endowment for Peace and the Project for a New American Century) (Kagan and Kristol 2001). In it, Kagan and Kristol proved incredibly sensitive to perceived moments of US humiliation in the eyes of potential rivals. In particular, their interpretation of the Sino-US diplomatic scuffle over the return of a crew from a crashed US surveillance aircraft asserted that the Chinese demand for an official apology from Washington was a blatant attempt to 'inflict upon the United States a public international humiliation' (ibid.). According to Kagan and Kristol, giving into this pressure and apologizing would have been a major mistake. In their words, apologizing put 'the United States on the path to humiliation'; 'for a great power, not to mention the world's sole superpower, humiliation is not a matter to be taken lightly. It is not just a petty issue of 'face' (ibid.: 12). They therefore excoriated Colin Powell's diplomatic statements of regret (even though Powell made it clear they were not an apology) and sadly noted: 'President Bush has revealed weakness. And he has revealed fear' (ibid.). This 'American capitulation', they claimed, would both allow China to be more aggressive regarding Taiwan and would 'also embolden others around the world' to challenge US interests. They categorically opined: 'this defeat and humiliation … must not stand' (ibid.).

Perhaps equally important, deep and widespread feelings of anger, fear, outrage and humiliation also seem to have characterized post-9/11 US public opinion. While there has been much debate in IRT about the relevance of domestic factors for the creation of foreign policy, most commentators recognize that public and national expectations, emotions and judgments are becoming increasingly critical influences on foreign policy formulation (Wittkopf and McCormick 2004). Arguably, many of same commitments and emotional responses of humiliation that were influential in the community of key decision makers were also operative (although in different ways) in the wider US public.

For example, with appropriate qualifiers, we would hold that there are some widely (albeit not universally) held commitments and self-understandings (which become particularly solidified in times of crisis) that closely link the core identity of the United States as great power to notions of masculinity – like strength, invulnerability, determination, resolution. Moreover, this popular self-perception of the USA as invulnerable has also been fused with conceptions about the 'American dream' and 'American exceptionalism' (Wooldridge and Micklethwait 2004). Robert Jay Lifton, for example, synthesizes the resulting identity when he suggests that a significant element of US public consciousness is defined by a 'superpower syndrome' which holds not only that the USA is omnipotent – but that it is entitled to expect respect, deference and indeed receive special 'dispensation' for its actions American Apocalypse' (Lifton 2003)

If this is the case, then as a nation, popular consciousness in the USA seems primed to interpret any lack of proper respect for the country's omnipotence as a profound humiliation. It is thus hardly surprising to find expressions of an aggressive reaction against this humiliation in the back-and-forth between Bush and the crowds on his first visit to the site of the fallen towers of the World Trade Center days after the attack. (George W. Bush – 9/11 Bullhorn Speech 2009)

For what is conveyed in this interaction is not only the sorrow, anger and patriotism of a group determined to make their country safe again. We can also hear the overtones of a deep anger that seeks to reassert national pride and self-respect in the face of this humiliation. Bush's choice of words is revealing. For he did not merely thank the rescue workers for their hard work, exceptional self-sacrifice and success in saving lives. He also made a point of thanking them for 'making the nation proud'. In so doing, Bush instinctively tapped into and expressed a deep desire to rebel against and overturn the humiliation of 9/11.

Arguably, this emotional context is crucial to understanding some of the key events of global politics in the first several decades of the 21st century. At the macro-level, understanding feelings and practices of humiliation and counter-humiliation helps illuminate important elements of the overall dynamic of US – Middle East relations. It is a truism – but no less valid for that – that many religious and political groups in the Middle East explicitly interpret and understand U.S policy towards Palestine and the Arab world as a humiliation of Islam (Telhaim 2003, 2013). In this context, it would seem plausible to see feelings of being humiliated as an important part of the story that explains not only the motivations of the al-Qaeda attacks – but also why their cause has resonated in various populations across the Middle East, including among some groups that are largely anti-Islamist. Understanding the feeling of, and reactions to, emotions like humiliation is essential for grasping this.

Understanding the emotional force of humiliation also helps us understand why the attacks were almost immediately viewed through the lens of a 'clash of civilization', and were translated into the language of good and evil with Bush's accompanying analogies to the Crusades. Can we explain the resonance of the language of the clash of civilizations in the broader US population and the willingness to use and accept the language of evil simply by reference to Bush's religious views or the 'Orientalist/Islamophobic' nature of American public culture, as some commentators suggest? Or is part of the reason why this language resonated so widely is that it spoke to the emotional depths of the wounds of national humiliation, feelings shared well beyond the percentage of the population who identify themselves as deeply and fundamentally religious?

Consider a very different conflict, the recent Syrian crisis, and US President Obama's response. In many ways, Obama appeared to be confronted by a serious foreign policy dilemma when, after having claimed that the use of chemical weapons in the civil war was a 'red line' that would automatically trigger US involvement, evidence emerged that the Assad regime had indeed employed chemical weapons. The analysis offered by many pundits was similar. Obama had made an unequivocal commitment. If he failed to act on it, this would not only show him to be weak and indecisive, but would also humiliate Obama himself and the country and provoke further challenges to US interests and power. Given the fact that Democrats have traditionally been accused of being weak on foreign policy, this placed Obama in a particularly difficult position. If he did nothing, he would be painted as a coward who had allowed the nation to be profoundly humiliated. As such, although the Syrian crisis was much less emotional for much of the US population than was 9/11, it was likely an intensely emotional issue with deeply personal stakes for the main decision makers in Washington.

Yet Obama not only avoided using force (even a low-cost version of responding with a symbolic amount of force), but also remained open to a diplomatic solution and dialogue process with Russia – even though doing so opened Obama up to critique as being weak and allowed a rival like Putin to gain crucial political capital on the world stage. How did this come about? One reading of this (a version of the dialogue idealist thesis) is that Obama, as the quintessential cerebral lawyer, simply eliminated emotions from his calculus and was able to see the issue more clearly and rationally than his critics. While that may be part of the picture, this explanation seems insufficient. In fact, insider reports do *not* portray Obama as rejecting the emotional dimensions of the decision. Instead, they indicate that Obama found a different way to frame the issue, one that allowed key figures to feel pride in their decision to avoid using force, even if it was criticized by many in the political establishment. For example, Ben Rhodes, Deputy National Security Advisor for Strategic Communication, has suggested that Obama viewed the decision not merely through the prism of a simplistic analysis of the immediate stakes of the crisis and the likely effect on his own presidential strategic credibility – as one of Obama's advisors noted, it was important to challenge the schoolyard logic and remember that 'you don't go to war in Syria to send a message to Russian not to invade Crimea' (Burleigh 2014). Rather, according to Rhodes, the key point was that Obama reframed the question more broadly in reference to the type of leadership and power that he believed presidents should, and should not, exercise:

> Only someone who had been president for several years could have been making the argument he was making. He cited previous decisions of his own. He cited the sense of the country and how public opinion needed to be better reflected in his decision-making and how he wanted to leave things for whoever comes next. I think he would have been far less likely to come to that decision in the first year of his presidency (ibid.).

It has since come to light that the ultimate solution to the crisis emerged as a result of both a long-standing policy planning process that valued and believed in the importance of continued diplomacy and set of impromptu, but probably not coincidental, remarks made by John Kerry in the form of a hypothetical continuation of ongoing dialogue about potential ways to avoid military confrontation (Terkel 2013).

This suggests that both intellectual self-reflexivity and emotional maturity – as well as a conscious valorization of dialogue – were crucial in allowing Obama to recast the emotional dimension of the crisis and its potential dialogue solution in ways that could be emotionally empowering to the President. It was not the absence of emotion that allowed dialogue to remain a diplomatic option for the USA. It was the reframing of certain traditional emotional narratives and understandings in ways that allowed diplomatic dialogue to become an emotionally compelling solution that the administration could be proud of. This, combined with a willingness to continue employing diplomatic processes of dialogue long after they appeared to be useful, created the opening that allowed for a resolution that did not require military intervention.

In a context where cries of 'appeasement' and references to Neville Chamberlain and Nazi Germany have been common staples, the Obama administration's ability to achieve this is no mean feat. This suggests that a foreign policy that works hard to remain open to the possibility that dialogue can provide key constructive potential solutions in even the most apparently intractable conflicts (as with the Cuban Missile Crisis). Further, a foreign policy that recognizes the importance of emotional elements (as factors often pushing towards the use of military force, and as a dimension that must be positively framed in the championing of diplomatic and dialogue related strategies) may be an important ideal to aim for, even if its actual application in practice may be difficult and challenging to achieve.

Conclusions

In this chapter, we have sought to make several points about why observers and participants of international politics need a better understanding how emotions and dialogue are crucial to modern global politics. First, we have shown that many scholars and practitioners of international politics have systematically ignored the role that emotions play in global politics and, partially as a function of this, have tended either to dismiss dialogue as a legitimate foreign policy option, or to view it as a relatively straightforward tool whose success depends on the ability to focus on core interests and exclude all emotional and other 'peripheral' investments.

Second, we have sought to demonstrate that these approaches are misguided. We have argued that understanding emotions and their impact on decision making at all levels is crucial for understanding and navigating in international politics today. In particular, we have shown how emotional dimensions have influenced some of the most important historical and contemporary events in international politics. We have also tried to show that how policymakers and decision makers understand and respond to these emotional dimensions have a significant impact on whether moments of tension and conflict can be successfully resolved.

Third, we have shown that processes of dialogue are crucial tools that can aid in managing and navigating the emotionally charged world of global politics and that both Track I and Track II types of dialogue can play significant roles in understanding and managing emotionally charged situations in international politics. Further, we have also argued that these practices of dialogue can be important on different 'levels' of international politics. They can help in terms of individual as well as group interactions at the elite level since they can prove crucial in helping to mitigate the distrust, animosity and other negative personal feelings often present in tense situations. These practices can also have an important role in mitigating broader collective emotional sentiments in public opinion. In contemporary global politics, these domestic pressures are often an important context for, and influencing factor on, foreign policy decisions.

Fourth, although there has not been enough space to investigate this in detail here, we believe that our findings have implications for how dialogue may be used to reduce the intensity of major intercultural, or inter-civilizational, global tensions and conflicts. Once we understand the central role that emotions play in global politics – especially regarding global identity politics and the fact that much of the world perceives US (and Western) military interventions as colonial, disrespectful and humiliating – it becomes clear that many of the Western foreign policy choices of recent decades have been particularly misguided, serving only served to heighten the emotional stakes of certain tensions. One example of this can be found in the responses of the USA to the events in Egypt following the 2011 Arab Spring. It is clearly no longer enough for the West to engage in rational elite negotiations and make policy decisions based on these considerations. The USA in particular would have greatly benefited from engaging the local citizenry in a much deeper and wider public diplomacy in Egypt through various Track I and II dialogue efforts. That would have offered the possibility of actively and concretely combating widespread anti-American sentiments – which in turn could have expanded US influence not only in Egypt, but also possibly more widely across the Middle East. Instead, US decision makers chose to largely ignore this aspect – leaving them in a much weaker place of influence.

This reality is certainly not limited to Egypt. It seems clear that most of the 'intractable' conflicts that exist in the world become underpinned and further intensified by a range of emotional factors. Creating a sustainable resolution to the question of Israel and Palestine, for example, is unimaginable unless there can be an active understanding of the emotional components and a very concrete plan for dealing with these dimensions – both in the lead-up to any real peace negotiations, and for any lasting settlement. Otherwise, any long-term solution will not only be unsustainable: it will not even be born. The distrust and animosity is so deep and intense that merely getting to a place of negotiation is impossible.

That is not to say that once we understand the role of emotions and the importance of processes of dialogue, it will be possible to navigate easily, and resolve all crises and tensions in the world. Far from it. Conflict resolution and mediation are incredibly difficult and delicate endeavours that may fail for many, many reasons. However, a better understanding of the importance of the emotional dimension of international politics – and the way that dialogue processes can address these elements – may help practitioners resolve conflicts more successfully than they otherwise would.

References

Ahmed, S. 2004. *The Cultural Politics of Emotions*. New York: Routledge.

American Apocalypse, *The Nation* [Online 22 December]. Available at: http:// www.thenation.com/article/american-apocalypse [accessed: 25 July 2014].

Ashley, R. 1990. The Poverty of Neorealism, in *Neorealism and its Critics*, edited by R. Keohane. New York: Columbia University Press.

Barbalet, J.M. 2003. *Emotions and Sociology*. Oxford: Blackwell.

Barbalet, J.M. 2001. *Emotion, Social Theory, and Social Structure*. Cambridge: Cambridge University.

Burleigh, N. 2014. Obama vs. the Hawks, *Rolling Stone*, 10 April, 36.

Bush, G.W. 2009. 9/11 Bullhorn Speech [Online]. Available at: http://www. youtube.com/watch?v=x7OCgMPX2mE [accessed: 25 July 2014].

Campbell, D. 1998. *Writing Security: United States Foreign Policy and the Politics of Identity*. Minneapolis, MN: University of Minnesota Press.

Campbell, D. 1998. *National Deconstruction*. Minneapolis, MN: University of Minnesota Press.

Cohn, C. 1987. Sex and Death in the Rational World of the Defense Intellectuals, *Signs*, 687–718.

Coker, C. 1994. *War and the 20th Century: The Impact of War on the Modern Consciousness*. London: Potomac Books.

Connolly, W.E. 2005. *Pluralism*. Durham, NC: Duke University Press.

Connolly, W.E.2002. *Neuropolitics*. Minneapolis, MN: University of Minnesota Press.

Connolly, W.E. 1991. *Why I am Not a Secularist*. Minneapolis, MN: University of Minnesota Press.

Cooke, M. 1993. War, Wimps and Women, in *Gendering War Talk*, edited by M. Cooke and A. Woollacott. Princeton, NJ: Princeton University Press, 227–46.

Cox, R. 1990. Social Forces, State and World Orders, in *Neorealism and its Critics*, edited by R. Keohane. New York: Columbia University Press.

Crawford, N.C. 2000. The Passion of World Politics, *International Security*, 24(4) 116–65.

Doty, R.L. 1996. *Imperial Encounters*. Minneapolis, MN: University of Minnesota Press.

Ducat, J. 2004. *The Wimp Factor*. Boston MA: Beacon Press.

Edkins, J. 2002. Forget Trauma? Responses to 9/11, *International Relations*. 16(2), 243–56.

Edkins, J. *2003. Trauma and the Memory of Politics.* Cambridge: Cambridge University Press.

Enloe, C. 1989. *Bananas, Beaches, and Bases: Making Feminist Sense of International Politics.* Berkeley: University of California Press.

Enloe, C. 1993. *The Morning After: Sexual Politics at the End of the Cold War* Berkeley: University of California Press.

Fisher, R. and Ury, W. 1991. *Getting to Yes: Negotiating Agreement Without Giving In.* New York: Penguin Books.

Flathman, R. 1993. *Thomas Hobbes: Skepticism, Individuality and Chastened Politics* Newbury Park, CA: Sage.

Frost, S. 1993. Faking It: Hobbes' Thinking-Bodies and the Ethics of Dissimulation, *Political Theory*, 21(1), 30–57.

Goldstein, J.S. 2001. *War and Gender: How Gender Shapes the War System and Vice Versa.* Cambridge: Cambridge University Press.

Huntington, S. 1993. Clash of Civilizations, *Foreign Policy*, 72(3), 22–49.

Huntington, S. 1996. *Clash of Civilizations.* New York: Simon & Schuster.

Kagan, W. and Kristol, R. 2001. National Humiliation, *Weekly Standard*, April 9, 2001, 11–15.

Kahneman, D. 2011. *Thinking Fast, Thinking Slow.* New York: Farrar, Straus & Giroux.

Keynes, J.M. 1919. *The Economic Consequences of the Peace*, New York, Harcourt: Brace & Howe.

Lewis, B. 1990. The Roots of Muslim Rage, *The Atlantic Monthly*, 266(3) 47–60.

Lifton, R.J. 2003. *Superpower Syndrome: America's Apocalyptic Confrontation with the World.* New York: Nation Books.

Lifton, R.J. 2005. Americans as Survivors, *New England Journal of Medicine.* 352, 2263–5.

Mercer, J. 2005. Rationality and Psychology in International Politics, *International Organization*, 59, 97–8.

Neumann, I. 1998. *Uses of the Other: The East in European Identity Formation.* Minneapolis, MN: University of Minnesota Press.

Ross, A. 2005. *Affective States: Rethinking Passion and Global Politics*, Ph.D. dissertation, Johns Hopkins University.

Ross, A. 2006. Coming in from the Cold: Constructivism and Emotions, *European Journal of International Relations*, 12(2), 197–222.

Said, E.W. 1979. *Orientalism.* New York: Vintage.

Saurette, P. 2000. International Relations' Image of Thought: Collective Identity, Desire, and Deleuzian Ethology, *International Journal of Peace Studies*, 5(1).

Saurette, P. 2006. You Dissin' Me? Humiliation and Post 9/11 Global Politics, *Review of International Studies*, 32, 495–522.

Telhami, S. 2013. Is Kerry Right to Put Peace First' *Foreign Policy* [Online, 22 July]. Available at: http://www.foreignpolicy.com/articles/2013/07/22/why_

israel_palestine_still_number_one_issue_in_the_middle_east [accessed: 25 July 2014].

Telhami, S. 2003. History and Humiliation, *Washington Post* [Online 28 March]. Available at: http://www.brookings.edu/research/opinions/2003/03/28iraq-telhami [accessed: 25 July 2014].

Terkel, A. 2013. John Kerry's Syria Solution in the Works for Months, *Huffington Post*, [Online, 10 September]. Available at: http://www.huffingtonpost.com/2013/09/10/john-kerry-syria-solution_n_3901863.html [accessed: July 25 2014].

The Fog of War (dir. Morris, E.) [Online]. Available at: http://www.sonyclassics.com/fogofwar [Accessed 27 July 2014].

Turner, J. and Spets, J. 2005. *The Sociology of Emotions*. Cambridge: Cambridge University Press.

Weber, C. 1990. *Faking It: U.S. Foreign Policy in a Post-Phallic Era*. Minneapolis, MN: University of Minnesota Press.

Weber, C. 1994. *Simulating Sovereignties*. Cambridge: Cambridge University Press.

Westen, D. 2007. *The Political Brain*. New York: PublicAffairs.

Chapter 5

What Makes Dialogue and Diplomacy Work or Not? Russia – Georgia and Russia – Ukraine

Jakub M. Godzimirski

Introduction

This chapter investigates the role of diplomatic efforts at conflict prevention and solution in the context of two gravest conflicts in the recent history of Europe – the five-day war between Georgia and Russia in August 2008, and the conflict between Russia and Ukraine in 2014. The outbreak of open hostilities on the night of 7/8 August 2008 resulted in a full-scale military conflict between Georgia and Russia. In the case of the spring 2014 Ukrainian-Russian conflict, the most tense phase began on 1 March 2014, when Russian President Vladimir Putin won parliamentary approval to send Russian troops to Ukraine, and thousands of heavily armed 'green men' without insignia emerged in various locations in the Autonomous Republic of Crimea. However, unlike the situation in Georgia, the outbreak of open hostilities and full-scale war between Russia and Ukraine was prevented in this case. That was due in part to the reluctance of Ukrainian decision makers to respond to the Russian invasion of the Crimea peninsula with military resistance, and partly to diplomatic pressure exerted on Russia by certain Western powers that saw Russia's intervention as a grave violation of international law and the direct threat to the post-Cold War order in Europe.

In both instances, the Russian official justification was the need to protect ethnic Russians, Russian citizens and/or Russian-speakers in the conflict area. In the case of Georgia, Russia acted, as President Medvedev himself put it, 'to coerce Georgia to peace'. In the case of Ukraine, Russian officials justified the intervention by the need to protect ethnic Russians from the fascist threat stemming from the illegitimate government in Kiev that had taken power from President Viktor Yanukovych after a bloody coup supported by the West.

The two conflicts stand as watershed events in the recent history of Russia's relations with the post-Soviet states and the West, and as such deserve academic attention. Although diplomacy, dialogue and negotiations failed to prevent the outbreak of the conflicts, diplomatic efforts – first and foremost in the form of Track I diplomacy – played a major part in putting an end to open interstate hostilities and in preventing the local conflicts from spiralling out of control. It is therefore important to explore the role of diplomacy and dialogue in that context.

This study aims at answering questions concerning the role of dialogue and diplomacy in conflict prevention and containment in the cases of Russia/ Georgia and Russia/Ukraine/Crimea, as noted above. The first section briefly presents the historical background to the conflicts and turning points in their development. In the next section we examine the failed attempts at finding a peaceful solution. In the third part we explore the role of dialogue and diplomacy in putting an end to the armed phase of the conflicts. For both conflicts, the focus will be on the strategic rationales of the actors involved. However, because war propaganda stirred up emotions, making a solution more difficult, we also pay attention to the role of these emotional elements, dealt with by Paul Saurette and Henrik Thune in their chapter in this volume (see also Moïsi 2009). The two cases studied here can provide insights into what makes dialogue and negotiations work or not when actors misread each other's intentions or are unwilling to engage in dialogue because the stakes are too high, strategic positions irreconcilable and emotions too difficult to control.

Georgia, Ukraine and Russia: Historical Background and Turning Points

Both conflicts have deep historical roots, dating back to the period of the collapse of the Soviet Union and its aftermath. In the case of Georgia, the main bone of contention has been the status of two regions on the territory of the newly re-established Georgian state. However, the conflict has also had broader strategic ramifications, as it also concerned relations between the newly established Russia and 14 other post-Soviet states, and how those 15 actors were to relate to other centres of global and regional power – in particular, the integrating Europe under the EU, and the trans-Atlantic community.

This second dimension has been even clearer in the case of the conflict between Ukraine and Russia that broke out after the Maidan revolution in Ukraine in November 2013. Ukrainian President Viktor Yanukovych's decision to withdraw from negotiations with the EU and instead strengthen relations with Russia triggered a wave of protests that ended in bloodshed on the streets of Kiev, followed by Yanukovych being ousted from power. After having signed the agreement with the opposition on 21 February 2014 that was to put an end to the slaughter, Yanukovych decided to flee the country. The Ukrainian Parliament voted to remove him from power in a move that was contested by Russia. The new Ukrainian authorities were recognized and supported by the West, while Russia refused to accept this change: Moscow held that the new government lacked legitimacy, and saw Yanukovych as the president of the country. Developments in Ukraine have been interpreted as a conflict over influence in which Russia decided to respond to what the Kremlin saw as Western incursion in the Russian zone of exclusive interests. Russia responded by deploying 40,000 troops close to Ukrainian border, deploying unmarked troops to Crimea, and helping to stage a non-recognized referendum that was used on 18 March 2014 as official justification for Russia's annexation of this territory.

There is no point in analysing all the phases of the conflict in Georgia, given the abundant literature on the topic (Flikke and Godzimirski 2007, Blandy 2009, Independent International Fact-Finding Mission on the Conflict in Georgia 2009, Asmus 2010, Pukhov and Glantz 2010, Charap and Welt 2011). As regards Ukraine, there are many analytical texts describing the most recent phases, but the conflict is at the time of writing far from being resolved.

These conflicts that erupted in 2008 and 2014 had been in the offing for many years. In the case of Georgia, the armed clashes that started on 7 August were, as clearly stated in the IIFFM report, 'only the culminating point of a long period of increasing tensions, provocations and incidents' (Independent International Fact-Finding Mission on the Conflict in Georgia 2009: 11). In the case of Ukraine, the roots of the conflict go back to 1991, when Ukraine voted for independence, and the Ukrainian president, together with his Russian and Belarusian counterparts, gave the *coup de grâce* to the Soviet project. As the collapse of the Soviet Union was described by President Putin as the greatest geopolitical catastrophe of the twentieth century, reversing the negative consequences of that momentous event became an important strategic goal of the Putin regime. In Russia as well as in the West, Ukraine is widely seen as the most important geopolitical brick in the post-Soviet space. Control over Ukraine is therefore deemed crucial by those who want to strengthen links between the former Soviet republics and by those who hold that Russia cannot succeed in an imperial revival without securing control over Ukraine. Developments in Ukraine in 2013 and 2014 have therefore been interpreted by both Russia and the West as a zero-sum geopolitical game (White et al. 2010, Flikke 2013, Rywkin 2014). In November and December 2013 Putin could celebrate a victory over the West in the contest for Ukraine; however, as of February 2014, the West appeared to be getting the upper hand, and it seemed that Putin would have no other option than to swallow the bitter Ukrainian pill, as he had done in 2004 in the wake of the Orange Revolution. Instead, however, Putin decided to get tough. The conflict escalated – first in Crimea and then in the eastern part of Ukraine.

Unconventional Wars and Conventional Diplomacy?

Georgia

Full war in the Caucasus was a fact on 7 August 2008, but from the outset of the armed phase of the conflict, new diplomatic efforts were made to put an end to hostilities and prevent the conflict from spiralling out of control. The first to propose a ceasefire was US Secretary of State Condoleezza Rice, who already on 8 August presented a three-point ceasefire plan during her talks with Russian MFA Sergei Lavrov (Asmus 2010: 40). On 9 August 2008 the French Foreign Minister Bernard Kouchner, acting on behalf of the whole EU and accompanied by the Finnish Foreign Minister Alexander Stubb representing the OSCE, visited Tbilisi and presented a draft ceasefire agreement to Georgia's President Saakashvili, who accepted the proposal. However, Moscow rejected the idea and continued its military operations. It was not until 12 August that President Medvedev ordered Russian troops to halt their operations in Georgia.

The parties agreed on a six-point plan to put an end to hostilities. The plan provided for (1) the commitment to the non-use of force; (2) a permanent end to all military operations; (3) ensuring free access to humanitarian aid; (4) the return of Georgian armed forces to their normal deployments; (5) the withdrawal of Russian Federation armed forces to their positions from before the start of offensive operations; pending the development of 'international mechanisms', the Russian peacekeeping forces (i.e. the armed forces of the Russian Federation) were to undertake 'additional security measures'; (6) the opening of an international debate on the status of South Ossetia and Abkhazia, and on means to ensure their security.

In the course of one week – between 7 and 12 August – the world saw both a failure and a success of diplomacy. Diplomacy and negotiations had not been able to prevent the outbreak of the Georgian-Russian war; but they succeeded in putting an end to the armed clashes and in preventing the situation from spiralling out of control and developing into a conflict between Russia and the West.

Ukraine 2014

The situation in Ukraine developed differently. After what Russian officials described as a coup in Kiev, on 1 March 2014 the Russian Parliament approved Putin's request for sending troops to Ukraine in connection with the developing Crimean crisis. As Russia had 40,000 troops deployed close to its borders with Ukraine, it was feared that a full-scale invasion of Ukraine was a matter of hours or days. However, what ensued was not such an invasion but a new type of asymmetric, hybrid warfare – thousands of 'green men' surfaced in various locations on the Crimean peninsula, taking control over the most important buildings and surrounding the Ukrainian troops stationed there. According to Putin, these green men were local self-defence militia units who bought their uniforms and weapons in local shops. They supposedly decided to defend the local population against the attacks of right-wing activists from the Kiev Maidan, presented by Russian official propaganda as fascists and bloodthirsty enemies of the Russian people. Putin and other Kremlin officials denied that Russia had anything to do with the developments in the Crimea. Ukrainian troops in the Crimea – and decision makers in Kiev – were apparently taken aback. Also policymakers in the West had problems in finding a way of dealing with what was sometimes interpreted as implementation of Yevgenii Messner's ideas on the new type of rebel wars (Messner 1999).

Due to a combination of various factors – the reluctance or the inability of the Ukrainian troops in the Crimea to respond to the challenge with violence, support among the local (nearly 60 per cent Russian) population for Crimea's return to Russia, the West's reluctance to confront Russia, and Russia's formal distancing itself from the events in the Crimea – it was possible to avoid massive bloodshed in the region. However, the result was devastating for Ukraine – the rigged referendum conducted in the region on 16 March 2014 produced results that were quickly used by Russia to justify annexation.

This development – and most probably direct and indirect instigation on the part of Russia – then led to the outbreak of violent conflict in the Lugansk and Donetsk regions of eastern Ukraine. Russia treated the new Ukrainian government as illegitimate, played the Yanukovych card, and refused to enter into direct dialogue with the government in Kiev, which Russian media presented as a bunch of fascists backed by Russia's enemies in the West. It took weeks of shuttle diplomacy, and several telephone conversations between Russian and Western diplomatic and political heavyweights before direct talks between Russian and Ukrainian decisionmakers could start in Geneva on 17 April 2014.

The four parties taking part in the Geneva meeting – Russia, the EU, the USA and Ukraine – agreed that all sides must refrain from violence, intimidation or provocative action of any kind; that all illegal armed groups must be disarmed; all illegally seized buildings must be returned to their legitimate owners; all illegally occupied streets, squares and other public places in Ukrainian cities and towns must be vacated. It was also agreed that amnesty would be granted to protestors and to those who had left buildings and other public places and had surrendered their weapons, with the exception of those found guilty of capital offences. The OSCE would deploy a Special Monitoring Mission that was to play a leading role in assisting the Ukrainian authorities and local communities in the immediate implementation of these de-escalation measures. The EU, Russia and the USA committed themselves to support this mission. It was also announced that constitutional process would be inclusive, transparent and accountable. Further, participants underlined the importance of economic and financial stability in Ukraine, and expressed readiness to discuss additional support (RT 2014, Borger 2014).

The Geneva Accord proved short-lived, and tensions in eastern Ukraine escalated. The Ukrainian authorities launched what they labelled 'an anti-terror operation', trying to put an end to the rebellion. The separatists refused to lay down their arms. The West accused Russia of not being cooperative in addressing the challenges in Ukraine. Russia responded by accusing Ukraine of taking bloody punitive measures against peaceful populations in the eastern part of the country and the West of supporting the illegitimate regime in Kiev. Less than three weeks after the Geneva negotiations, on 11 May 2014 the rebelling regions of Lugansk and Donetsk organized referenda on separation from Ukraine – although Putin had recommended postponing the move. On 25 May 2014 Ukraine itself organized presidential elections, won in the first round by Petro Poroshenko. The fact that Poroshenko received overwhelming support from the majority of Ukrainians – although those living in Donetsk and Lugansk could not take part in the elections – gave him renewed legitimacy.

On 5 June 2014 it was announced that the Russian ambassador to Kiev, Mikhail Zurabov, who had been called back to Moscow on 24 February, was to return to the Ukrainian capital. On 6 June, the newly elected Poroshenko met Putin during D-Day celebrations in France, and in the following weeks the two presidents held several rounds of telephone conversations on the crisis in Ukraine (Lenta 2014a, President of Russia 2014).

Interpreting the Conflicts

Both conflicts broke out partly because the involved parties had failed to engage in a dialogue with a win–win potential, in turn caused by the fact that their strategic goals seemed to be at least partly irreconcilable. Also other factors played a role – for instance, the personalities of the leaders involved and the choice of information strategies that stirred up emotions in both Russia and the West that made it impossible to enter into direct dialogue with those who were accused of genocide and other crimes on the one hand, and of blatant violation of international rules and norms on the other hand.

All key parameters of these two conflicts were set soon after the collapse of the Soviet Union in December 1991. Georgia lost control over the Abkhaz and South Ossetian territories in the wake of wars fought in 1992 and 1993. The re-establishment of Georgian sovereignty over those areas has become a key point on the Georgian political agenda. Russia has adopted a rather ambiguous position in that conflict: it was expected to act as an impartial peacekeeper acting on behalf of the whole CIS but was also suspected of having its own political and strategic agenda in the region (Nodia 2007, Halbach 2009). Georgia suspected Russia of undermining its position in the region and of seeking closer cooperation with breakaway regions as a means of preventing Georgia's closer cooperation with West; the Kremlin in turn suspected Georgia of undermining Russia's position in the whole post-Soviet space by proposing another model of political culture that could have (and indeed had) an appeal in other parts of the post-Soviet space and of being a Western 'agent' and instrument for undermining Russia's geopolitical position in an area where it felt vulnerable (Scott 2007). These Russian suspicions led Russia to treat the conflict between Georgia and Abkhazia/South Ossetia in an instrumental manner, using it to gain a strategic upper hand over Georgia and to obstruct Georgia's chances of becoming a full-fledged member of Western institutions, first and foremost NATO.

In the case of Ukraine the situation was far more complex, with a wide range of factors influencing developments in and around the country. The sheer size of the territory and its location between Russia and the enlarging West was one of these factors. The second factor was Ukraine's dependence on energy imports from Russia. The third factor influencing Ukrainian policy was the fact that approximately 18 per cent of the country's inhabitants were ethnic Russians. The fourth important factor was the evolution of the political system in Ukraine itself and deep internal divisions, as confirmed by the results of elections in the country (Katchanovski 2006, Kulyk 2011, Olszański 2014). Portions of the elite, especially from the predominantly Russian-speaking eastern part of the country, held that Ukraine should continue close political and economic cooperation with Russia; others, especially those from the central and western regions, opted for closer cooperation with the West as the best way of securing its long-term national interests.

All Ukrainian presidents after 1991 have had to balance the interests of various groups in the country, managing relations with both Russia and the West (Wilson 2005, D'Anieri 2010, Moshes 2013). Yanukovych, who won a slight victory over Tymoshenko in 2010, promised to conduct a balanced policy towards Russia and the West. In April 2010 he was accused of giving in to Russian demands by signing the controversial Kharkiv Accord that extended the period of stationing the Russian Black Sea Fleet in Crimea to 2042 in exchange for lower gas prices (Sherr 2010). However, he also engaged in dialogue with the EU on a comprehensive European Union Association Agreement (Sherr 2013). Only one week before the EU Eastern Partnership summit in Vilnius (28–29 November 2013), the Ukrainian authorities announced however that the signing of the association agreement would be suspended. This decision triggered a wave of protests in Kiev, with the ensuing Maidan revolution that resulted in Yanukovych's removal from power on 22 February 2014. The Kremlin decided to act to defend – as it was put officially – the rights and lives of ethnic Russians and Russian-speakers in Ukraine (Casula 2014). Thus, Russia used the same arguments when intervening in Ukraine in 2014 as it had in 2008, when the intervention in Georgia was officially presented as an operation to protect lives of Russian citizens and Russian-speakers in the area.

It seems, however, that what Russia did in both cases was not aimed solely at the protection of Russian citizens, but was also a reaction to what Kremlin policymakers interpreted as Western interference in Russia's exclusive sphere of interests. The West – the USA in particular – was, in the opinion of Russian policymakers, part of the problem in both Georgia and Ukraine. The West had established a stronger presence in the Caucasus by supporting Georgia's aspirations to join NATO and the EU (Larrabee 2009, Lukyanov 2009, Missiroli 2009). Likewise in Ukraine, which had embarked – especially after the Orange Revolution – on closer cooperation with the West, through the Partnership for Peace Programme with NATO and the Eastern Partnership and Neighbourhood Policy with the EU (Bátora and Navrátil 2014, Rieker 2014). The growing strategic presence of the West in what Russia perceived as its own strategic backyard annoyed circles in Moscow (Stepanova 2008, Bratersky 2014). Already in February 2007 then-President Vladimir Putin fired a heavy anti-Western salvo at the 43rd Munich Conference on Security Policy, accusing the West of seeking to establish a global system with 'one centre of authority, one centre of force, one centre of decisionmaking', of imposing new dividing lines and walls and of 'trying to transform the OSCE into a vulgar instrument designed to promote the foreign policy interests of one or a group of countries'. Putin did not mention the USA and the Western support for Georgia or Ukraine directly, but the situation in Georgia had been one of the core problems in Russia–Western relations ever since the OSCE Istanbul Summit in 1999. In the case of Ukraine it was the West's role in the Orange Revolution in 2004 that apparently provoked Putin and let him to make those remarks (Tsygankov 2006).

The conflicts between Russia/Georgia and Ukraine/Russia have developed from post-Soviet regional issues to problems that have been interpreted in a much broader context, especially after Georgia and Ukraine were given the promise of becoming full members of NATO (Dyakova 2010). The five-day war in 2008 was to a certain degree Russia's war by proxy with the West, caught unprepared and with evident problems in finding answers to the new and surprising developments (Klussmann 2009). Saakashvili's action and Russia's reaction to it strained relations between Russia and the USA/NATO, thereby directly impacting on relations between the most important elements of the international system (Chatham House 2008, Gahrton 2010, Astrov 2011). It was not only Georgia that lost in that five-day war – also the West's will and ability to contain Russian power and to manage conflicts in the post-Soviet space were put in question (Alexandrov 2010). In that sense, the 2008 conflict in Georgia and the West's reluctance paved the way for 2014 and the conflict in Ukraine, where Russia again decided to test the West's strategic response and its coherence.

When the conflicts between Georgia and Russia, and Ukraine and Russia, entered the most intense and heavily armed phase in August 2008 and in March 2014, respectively, the parties directly involved in these conflicts held completely different strategic perspectives. For Georgia and Ukraine, it was a question of the survival of the national – or at least the current – regime, and the protection of territorial integrity; for Russia it was a matter of retaking the lead, showing strategic capability and resolution, and also a way of containing the Western advances and demonstrating the limits of the waning US power (Felgengauer 2008).

Geopolitical factors made talks between Russia on the one hand and Georgia and Ukraine on the other more difficult. Russia has treated the area as its own strategic backyard, and has not been willing to let other powers enter and play a more important role in setting the regional agenda. Georgia's and Ukraine's drive for NATO membership and, in more general terms, closer cooperation with the West was therefore viewed by Russia as a strategic challenge (German 2012, Rywkin 2014).

However, the outbreak of hostilities in Georgia on 7 August 2008 was not solely the result of the diverging interests and policies of the parties directly involved in the conflict: it was also the consequence of what the report of the independent international commission described as 'the failure of the international community, including the UN Security Council, to act swiftly and resolutely enough in order to control the mounting tensions prior the outbreak of armed conflict'(Independent International Fact-Finding Mission on the Conflict in Georgia 2009: 12). Similarly, another commentator wrote: 'from the point of view of successful great power management … this war should not have happened in the first place' (Astrov 2011: 2).

Most Western observers and experts agreed that Russia's actions in Georgia were intended to prevent the West from establishing a strategic bridgehead in the Caucasus, but some underlined the lack of strategic intelligence and restraint on the part of Mikhail Saakashvili as a contributing factor (Allison 2008 and 2009, Klussmann 2009). However, when in March 2014 the Ukrainian leadership did show amazing restraint in dealing with the Russian threat in Crimea, and managed to avoid a full-scale military confrontation and bloodshed, it did not prevent the loss of the territory to Russia.

What complicated situation on the ground even further was the ascent to power of a new generation of politicians. Saakashvili advocated further democratization of Georgia and strengthening of ties between Georgia and Western institutions, while Putin embarked on a political project that resulted in a hybrid semi-authoritarian regime and the worsening of Russia's relations with the West. In the case of Ukraine, the fact that the new post-Yanukovych government embarked on a policy of quick rapprochement with the West was also an important factor behind Putin's decisions.

What proved be yet an additional element complicating relations between Georgia and Russia, preventing them from entering into constructive dialogue, was the personality of the two leaders. Even Saakashvili's friends in the West described him as having hard time practising patience (Asmus 2010: 85). Putin was also known for his hot temper and being vindictive and unforgiving, as well as calculating and unscrupulous. The diverging political agendas and these personal traits resulted in bad personal chemistry between Saakashvili and Putin, and they did not trust each other (ibid.: 56).

Regarding Ukraine, the Russian leaders consistently portrayed the new leadership in Kiev as illegitimate and fascist, and refused to enter into dialogue with either the new prime minister, Arseniy Yatsenyuk, or the acting president, Oleksand Turychynov. Instead Putin, who had openly criticized Yanukovych for his spinelessness and lack of decisive action, decided to 'resuscitate' the former President of Ukraine, giving him a platform from which he could attack the new authorities and help Russia justify its intervention in Ukraine.

An important role in conflict escalation was also played by heavy propaganda and information strategies chosen by opponents, stirring up emotions in all three societies (Zharov and Sheviakov 2009). Russian official propaganda depicted Saakashvili as an irresponsible 'madman' and hothead with serious mental problems (Ruchkin 2008a); in turn, Tbilisi presented Putin as an imperialist and the worst enemy of the young Georgian democracy (Georgia 2009), as did much of the Western interpretation of developments in the conflict area (IISS 2008, Blandy 2009). In the case of conflict with new government in Ukraine in 2014, the Russian propaganda machinery played also a crucial part, labelling the new Ukrainian leadership a fascist junta and accusing it of committing genocide of Ukrainian Russians in Donbas (Darczewska 2014).

What Were the Obstacles and What Made Diplomacy Work?

According to Irina Papkova, armed conflict was perhaps the inevitable outcome once these incompatibilities came to the fore in Georgia, where both sides were pursuing interests defined in terms of their conflicting self-understanding in an atmosphere already burdened with the negative legacy of the Cold War (Papkova 2011: 58). The actors involved were so far apart in strategic terms that dialogue was almost impossible: the conflict could be therefore defined as belonging to that 5 per cent of intractable conflicts that are highly destructive, never-ending, and virtually insoluble (Coleman 2011). In such a situation a leader may decide that fighting is a better option than negotiation (Mnookin 2010). However, when making such a decision a leader should act with prudence and consider all pros and contras – which was probably not the case with Saakashvili on the night of 7 August (Asmus 2010).

In the case of Ukraine the situation was highly complicated. Russia did not recognize the power shift in Kiev on 22 February 2014, describing the whole process as a coup supported by the West, and the new government was consistently labelled as illegitimate and fascist. In addition, the open conflict erupted during the most important PR effort launched by Russia, the Winter Olympic Games in Sochi – which were meant to improve Russia's international image and prestige. Russia had invested considerable diplomatic efforts, as well as (according to various estimates) some USD 50 billion in order to improve its image, which had been tarnished by Putin's return to power. It was therefore not easy for the Kremlin to launch any anti-Western and anti-Ukrainian countermeasures that could be expected to have negative impacts on Russia's relations with its most important economic and political partner, the West. However, the decision to challenge Ukraine's territorial integrity in Crimea was made by Putin and a small group of his closest acolytes: Sergei Ivanov, head of the presidential administration, Kremlin strategist Vyacheslav Volodin, Kremlin aide Vladislav Surkov, Foreign Minister Sergei Lavrov and the heads of the security services (Reuters and Piper 2014). Within days, just after the end of Sochi Olympics, Russian forces went to action.

Diplomatic (Re)actions

Once the war in Georgia broke out on 7 August 2008 the international community embarked on a more active policy of conflict management, and a negotiated solution was found. The indirect dialogue between Russia and Georgia, initiated by the French diplomats acting on behalf of the EU, probably combined with a more active US role behind the scenes, made the parties understand that the political and human costs of continuing the war could be higher than what they could accept.

The dialogue that succeeded in putting an end to the armed phase of the conflict was not a direct dialogue between Georgia and South Ossetia/ Abkhazia/Russia, but a series of bilateral talks involving the French negotiators and Georgia, Russia, South Ossetia and Abkhazia, with the results communicated to other parties by the French team. With no direct contact between the two warring parties, and the pressing need to prevent conflict escalation, there was no time to embark on Track II diplomacy, with its extensive use of dialogue involving members of the academic community and various active and non-active officials and other public figures – not official diplomats. Instead, professional diplomats and political heavyweights had to enter the stage to secure de-escalation of the conflict, and several rounds of formal and informal negotiations followed. Direct talks between the French Minister of Foreign Affairs Bernard Kouchner and OSCE Chairman-in-Office Alexander Stubb, supported by Sarkozy, with Saakashvili and the Medvedev/Putin tandem, played a crucial role in preventing escalation of the conflict in August 2008. The negotiators persuaded the warring parties to accept a set of conditions and concessions as a precondition of the ceasefire. Georgia agreed to accept the effective loss of control over territories that had been out of its reach since the early 1990s. Despite that – and the military defeat – the incumbent Georgian president stayed in power and was not ousted – obviously Russia's concession to the French negotiators. In addition Russia decided to stop the movement of its forces towards Tbilisi and to pull out its troops from the undisputed Georgian territory. A further factor that facilitated this negotiated solution was probably the fact that Russia had by that time achieved most of its war objectives, Georgia was on the brink of collapse and had to accept the harsh conditions, and the French negotiators had good contacts in Moscow and in Tbilisi.

The situation in Ukraine in 2014 was both less and more dramatic than in Georgia in 2008. It was less dramatic, because at the time of the Russian annexation of Crimea, there had not been many casualties in the Crimean 'war' between Russia and Ukraine. On the other hand, it was more dramatic because the conflict involved two countries with a combined population of almost 200 million – one of them a great power with a huge nuclear arsenal and a main supplier of energy to Europe; and the other one far more capable than Georgia of mounting a stiff opposition to any Russian incursion, as well as being the main transit area for Russian gas to the EU. Moreover, the West – the EU, the USA and NATO – became involved in the conflict, due to what Russia saw as its dubious role in the Maidan revolution. The West could not act as an intermediary between Russia and Ukraine, but had to side with Ukraine, which from the outset was presented in the West as an innocent victim of Russian aggression.

This was also clearly reflected in the Track I diplomatic efforts undertaken by the EU, NATO and the USA, acting largely on behalf of Ukraine. The goal of the West was twofold – to deter Russia from any further steps that could escalate the conflict, and to get Russia into direct dialogue with the new Ukrainian government that the Kremlin had refused to recognize. The West used a combination of sticks and carrots in getting Russia to reconsider its policy and actions towards Ukraine. US Secretary of State John Kerry held several rounds of telephone and direct negotiations with his Russian counterpart Sergey Lavrov. Both parties used the entire arsenal of diplomatic means and their country-specific negotiation strategies.[1] Lavrov, whose professional

---

1 On the permanent aspects of Russian diplomacy see Whelan 1979: 513–25; on American style of negotiations see Solomon and Quinney 2010.

background dated back to Soviet times, apparently recognized the lessons learned. His comprehensive negotiating strategy, closely controlled by the real policymakers in the Kremlin, could be therefore described as a combination of realism, toughness and a *quid pro quo* approach so characteristic of the old Soviet school (Whelan 1979: 522–5). Also important were the German and French Ministers of Foreign Affairs, who were directly involved with their Polish counterpart Radoslaw Sikorski in the process that resulted in the 21 February 2014 agreement between Yanukovych and the Ukrainian opposition.

Other Western leaders were also involved in diplomatic efforts aimed at getting Russia to rethink its decision to intervene directly in Ukraine and stop its direct and indirect support to separatists in eastern Ukraine, who from 7 April 2014 had started seizing key buildings in the Lugansk and Donetsk regions. US President Barack Obama had several telephone talks – on 21 February, 1 March, 6 March, 16 March, 28 March, 14 April – with his Russian counterpart Vladimir Putin in which he tried to persuade the Russian leader to show restraint, and warned of actions against Russia if the situation in Ukraine were to deteriorate. The two had also a brief informal meeting on 6 June during D-Day celebrations in France, also the scene of the first direct contact between Putin and the newly elected president of Ukraine Petro Poroshenko. In Europe it was German Chancellor Angela Merkel who took the lead in the work on finding a political solution to the conflict – it is said that by the end of November 2014 she had conducted no less than 35 telephone conversations with Putin and met him for lengthy direct talks in both Milan during the EU–Asia summit and in Brisbane at the G20 summit in November 2014. The effects of these direct and indirect talks are difficult to measure but it was important to use all channels available to convey the united West's message to Putin.

These rounds of talks between Russian policymakers and their Western counterparts finally yielded some positive results. Russia – and Vladimir Putin – decided to recognize *de facto* the new Ukrainian president, who had been elected on 25 May, and a direct dialogue on solving the Ukrainian crisis could begin. The April talks in Geneva, during which the principles of solving the conflict had been formulated, were followed by several rounds of telephone contacts between Poroshenko and Putin (on 12, 17 and 19 June 2014 (Lenta 2014b)). Putin's (reluctant) support for Poroshenko's peace plan for Ukraine was announced on 21 June 2014 (Lenta 2014c). On 23 June 2014, the first round of talks between the separatists and the Ukrainian central authorities was held. The Ukrainian side was represented by the former president Leonid Kuchma. The Russian side was represented by Ambassador Mikhail Zurabov; from the OSCE came Ambassador Heidi Tagliavini of Switzerland, who had been the main author of the EU's report on the war in Georgia in 2008; and the separatists were represented by Aleksandr Boroday, Oleg Tsariev, and Viktor Medvedchuk (Lenta 2014d).

The two presidents also met at the meeting organized in Minsk on 26 August 2014 to discuss questions of mutual interest together with representatives of the EU and Eurasian Customs Union. On 5 September 2014 Minsk was also a scene of another important meeting at which parties to this conflict agreed an immediate ceasefire and decided to begin a political process. This agreement was to put an end to the military phase of the conflict that escalated in the end of August 2014 because of Russian direct military intervention that changed the balance of power on the ground in Ukraine's disfavour forcing the Ukrainian leadership to seek a negotiated solution. Although the Minsk Agreement brought some positive results it did not put an end to open hostilities – according to most recent UN report on situation in Ukraine published in November 2014 almost 1000 people lost life in the two following months (UN News Center 2014).

In both cases, it seems that the relative success of the indirect and direct talks was due to the fact that the parties involved in this indirect dialogue followed the '7 steps of principled negotiations' (Fisher and Ury 1991). The parties to the conflict managed to identify key interests. What was at stake for Georgia and then for Ukraine was their territorial integrity and survival as independent nations. For Russia the key interest was to retain control in its strategic backyard and prevent direct involvement of other great powers – achieved only partly in both Georgia and Ukraine. However, Russia must pursue a long-term strategy in which various priorities have to be weighed against each other. Black (1962), Lomagin (2004) and Rieber (2007) argue that Russia has some 'persistent' goals in its foreign policy. Black (1962) lists four of them – stabilization of frontiers, assurance of favourable conditions for economic growth, unification of Russian territories, and participation in alliance systems and international institutions. Russia could apparently not ignore the costs that open conflict with the West supporting Georgia and Ukraine would have for its own long-term political and economic interests. Although there was no personal trust between Saakashvili and Putin/Medvedev, and Russia was for a long time unwilling to recognize the new Ukrainian government, other actors could act as intermediaries between the warring parties. France's Sarkozy managed to bridge that personal gap in a strained situation when the stakes – regime/state survival – became high for Georgia, and the costs – strained relations with Russia's most important economic partner, the EU – of continuing military operations in Georgia proved higher than the possible strategic gains for Russia. In the case of Ukraine, a similar role was played by the orchestrated efforts of Western leaders, first and foremost Barack Obama of the United States, and Angela Merkel representing the EU.

When agreement was reached in 2008, Georgia's reservation point had been pushed so hard that Tbilisi had to accept the conditions proposed by the French negotiators and accepted by Moscow. For Georgia the desired solution would have been regaining control over Abkhazia and South Ossetia and repealing the

Russian intervention, but after defeat on the battlefield Georgia was forced to 'move' its reservation point and accept the harsh conditions. At the same time Russia seemed satisfied with the solution achieved, even though the Saakashvili regime was not removed from power. Moreover, faced with a concerted effort of the EU, supported indirectly by the USA, Russia decided to 'shift' its reservation point, broadening the zone of possible agreement with the West. Those two acts of unwilling moving of reservation points made it possible to agree to the cessation of hostilities in 2008. The same logic and almost same actors were also involved in the process that prevented the outbreak of full-scale war between Russia and Ukraine in 2014.

It seems that in the wake of the five-day war in 2008, the situation in the region could be best described as a stalemate where Georgia could not find a mutually acceptable solution and Russia was not interested. Another important element facilitating a negotiated settlement was also the fact that Russia was aware that this local conflict could have global implications and develop into a new conflict between Russia and the West. In the case of Ukraine, the situation is still unclear. Ukraine will probably have to accept the loss of Crimea in return for Russia's withdrawal of overt support for the separatist movement in eastern Ukraine and very likely some other concessions to Russian strategic interests, such as the declaration of the Ukraine's status as a formally non-aligned state.

Different core interests, apparently irreconcilable, seem to be at stake and in conflict. For Georgia the question of national survival, territorial integrity and inviolability of the country's borders was at stake at the outbreak of war, but after five days the question boiled down to the issue of state's survival and Georgia had no option but to accept the conditions of the proposed ceasefire. In the case of Ukraine, similar concerns have been involved, but Ukraine could also play the Budapest 1994 memorandum card, giving it more chances to engage the West on its side. For Russia the key question has been the preservation of its status as a great regional and global power, a power that does not accept other direct or indirect presence of other powers in what Russia sees as its own strategic zone of 'privileged interests'. In both conflicts, Russia claimed to have legitimate goals – protection of Russian citizens/ethnic Russians/Russian-speakers and prevention of genocide. Once these goals were achieved, Russia was ready to accept (albeit reluctantly) the conditions proposed by the EU and the USA. The fact that the Kremlin could not act freely but had to take into consideration what the West described as 'the costs' clearly shows the limits of Russia's power, even in the post-Soviet space.

However, its actions in Ukraine, especially the outright annexation of Crimea, have dealt a heavy blow to relations between Russia and the West, leading many to talk about the advent of a new Cold War era (Karaganov 2014, Legvold 2014).

All parties directly involved in the Georgian conflict decided to accept the commitments proposed by negotiators. Georgia that had suffered a military defeat and could not count on any external support, had no other option but to accept. By contrast, Russia decided to accept the set of commitments because it had achieved most of its strategic and local objectives; moreover, the cost of confrontation with the West that would follow had Russia continued its march towards Tbilisi would have been prohibitive in political terms, perhaps also in military ones. The same logic was also on display in the case of the Ukrainian crisis in 2014.

Direct communication between the warring parties was effectively breached on the day the Georgian President decided to send in troops to retake Tskhinvali on 7 August 2008, or even earlier (Ruchkin 2008b, Yakobashvili 2009). In the case of Ukraine, communications between Kiev and Moscow were severed when Ukrainian President Yanukovych was removed from power on 22 February 2014, and were not restored until the Geneva talks on 17 April. The success of negotiations was, however, secured by a clear communication strategy on the part of the teams of professional negotiators who made it clear to both parties that the alternative to a negotiated settlement was complete annihilation of the Georgian state and the effective breakdown in relations between Russia and the West, as already signalled by NATO's decision to withdraw from cooperation with Russia. It was especially Sarkozy's persuasive skills and his determination to get the parties to understand that they had no better alternative to that negotiated agreement that made it work.

In the case of Ukraine 2014, it was the concerted effort of the Western leaders that prevented the escalation of the conflict into a full-scale war between Russia and Ukraine with consequences that were impossible to predict. However, the situation in eastern Ukraine is still at the time of this writing – November 2014 – very volatile, especially after the downing of the Malaysian MH17 flight over this war-torn part of Ukraine on 17 July 2014 that claimed lives of almost 300 European, Australian and Malaysian citizens and contributed to further internationalization of this conflict.

In both cases, communication between the warring parties was difficult because the war propaganda – especially in Russia, but also in the West, in Georgia and in Ukraine – managed to set in motion very strong emotions in the societies in question and in policymaking circles. Pictures of soldiers and civilians killed on the streets of Kiev and Tbilisi, and the humiliation of both Georgian and Ukrainian troops facing better-equipped Russian units, unleashed such strong emotions and feelings that it will take long time for the mental wounds of the warfare to heal. The massive anti-Ukrainian campaign in major Russian media and TV channels presenting pro-European Ukrainians as Fascists and Nazis committing crimes against humanity has done severe, perhaps irreparable, damage to bilateral relations. Here it is essential to bear in mind the emotional side of the conflicts, as studied by Moïsi (2009), and the impact on diplomatic efforts, as dealt with in the chapter by Paul Saurette and Henrik Thune in this volume.

Concluding Remarks

This brief study has sought answers to several questions on the utility of dialogue and diplomacy in conflict prevention and settlement, focusing on the cases of Georgia/Russia and Ukraine/Russia. The 2008 conflict between Georgia and Russia could escalate because the distance between the parties involved had grown so great that calls for dialogue had no chance of reaching the ears of those in charge. In addition came the visible lack of mutual trust, indeed a sense of hostility, between the Georgian and Russian leaders and the lack of commitment on the part of the international community to prevent the conflict from escalating. On top of that, a series of misjudgements and miscalculations triggered the outbreak of open hostilities. In Ukraine in 2014, similar combination of factors played a role in the development of the conflict, although the West was more active throughout than it had been in the case of Georgia, due not least to the fact that Russia's actions – especially the annexation of Crimea – were seen as posing a more serious threat to peace in Europe.

The immediate tipping points beyond which the direct dialogue was no longer possible came with the Georgian troops' shelling of Tskhinvali and the Russian violation of Georgian sovereignty and territorial integrity in the case of Georgia; and the ousting of the pro-Russian president Yanukovych in the case of Ukraine. The shelling of Tskhinvali gave Russia a pretext for intervention that resulted in military defeat for Georgia and the apparent undermining of the credibility of the West as a provider of security in the post-Soviet space. In the case of Ukraine, the ousting of Yanukovych was read by the Kremlin as an anti-Russian coup supported by the West and conducted by fascist forces in Ukraine.

What the Georgians read as Russia's violation of Georgian sovereignty left Saakashvili with no other option but to fight. At that point, dialogue was not an option any of the parties involved was willing to consider. For dialogue to become relevant again the situation on the ground had to change and the involvement of new actors was apparently needed in order to the get the warring parties to silence their guns. In Ukraine, Russia chose to react to counter what the leadership saw as a negative development in its strategic backyard and as a Ukrainian-cum-Western anti-Russian conspiracy for changing the strategic balance in the Eurasian space. According to that realist logic, Russia had no other option but to react, to prevent that from happening – or at least to punish the new Ukrainian leadership and boost support for the Putin regime at home.

Due largely to the disparity in military potentials available and engaged in the military conflict phase, the situation changed dramatically in the course of a few days. This made other actors (the EU, the OSCE, USA) who realized the gravity of the situation, to get involved in attempts at finding a negotiated solution. With the involvement of new actors, the strategic calculus of the parties directly involved in the conflict changed. The dialogue and diplomacy proved again a relevant option as a way out of the war deadlock. After several rounds of negotiations, an agreement on immediate ceasefire was reached on 12 August 2008.

Negotiations have brought an end to the armed phase of the Russo-Georgian and prevented – for the time being – the Russo-Ukrainian conflicts from spiralling out of control. However, the underlying problems have not been resolved. Relations between Russia and Georgia and between Russia and Ukraine remain tense and appear unlikely to improve soon. The wars examined here have shown that such conflicts do not have a military solution. The only way to address them is through negotiations and dialogue, which will probably take a long time and may even end in a new failure. That said, most people who have learnt the painful lessons of war would agree that even a poor and difficult dialogue with no guarantee of success is far better an option than a new, low-scale and not necessarily victorious war.

References

Alexandrov, M. 2010. *Bitva za Kavkaz, 2004–2008: Institut stran SNG v bor'be za natsional'nye interesy Rossii na Iuzhnom Kavkaze.* Moscow: Institut stran SNG.

Allison, R. 2008. Russia Resurgent? Moscow's Campaign to 'Coerce Georgia to Peace', *International Affairs*, 84(6), 1145–71.

Allison, R. 2009. The Russian Case for Military Intervention in Georgia: International Law, Norms and Political Calculation, *European Security*, 18(2), 173–200.

Asmus, R.D. 2010. *A Little War that Shook the World: Georgia, Russia, and the Future of the West.* New York: Palgrave Macmillan.

Astrov, A. 2011. Great Power Management Without Great Powers? The Russian–Georgian War of 2008 and Global Police/Political Order, in *The Great Power (mis)Management: The Russian Georgian War and its Implications for Global Poliitcal Order*, edited by A. Astrov. Farnham: Ashgate, 1–23.

Bátora, J. and Navrátil, M. 2014. The Socially Conditioned Dynamics of Security Community Building Beyond EU Borders: The Case of Ukraine, *NUPI Working Paper* 834, Oslo: NUPI [Online]. Available at: http://english. nupi.no/index.php/content/download/494798/1644906/version/2/file/ NUPI+WP-834+Batora+and+Navratil.pdf [accessed: 1 July 2014].

Black, C.C. 1962. The Pattern of Russian Objectives, in *Russian Foreign Policy: Essays in Historical Perspective*, edited by I. Lederer. New Haven, CT: Yale University Press. 3–38.

Blandy, C.W. 2009. Provocation, Deception, Entrapment: The Russo-Georgian Five Day War, *Advanced Research and Assessment Group, Caucasus Series* (09/01).

Bratersky, M. 2014. Transformation of Russia's Foreign Policy, *Russia in Global Affairs Online* [Online]. Available at: http://eng.globalaffairs.ru/number/Transformation-of-Russias-Foreign-Policy--16706 [accessed: 1 July 2014].

Borger, J. 2014. Ukraine Crisis: Geneva Talks Produce Agreement on Defusing Conflict, *The Guardian*, 17 April [Online]. Available at: http://www.theguardian.com/world/2014/apr/17/ukraine-crisis-agreement-us-russia-eu [accessed: 1 July 2014].

Casula, P. 2014. The Road to Crimea: Putin's Foreign Policy Between Reason of State, Sovereignty and Bio-Politics, *Russian Analytical Digest*, 148, 2–5.

Charap, S. and Welt, C. 2011. *A More Proactive U.S. Approach to the Georgia Conflicts*. Center for American Progress [online]. Available at: http://www.americanprogress.org/issues/2011/02/pdf/georgia-report.pdf [accessed: 1 July 2014].

Chatham House 2008. Whither Georgia: The Impact of Russian Actions since August 2008, *Russia and Eurasia Programme Seminar Summary* [Online]. Available at: http://www.chathamhouse.org/sites/default/files/public/Research/Russia%20and%20Eurasia/151208summary.pdf [accessed: 1 July 2014].

Coleman, P. 2011. *The Five Percent: Finding Solutions to Seemingly Impossible Conflicts*. New York: Public Affairs.

D'Anieri, P.J. 2010. *Orange Revolution and Aftermath: Mobilization, Apathy, and the State in Ukraine*. Washington, DC: Woodrow Wilson Center Press/Baltimore, MD: Johns Hopkins University Press.

Darczewska, J. 2014. The anatomy of Russian information warfare. The Crimean operation, a case study, *OSW Point of View* 42, Warsaw: OSW [Online]. Available at: http://www.osw.waw.pl/sites/default/files/the_anatomy_of_russian_information_warfare.pdf [accessed: 1 July 2014].

Dyakova, N. 2010. Voyennaya politika SSha v otnosheni Ukrainy i Gruzii (2004–2010 gg), *Ssha Kanada. Ekonomika, politika, kultura*, 10, 90–107.

Felgengauer, P. 2008. This Was Not a Spontaneous but a Planned War, *Novaya Gazeta*, 14 August.

Fisher, R., Patton, B., Ury, W. 1991. *Getting to Yes: Negotiating Agreement Without Giving In*. New York: Penguin.

Flikke, G. 2013. Ukraine in Europe – Europe in Ukraine, *NUPI Report*, Oslo: NUPI [Online]. Available at: http://english.nupi.no/index.php/content/download/440122/1475320/version/1/file/Ukraine+in+Europe-Europe+in+Ukraine.pdf [accessed: 1 July 2014].

Flikke, G. and Godzimirski, J.M. 2007. Words and Deeds: Russian Foreign Policy and post-Soviet Secessionist Conflicts, *NUPI Report*. Oslo: NUPI [Online]. Available at: http://www.nupi.no/content/download/1101/30323/version/2/file/Words+and+Deeds-report1.pdf [accessed: 1 July 2014].

Gahrton, P. 2010. *Georgia Pawn in the New Great Game*. London: Pluto Press.

Georgia 2009. *Report by the Government of Georgia on the Aggression by the Russian Federation against Georgia*. New York: United Nations.

German, T. 2012. Securing the South Caucasus: Military Aspects of Russian Policy Towards the Region since 2008, *Europe-Asia Studies*, 64(9), 1650–66.

Halbach, U. 2009. The Longer 'Countdown to War': Growing Confrontation between Georgia and Russia 2004–2008, *Caucasus Analytical Digest*, 10, 2–4.

IISS 2008. Georgia: The war in words. Key quotes from the crisis, *IISS Strategic Comments Georgia Crisis Special Issue*, 14.

Independent International Fact-Finding Mission on the Conflict in Georgia 2009. *Independent International Fact-finding Mission on the Conflict in Georgia*. IIFFMCG [Online]. Available at: http://www.ceiig.ch/Report.html [accessed: 1 July 2014].

Karaganov, S. 2014. Europe and Russia: Preventing a New Cold War, *Russia in Global Affairs online* [Online]. Available at: http://eng.globalaffairs.ru/number/Europe-and-Russia-Preventing-a-New-Cold-War-16701 [accessed: 1 July 2014].

Katchanovski, I. 2006. Regional political divisions in Ukraine in 1991–2006, *Nationalities Papers*, 34(5), 507–32.

Klussmann, U. 2009. Georgia's Murky Motives: Saakashvili under Pressure from EU Probe, *Der Spiegel*, 23 March [Online]. Available at: http://www.spiegel.de/international/world/0,1518,615160,00.html [accessed: 1 July 2014].

Kulyk, V. 2011. Language Iidentity, Linguistic Diversity and Political Cleavages: Evidence from Ukraine, *Nations and Nationalism*, 17(3), 627–48.

Larrabee, F.S. 2009. The United States and Security in the Black Sea Region, *Southeast European and Black Sea Studies*, 9(3), 301–15.

Legvold, R. 2014. Managing the New Cold War: What Moscow and Washington Can Learn from the Last One, *Foreign Affairs* (July/August 2014), 74–84.

Lenta 2014a. Порошенко рассказал Путину о планах урегулирования на юго-востоке Украины. *Lenta*. 12 June [Online]. Available at: http://lenta.ru/news/2014/06/12/callingputin [accessed: 1 July 2014].

Lenta 2014b. Порошенко раскрыл Путину детали своего мирного плана. Lenta. 20 June [Online]. Available at: http://lenta.ru/news/2014/06/20/porosh_putin [accessed: 1 July 2014].

Lenta 2014c. Путин поддержал решение Порошенко о прекращении огня. Lenta. 21 June [Online]. Available at: http://lenta.ru/news/2014/06/21/putin [accessed: 1 July 2014].

Lenta 2014d. Начались переговоры по урегулированию конфликта в Донбассе. Lenta. 21 June [Online]. Available at: http://lenta.ru/news/2014/06/23/talks [accessed: 1 July 2014].

Lomagin, N. 2004. Persistent Factors of Russian Foreign Policy: Ideas of Hegemony and the Stabilisation of Frontiers, Paper for *The Annual Meeting of the International Studies Association*, 17 March. Le Centre Sheraton Hotel, Montreal, Quebec.

Lukyanov, F. 2009. The South Caucasus in the International Spotlight, *Caucasus Analytical Digest*, 10, 16–19.

Messner, Y. 1999. Myatezhvoyna, *Nezavisomoye Voyennoye Obozreniye*, 5 November [Online]. Available at: http://nvo.ng.ru/history/1999-11-05/7_rebelwar.html [accessed: 1 July 2014].

Missiroli, A. 2009. Georgia on the EU Mind, *Caucasus Analytical Digest*, 10, 10–12.

Mnookin, R. 2010. *Bargaining with the Devil: When to Negotiate, When to Fight*. New York: Simon & Schuster.

Moïsi, D. 2009. *The Geopolitics of Emotion: How Cultures of Fear, Humiliation and Hope are Reshaping the World*. New York: Random House.

Moshes, A. 2013. A marriage of unequals: Russian-Ukrainian relations under president Yanukovich, in *Economization versus Power Ambitions: Rethinking Russia's Policy Towards Post-Soviet States*, edited by S. Meister. Berlin: Nomos. 59–72.

Nodia, G. 2007. Have Russian-Georgian Relations Hit Bottom or Will They Continue to Deteriorate?, *Russian Analytical Digest*, 13, 15–17.

Olszański, T.A. 2014. Unity Stronger than Divisions: Ukraine's Internal Diversity, *OSW Point of View* 40, Warsaw: OSW [Online]. Available at: http://www.osw.waw.pl/sites/default/files/pw_40_unity_stronger_than_divisions_net.pdf [accessed: 1 July 2014].

Papkova, I. 2011. Great Power Misalignment: The United States and the Russian-Georgian Conflict, in *The Great Power (mis)Management: The Russian Georgian War and its Implications for Global Political Order*, edited by A. Astrov. Farnham: Ashgate, 43–58.

President of Russia, 2014. *Telephone conversation with President of Ukraine Petro Poroshenko*. President of Russia [Online]. Available at: http://eng.kremlin.ru/news/22498 [accessed: 1 July 2014].

Pukhov, R. and Glantz, D.M. 2010. *The Tanks of August*. Moscow: Centre for Analysis of Strategies and Technologies.

Reuters and Piper, E. 2014. From loyal aides and 'inner voice', Putin hears no Crimea dissent [Online]. Available at: http://www.reuters.com/article/2014/03/11/us-ukraine-crisis-putin-analysis-idUSBREA2A1DH20140311 [accessed: 1 July 2014].

Rieber, A.J. 2007. How Persistent Are Persistent Factors?, in *Russian Foreign Policy in 21st Century: The Shadow of the Past*, edited by R. Legvold. New York: Columbia University Press, 205–71.

Rieker, P. 2014. The European Neighbourhood Policy: An Instrument for Security Community Building, *NUPI Working Paper* 832, Oslo: NUPI [Online]. Available at: http://english.nupi.no/index.php/content/download/494795/1644856/version/1/file/WP-832-Rieker.pdf [accessed: 1 July 2014].

Ruchkin, V. 2008a. Virus vozhdizma, *Krasnaya zvezda*, 13 August [Online]. Available at: http://old.redstar.ru/2008/08/13_08/4_06.html [Accessed 1 July 2014].

Ruchkin, V. 2008b Protivostayanie narastayet, *Krasnaya zvezda*, 8 August [Online]. Available at: http://old.redstar.ru/2008/08/08_08/1_03.html [Accessed 1 July 2014].

Rywkin, M. 2014. Ukraine: Between Russia and the West, *American Foreign Policy Interests*, 36(2), 119–26.

Scott, E.R. 2007. Russia and Georgia After Empire, *Russian Analytical Digest*, 13, 2–5.

Sherr, J. 2010. *The Mortgaging of Ukraine's Independence*. London: Chatham House.

Sherr, J. 2013. Ukraine and Europe: Final Decision?, *Russia and Eurasia* 2013/05, London: Chatham House [Online]. Available at: http://www.chathamhouse.org/sites/files/chathamhouse/public/Research/Russia%20and%20Eurasia/0713pp_sherr.pdf [accessed: 1 July 2014].

Solomon, R.H. and Quinney, N. 2010. *American Negotiating Behavior: Wheeler-dealers, Legal Eagles, Bullies, and Preachers*. Washington, DC: United States Institute of Peace.

Stepanova, E. 2008. South Ossetia and Abkhazia: Placing the conflict in context, *SIPRI Policy Brief* [Online]. Available at: http://kms1.isn.ethz.ch/serviceengine/Files/ISN/95693/ipublicationdocument_singledocument/58604569-366d-497a-aab0-04137deefd92/en/SIPRIPB0811.pdf) [accessed: 1 July 2014].

Tsygankov, A.P. 2006. New Challenges for Putin's Foreign policy, *Orbis: A Journal of World Affairs*, 50(1), 153–67.

UN News Center (2014) In latest report, UN rights office says nearly 1,000 dead amid shaky Ukraine ceasefire, UN News Center with breaking news from the UN News Service [Online]. Available at: http://www.un.org/apps/news/story.asp?NewsID=49393#.VHuD_PTF_6c [accessed: 1 Desember 2014].

Whelan, J.G. 1979. *Soviet Diplomacy and Negotiating Behavior: Emerging New Context for U.S. Diplomacy*. Special Studies Series on Foreign Affairs Issues, 1; Washington, DC: Committee on Foreign Affairs of the US Congress.

White, S., McAllister, I., and Feklyunina, V. 2010. Belarus, Ukraine and Russia: East or West?, *British Journal of Politics & International Relations*, 12(3), 344–67.

Wilson, A. 2005. *Ukraine's Orange Revolution*. New Haven, CT: Yale University Press.

Yakobashvili, T. 2009. The Aggression by the Russian Federation against Georgia, *Caucasus Analytical Digest*, 10, 12–16.

Zharov, M. and Sheviakov, T. 2009. *Khroniki informatsionnoi voiny*. Moscow: Evropa.

Chapter 6
Nuclear Diplomacy: The Case of Iran

Sverre Lodgaard

Synopsis

This chapter examines ten years of diplomacy over Iran's nuclear programme. Why did it fare so poorly for so long, and what finally made it yield results? To facilitate the reading of a complex story, it starts with a synopsis of the process and the role of dialogue in it.

The negotiations started in the aftermath of the 2003 occupation of Iraq. The EU3 (France, Germany and the UK) and Iran turned to diplomacy to avoid another war. Iran made substantial offers aimed at solving the nuclear controversy, but the Europeans were restrained by the USA, which turned a cold shoulder to diplomacy. The parties obviously differed in terms of action space and ambitions, and when the talks broke down in 2005, the ensuing frustrations raised the level of conflict. These talks took place at Washington's unipolar moment: Iran was part of the Axis of Evil – and rather than negotiating with evil, the Bush Administration wanted to take action against it.

What followed was a period of unproductive posturing (2006–2009). The parties exchanged positions, not concessions. All the time, diplomacy was strictly limited to governmental diplomacy – Track I – and the negotiators were held on a short leash. On occasion, negotiators spoke with each other informally on the margins of their mandates, but these were exceptions, and they led nowhere. The negotiating format was Iran and the five permanent members of the UN Security Council plus Germany (P5+1). Sometimes, however, the conflict seemed to boil down to three states – Iran, the USA and Israel – the latter with privileged access to information about the talks and special status in the US political system.

When the Obama Administration took office in January 2009 diplomacy got a new chance, half-heartedly at first because of Iranian bickering and recalcitrance and Israeli opposition. In the autumn of 2009 the turbulence in Teheran after the presidential elections that year brought negotiations on confidence-building measures to naught – whereupon Obama continued where

Bush had left off, with top-down diplomacy backed by sanctions and threats of war.

Obama did not give up on the diplomatic track, however. Helped by the good offices of Oman, a US-Iranian back channel was established in 2012. Secrecy was a must: as long as Iran was seen to be unyielding, probes undertaken in public would have been easy prey for spoilers seeking to castigate the Obama Administration for being weak. However, it was not until Hassan Rouhani was elected president in Iran in 2013 that substantial progress was made. The nature of the game became distinctly win–win, and communicative action – defined as cooperative efforts based on mutual deliberation and argumentation (Habermas 1984) – paved the way for the interim agreement of 24 November 2013. This agreement, framed by Iran and the USA, was quickly endorsed by all P5+1, with some amendments.

The alternatives to a negotiated solution were discouraging. The nuclear programme continued unabated in spite of the sanctions, and war would be harmful to both. Another driver of diplomacy was overlapping national interests of Iran and the USA in the Middle East. The parties had agreed to limit the negotiations to nuclear issues, but the actual key to progress was overlapping national interests of Iran and the USA in other domains. To realize those interests, it was necessary to get the nuclear problem out of the way. It was not dialogue that created those commonalities of interest: there is no sign that the back-channel, or the formal meetings of Iran and the P5+1 between 2011 and 2013, changed the identities and interests of the parties in any significant way. It was developments in international affairs in the Middle East and beyond that did so.

When Rouhani took office with a mandate to give diplomacy a fair chance, the search for a negotiated solution was long overdue. It had been waiting for the right constellation of governments – and when that happened, the parties were quick to act. Fast progress also had the advantage of reducing the space for spoilers.

Now, a broad dialogue conducted at many levels, in secret and in public, formally and informally, unfolded in parallel with the outcome-oriented negotiations to prepare the domestic constituencies for a diplomatic solution. Rouhani and his team launched a confidence-building campaign: many of them knew from experience how to do it, for they had been involved in the talks of 2003–2005. This not merely facilitated the breakthrough: it was indispensable, for relations between Iran and the USA had been frosty, hostile and highly emotional ever since the Iranian revolution in 1979.

The chapter gives a brief review of the origin of the conflict. It then identifies the turning points of the diplomatic process and what characterized them. Finally, it analyses the role of dialogue from the beginning in 2003 until the breakthrough in 2013.

Origin of the Conflict

The Iranian fuel-cycle programme, which came to public attention in 2003, has a long history dating back to the Shah's investments in fuel-cycle works in the mid-1970s (Mousavian 2012: 39–51). After a period of neglect following the revolution in 1979, the programme was revived in the mid-1980s but kept secret until 2002, when an opposition movement revealed the conversion and enrichment facilities in Esfahan and Natanz and the heavy-water works in Arak.[1] These activities had not been declared to the International Atomic Energy Agency (IAEA), which, in February 2003, started the difficult process of reconstructing Iran's nuclear history.

At that time, the United States was in its unipolar moment, keen to convert its superior military might to political advantage. Having declared 'mission accomplished' in Iraq in the spring of 2003, Washington contemplated the use of force to solve the problem. President Bush was mulling the options: could a military attack on Iran arrest the nuclear programme and bring Iran back into the US sphere of influence?[2]

For Iran, the enmity toward the United States dated back to the coup against Muhammad Mossadeq in 1953. For the USA, the bitterness toward Iran began with the hostage crisis of 1979. Ever since, there has been fertile ground for punitive action. Diplomatic relations were cut and US sanctions introduced. For Iran, the USA became the great Satan, with Israel the lesser one. For the USA, Iran became a main enemy.

It was in that context of enmity that the nuclear issue emerged in 2002/2003. The timing could not have been worse. After the events of 9/11, Iran had cooperated with the US in removing the Taliban regime in Afghanistan, but that did not prevent the Bush administration from making Iran part of the 'the Axis of Evil' together with Iraq and North Korea. In Washington, the mantra was 'you don't talk to evil. You take action against it'. If talks were to be conducted, it would have to be on European initiative – and that is what the UK, France and Germany (EU3) set out to do. In October 2003 the EU3 foreign ministers went to Teheran to start a negotiation that faltered at first, but came on stream again with the Paris Agreement of October 2004 (Engelbrekt

---

1 In mid-August 2002, the National Council of Resistance in Iran (NCRI) – an Iranian opposition group based in Paris – held a press conference in Washington DC, disclosing these works. It is not known whether the disclosure was based on separate intelligence or on Western/Israeli intelligence.

2 When Norway's Prime Minister Kjell Magne Bondevik visited the White House in early summer 2003, George W. Bush brought this question up for reflection and discussion. Communication from Bondevik to the author.

and Hallenberg 2007). The USA let it happen, but never believed it would yield satisfactory results.

The conflict with Iran has been about much more than the nuclear programme, however. For the political elite in Washington, another grievance may have been more substantial than the humiliation over the hostages: the loss of a faithful ally in the Gulf. Iran had regained independence after almost three centuries of intrusion and humiliation by the big powers – by Russia, the UK and the USA first of all. Ever since the Islamic revolution, US administrations have therefore entertained the idea of regime change. In this century, however, they have not been clear about the relationship between nuclear reversal and regime change, and how to set priorities among these objectives – not until the diplomatic breakthrough of 2013, which gave priority to getting the nuclear issue settled.

The conflict is also about the role of Iran in the Middle East. Western powers and Sunni Arab governments have tried to constrain it as much as possible while Iran has sought acceptance of a role corresponding – somehow – to its size and importance in the region. Many times, it has called for a grand bargain to normalize relations with the West and solve the nuclear problem in that context. Throughout, Iran has been asking for justice and mutual respect.

For Israel, nuclear weapons in the hands of a hostile Iranian leadership are what the conflict is all about. Prime Minister Netanyahu and many other Israeli leaders have seen Iran as an existential threat. The Israelis are not ready to live with an Iranian programme that can be weaponized on short notice. The Iranians, on the other hand, are determined to continue their fuel-cycle works, invoking Art. IV of the nuclear Non-Proliferation Treaty (NPT) which gives member states the right to enrich uranium and reprocess plutonium under international safeguards (Miller 2007). For them, the nuclear programme is a high-technology prestige programme that cannot be discontinued without seriously compromising their hard-won sovereignty and independence. President Ahmadinejad, in particular, elevated the programme to national prominence and mobilized broad public support for it.

Under the leadership of Mohamed ElBaradei, the IAEA noted that up to 2003, Iran had failed to inform it about its fuel-cycle works. The Agency published a lengthy list of items that should have been reported. This underreporting was an obvious violation of the safeguards agreement, but not necessarily of the NPT.[3] However, a report of November 2011, prepared under the leadership

---

3 For that to be the case, the items would have to be unambiguously connected with a weapons programme, such as development and testing of triggering mechanisms and work on nuclear weapon designs. Or they would reveal assistance to others in the acquisition of nuclear arms, which is prohibited under Art. II of the NPT. To date, no proof of any of this has emerged.

of Yukio Amano, conveyed a different message. Now, the Agency said that Iran had conducted weapons-oriented activities up to 2003; that there were indications that such activities had continued after that year; and that some of them might still be going on (IAEA 2011). This report made extensive use of information provided by member states. The US National Intelligence Estimate (NIE) of 2007 had made a similar assessment of the period up to 2003, but claimed that the weapons-oriented works had stopped that year and had not been resumed (NIE 2007). Later Estimates have been broadly consistent with that of 2007.

Acquisition of fissile materials is the key to production of nuclear weapons. In this respect, Iran is obviously building a *capability* to produce weapons. However, there is broad agreement in intelligence circles that it has made no decision to weaponize the programme. This is far from unique: many NPT members have long had that option, without exercising it.

This century, it has been predicted, over and over again, that Iran may build nuclear weapons in anywhere between one and seven years. Such predictions have usually been phrased in a way that blurs the distinction between capability and intent (Sahimi 2010), alerting people to a seemingly imminent danger. Sometimes the alarm has been an expression of genuine concern; sometimes it has been hype aimed at underpinning the demand for stronger punitive measures and regime change. US sanctions legislation calls for the latter: the sanctions cannot be lifted unless a new regime is established, on terms described by the US Congress. Merely scrapping the nuclear programme will not do.[4]

Given the long and deep-rooted nature of the conflict, it will take a lot to lay the concerns to rest. In fact, however, this is precisely what the new diplomatic drive is trying to do. The Joint Plan of Action (JPA) of 24 November 2013 defined interim limitations on the nuclear programme, enhanced inspections, and renewed efforts to clarify Iran's nuclear history – in return for modest sanctions relief. All the same, even under the best of circumstances, it will take

---

4 US sanctions can be lifted only after the President *certifies to Congress* that the government of Iran has: (1) released all political prisoners and detainees; (2) ceased its practices of violence and abuse of Iranian citizens engaging in peaceful political activity; (3) conducted a transparent investigation into the killings and abuse of peaceful political activists in Iran and prosecuted those responsible; and (4) made progress toward establishing an independent judiciary. Further, the President must certify that 'the government of Iran has ceased supporting acts of international terrorism and no longer satisfies certain requirements for designation as a state sponsor of terrorism; and [that] Iran has ceased the pursuit, acquisition, and development of nuclear, biological, chemical, and ballistic weapons'. Initially, the unilateral US sanctions were imposed by executive orders, which can be eased or even waived at the President's discretion. In recent years, however, more and more sanctions have been enacted into law (Katzman 2014).

time to establish confidence in the peaceful nature of the programme. A final agreement would therefore have to run for many years.

Up to 2013, the Western powers had two main approaches to the problem: sanctions and threats of war. Diplomacy played a marginal role. Except for talks about a confidence-building measure in the autumn of 2009, the parties were nowhere near agreement on anything.

Four rounds of sanctions were mandated by the UN, and unilateral US and EU sanctions went much further. Cyber-attacks of various kinds have been launched and Iranian nuclear scientists have been killed. Drones have been flying over Iranian territory, and covert operations of many kinds have been reported. Efforts have been made to deprive Iran of supporters and allies, and all the time there have been threats of using force to halt the nuclear programme. Israel and/or the USA are assumed to be the architects of most if not all of these activities. While there has been much talk about sticks and carrots, the sticks have been strong and painful and the carrots few and modest.

Among the P5+1, the strongest supporters of diplomacy have been Russia and China, backed by Turkey and Brazil and the great majority of non-aligned states. These countries are less alarmistic about the Iranian nuclear programme, more understanding of Iranian behaviour than the West, and more critical of Western policies than the voting patterns in international organizations would indicate.[5] The common denominator for all of them is to prevent Iran from becoming a nuclear-weapon state. Geopolitically, the BRICS (Brazil, Russia, India, China, South Africa) countries and others do not want Iran to fall back into the Western sphere of influence. There is an important geopolitical fault line going by Iran.

In 2013, diplomacy took the front seat. Use of force was relegated to a back-up option in case negotiations failed. The bulk of the sanctions remained in place: they were kept as bargaining cards, and leaders hostile to Iran – some of them proponents of regime change – could use them to undermine the negotiations. Israel and the powerful The American Israel Public Affairs Committee (AIPAC) were lobbying the US Congress to define requirements that a final deal could not possibly meet: slowly but surely, however, they were pushed onto the defensive.

All the time, the talks were conducted against the backdrop of IAEA efforts to reconstruct Iran's nuclear history and clarify the nature of its nuclear programme. Agency negotiations with Iran have been conducted on a bilateral basis between the secretariat and Iranian authorities; to some extent they have been steered by its Board of Governors, which became politicized over this issue, sometimes passing decisions by majority vote rather than by consensus as had been normal within the IAEA; and from 2006 onwards the UN Security

---

5 As can be seen from the explanations of vote.

Council (UNSC) has also been involved. The JPA established a Joint Commission of Iran and the P5+1 which would work with the IAEA to facilitate resolution of past and present issues of concern. In effect, this recognizes that some of the issues may require political clarification.

Turning Points

From more than ten years of talks about Iran's nuclear programme, three turning points stand out very clearly: the breakthrough in Iranian transparency and the beginning of negotiations with the EU3/EU in the autumn of 2003; the breakdown of these talks and the resumption of fuel-cycle activities in Iran in August 2005, leading the IAEA Board of Governors to refer the Iranian file to the UNSC in February 2006 and to the imposition of UN sanctions; and the new impetus to diplomacy in 2013, leading to the JPA.

The first turning point occurred while Mohammad Khatami was President in Iran. When the nuclear programme was resumed in the mid-1980s, it was largely left to experts in the field to conduct. Full political attention did not come until 2002/2003, when the disclosure of the fuel-cycle works led to strong international reactions that necessitated a comprehensive governmental response. The second turning point coincided with the election of Mahmoud Ahmadinejad to the presidency, and was to some extent caused by him. Ahmadinejad pursued the nuclear programme vigorously and with a brazen rhetoric that exacerbated tensions with the West and with Sunni Arab states. The third turning point came in 2013, when Iran and the United States paved the way for the JPA, the first concrete fruit of diplomacy.

A glimpse of hope emerged in 2009, when Barrack Obama took office. During the presidential campaign, he had declared his readiness to talk with US adversaries, with no conditions. However, new obstacles came in the way, among them the unrest in Iran after the presidential elections in the summer of 2009 and the information that Iran was building a new enrichment facility at Fordow outside Qom, in the mountain to protect it from air attack. The facility had not been declared to the IAEA.

Later, it became known that, at about the same time, Obama had authorized sophisticated cyber-warfare against Iran known as Stuxnet, destroying hundreds of centrifuges in Natanz. Stuxnet was followed by other kinds of cyber-attacks.[6]

---

6 The exact timing of these decisions is not known. The US programme is led by a 4-star general, which indicates that it is a major one, but apart from that the secrecy is pervasive. The investments in cyber-warfare and the conduct of cyber-attacks are very much kept 'in the dark'. To the extent that specific attacks have come to public attention, the information has emerged long after the attacks were set in motion.

To allay Israeli fears of the Iranian programme and prevent Israeli bombing of Iranian facilities, the attacks were conducted in cooperation with Israel (Sanger 2012). At first, the change from Bush to Obama was therefore more at the declaratory level than at the level of action policy. A meeting between Iran and the P5+1 in Geneva on 1 October 2009, focusing on a specific confidence-building measure, came to nought partly because of domestic disagreements in Iran and partly because the US administration was labouring under tight time constraints. By the turn of 2009/2010, Obama seemed to be back on the Bush Administration sanctions track.

The diplomatic ambition had not been abandoned, however. In July 2012 and March 2013, bilateral meetings between Iran and the USA were held in Oman, in secret, under the good offices of Sultan Qaboos.[7] Behind his public stance, which maintained that the first step was for Iran to comply with the UN Security Council resolutions demanding that Iran stop all fuel-cycle works, accept the Additional Protocol (AP) and allow additional inspections to restore confidence in its nuclear programme, Obama tried hard to establish productive relations with Iran. Iran went along, testing the waters, presumably with growing interest as the sanctions took their toll. But there were no concrete results until Rouhani became president of Iran. Now the style was entirely different, and the seriousness in pursuing results likewise. After his inauguration, there were at least five rounds of bilateral talks between the USA and Iran in rapid succession, in Oman, New York and Geneva, preparing what became the JPA.

The Turnaround of 2003: A Golden Opportunity

On 16 October 2003, Iran's chief negotiator Hassan Rouhani told ElBaradei that Iran was ready to turn over a new leaf in its relationship with the IAEA and provide full disclosure of its nuclear activities. Iran was also ready to conclude an Additional Protocol (AP). Pending its entry into force the Agency would be allowed to go by its provisions (ElBaradei 2011: 120–21).

Two factors account for much of the turnaround, perhaps all of it. One was the threat of war, seriously contemplated by a US Administration in a mental state of hubris and supported by the Israelis. Radical measures to prevent this seemed necessary. Another was the public exposure of Qadeer Khan's supply network, which had delivered sensitive nuclear technology to Libya. Disclosure of Iran's purchases from the same network was a sure consequence, so there was really no option but to admit to it.

---

7 In March 2013, the Iranian delegation was led by Deputy Foreign Minister for European and American Affairs Ali Asghar Kanji and the US delegation by Deputy Secretary of State William Burns. There may have been more than one meeting in Oman in 2012.

Two more factors – of a speculative nature in the absence of documentation – may have worked in the same direction. First, when the nuclear programme was revived in the midst of the war with Iraq, Saddam Hussein was conducting a secret nuclear weapon programme. How much Iran knew about it is unclear, but after the First Gulf War the programme was disclosed. Today, we know that Saddam abandoned it and that it was dismantled by UNSCOM,[8] but that was not clear at the time. The Western powers were not ready to draw that conclusion and Saddam was still in power. In 2003, when the occupying forces did not find any weapons of mass destruction and Saddam was removed, whatever concerns the Iranians might have had about Iraqi nuclear weapons disappeared. Second, it has been argued that, by 2003, Iran had already done so much work on non-nuclear components of nuclear weapons that stopping was no big sacrifice.

The first attempt by the EU3/EU to keep Iran unambiguously non-nuclear was part and parcel of this re-orientation: not only did Iran promise to cooperate with the IAEA and become fully transparent, but on 21 October 2003 it also signed the Teheran Agreed Statement with the EU3/EU in which it undertook to suspend sensitive fuel-cycle works and negotiate a long-term solution to the controversy. The scope of the Agreement proved contentious, however, particularly with regard to Iran's uranium conversion facility at Esfahan. Iran continued work on this facility and began converting uranium oxide into hexafluoride.

When these negotiations fell apart, the parties signed another agreement, in Paris on 15 November 2004, building on the Teheran agreement. In the Paris agreement, suspension of all enrichment-related and reprocessing activities was agreed and specified in unambiguous language.[9] The IAEA was invited to verify and monitor the suspension. The EU3/EU recognized that the suspension was a temporary and voluntary confidence-building measure and not a legal obligation.

---

8 The United Nations Special Commission on Iraq, charged with implementing the disarmament provisions of UNSC Res. 687, the ceasefire resolution on Iraq.

9 Iran undertook to 'continue and extend its suspension to include all enrichment related and reprocessing activities, and, specifically: the manufacture and import of gas centrifuges and their components; the assembly, installation, testing or operation of gas centrifuges; work to undertake any plutonium separation, or to construct or operate any plutonium separation installation; and all tests or production of any uranium conversion installation' (IAEA 2004).

2005/2006: A Fatal Turn of Events

The long-term arrangement to be negotiated on the basis of the Paris agreement should provide 'objective guarantees that Iran's nuclear programme is exclusively for peaceful purposes'. In return, Iran would get 'firm guarantees on nuclear, technological and economic cooperation and firm commitments on security issues (IAEA 2004). However, the parties never agreed on the operative meaning of 'objective guarantees'. Iran emphasized that, according to the provisions of the NPT, full transparency and application of the AP is all that an NPT member can legitimately be asked to accept. The EU3/EU emphasized that exercise of the 'inalienable right' to develop nuclear energy for peaceful purposes must be in conformity with Articles I and II of the NPT, and argued that, given Iran's long record of concealment and non-compliance with international obligations, the only way the international community could be confident that Iran was not determined to produce nuclear weapons was for Iran to forego all enrichment and reprocessing activities for a period to be defined. They probably had in mind a moratorium of 20 years or so.

At the core of the Framework for a Long-Term Agreement offered by the EU3/EU on 5 August 2005 were assurances of fuel supply for Iranian power reactors in return for a halt to all fuel-cycle activities (Framework 2005). Although international supply arrangements can never be as reliable as domestic sources of supply – the proposed buffer store would be located outside Iran – the credibility of these assurances was high. They were made by a group of states and communicated to all interested parties through a reputed international organization (the IAEA), and so could not be withdrawn by any individual government.

The Framework recognized Iran's right to develop a nuclear power programme, but stopped short of offering Iran light-water reactors. Article IV of the NPT commits supplier states to facilitate access to technology for non-nuclear-weapon state parties, but the text of the Framework promised only 'not to impede participation in open competitive tendering' (NPT, Article IV, paragraph 19b).

In addition to ratifying the AP, Iran should undertake to cooperate pro-actively with the IAEA to solve all outstanding issues, including by allowing IAEA inspectors to visit any site or interview any person they deem relevant to their monitoring of nuclear activity in Iran. To this, Iran responded that such inspections would go beyond the Additional Protocol, and considered this demand an intimidating infringement of national sovereignty (Islamic Republic of Iran 2005).

According to the Paris guidelines, the long-term agreement 'will ... provide ... firm commitments on security issues'. The actual offer included nothing of the sort. Neither was it easy for the EU3/EU to do so, for the main threat to Iranian security came from the USA, which kept Iran under high pressure and was doing military contingency planning for an attack on it.

The EU3/EU kept Washington well informed about the negotiations. The US Government made two gestures that conveyed a semblance of support, while staying at a distance: they would no longer object to negotiations for Iranian membership in the World Trade Organization (WTO), and they were willing to provide spare parts for Iranian civilian aircraft. There is a long way, however, from the start of WTO negotiations to a successful conclusion, and talks may easily get derailed. Providing spare parts for civilian aircraft of US origin ought to be a matter of course: denying it put civilians at risk without in any way affecting Iran's nuclear programme. The US side did not invest in the talks, but as long as the Europeans remained committed to halting all fuel-cycle works in Iran they could do no harm.

For several months, expectations of major steps toward an overall diplomatic solution were high. At the March 2005 meeting of the IAEA Board Iran did not figure on the agenda – for the first time in almost two years. In Iran, however, criticism was mounting as the negotiations failed to make visible headway. Well before they received the European offer, Iranian officials had indicated that they would not continue with the full suspension (ElBaradei 2011: 144). On 1 August, they announced that uranium conversion at Esfahan would resume.

A few days later, the European offer was presented. The Iranian response was sharp: 'the proposal is extremely long on demands … (and) absurdly short on offers to Iran…(and) amounts to an insult to the Iranian nation (Islamic Republic of Iran 2005).

From then on, the conflict escalated rapidly. On 24 September, the IAEA Board characterized Iran's history of concealment and reporting failures as constituting 'non-compliance', a term that foreshadowed referral of the Iranian file to the UN Security Council. That happened on 4 February 2006, and the next day Iran withdrew from the Additional Protocol – as it had said it would do. Two months later, the updated US National Security Strategy named Iran as the single greatest threat to the United States.

2006–2009: Posturing Over a Vexing Problem

Between 2006 and 2009 there were virtually no formal negotiations that could have introduced constraints. Proposals were exchanged and the chief negotiators and others met, but there was only one brief official meeting between Iran and the P5+1 (held in Geneva in July 2008).

When Iran reverted to the standard safeguards agreement, the IAEA gradually lost overview of what was going on. On occasion, the Agency was allowed to go beyond the agreement, but only at Iran's discretion.[10] It could no longer follow the production of centrifuges, only register installation of them where fissile materials were used. In 2007, the problem was compounded by the fact that Iran also reverted to the original safeguards provision requiring states to notify the IAEA 180 days before a new facility would become operational. In 2003, it had accepted – as the last country to do so – the new code 3.1. of the subsidiary safeguards arrangements, which requires notification as soon as the decision to build a new facility has been made . Now it withdrew unilaterally – as the first to do that. From then on, construction of new enrichment plants could go far without the Agency being aware of it. Enrichment generally leaves weak signatures, so national intelligence services may also fail to register such activities.

On European initiative, the P5+1 presented a new proposal in June 2006 which was more generous than the previous one, in substance and in tone. Unlike the EU3/EU offer of August 2005, the big powers now committed to actively supporting the construction of new light-water reactors in Iran using state-of-the-art technology. They also offered to improve Iran's access to the international economy through practical support for full integration into international structures, including the WTO, and to create a framework for increased direct investment and trade with Iran, including a trade and economic cooperation agreement with the EU. Steps would be taken to improve access to key goods and technologies. These and other provisions were presented without the patronizing tone of the first offer. However, the proposal repeated the demand for suspension of enrichment as a precondition for negotiations, and left the impression that resumption of activities would be predicated on Western approval.

Iran waited until 22 August to respond. Domestic bargaining seemed as complex as ever. But the Western powers did not wait, and the other veto powers went along: in the end of July a new Security Council resolution was adopted, making suspension mandatory under Chapter VII of the UN Charter. What could not be agreed under the NPT was now made illegal by the Security Council.

Iran's chief negotiator, Ali Larijani, tried to find a way around the suspension problem by limiting enrichment to the one or two cascades already in operation, or to a total of no more than 3000 centrifuges. Another possibility was some form of suspension in return for security assurances. Complete suspension

---

10 The main example was the work plan agreed in the autumn of 2008, containing a timetable for resolution of all outstanding inspection issues. A few questions remained unclarified, chiefly those pertaining to the 'alleged studies' stemming from an Iranian laptop that had landed in US hands, the authenticity of which has remained in doubt.

upfront seemed out of the question, but in Washington this requirement was written in stone: not one centrifuge would be allowed.

At the July 2008 meeting in Geneva, the USA was for the first time represented by a high official, Undersecretary of State William J. Burns. Mousavian's summary of what the US side wanted to achieve seems accurate: to show agreement with the other members of the P5+1; to prove that Washington was in favour of diplomatic means; and to convince the other P5+1 that if negotiations failed, there would be no alternative to more sanctions (Mousavian 2012: 311). In September, the Security Council passed its third sanctions resolution, and a fourth one was soon to follow.

2009– : A Glimpse of Hope … and Further Escalation

When Obama became US Presidents, there was a radical change of tone and atmosphere. Here was the man who had declared his willingness to talk with US adversaries without preconditions. Ahmadinejad sent a letter to Obama, congratulating him on his election.

The United States and Russia came up with a promising idea. Iran would receive fuel for the Teheran Research Reactor, which had worked on 20 per cent enriched uranium provided by Argentina, in return for transferring most of its low enriched uranium abroad. Of the 1,500 kilograms of low-enriched uranium (LEU) that Iran had produced at the time, 1,200 would be sent abroad. This way, Iran could demonstrate that its enrichment programme was for peaceful purposes. For the sceptics, what would remain in Iran was – if further enriched to weapons-grade – less than one bomb's worth. Most importantly for Teheran, Iran was not asked to stop or suspend enrichment. The proposal had the potential to defuse the enrichment issue and pave the way for serious negotiations. As a confidence-building measure, such a swap made good sense.

On 1 October 2009, Iran and the P5+1 met in Geneva to discuss the proposal. On the margins of the meeting, Burns and Jalili met bilaterally – the highest-level bilateral meeting between the two states in 30 years. In principle, the parties agreed to pursue the fuel swap. Another meeting was to be convened three weeks later to hammer out the details.[11]

But in Iran, it was pay-back time. Ahmadinejad, who had undermined Larijani's efforts to limit the enrichment programme and pursue the diplomatic track, supported the proposal – but now Larijani opposed it. Mir-Hossein Mousavi, who had been prime minister in the 1980s when the nuclear programme was revived, and front figure of the 'Greens' during the 2009 presidential elections, did the same. In the aftermath of the contested re-

_____

11 For an analysis of the fuel-swap negotiations, see Parsi (2011).

election of Ahmadinejad, the rivalries between institutions and personalities in the exceedingly complex Iranian political system were more intense than ever.

At the Geneva meeting the parties were innovative in their search for modalities, well assisted by ElBaradei. Still they failed to agree, and not solely because of the rivalries in Iran. The USA did not show much flexibility either. ElBaradei summarized his fuel-swap experiences thus: 'the pattern was familiar: nothing would satisfy, short of Iran coming to the table completely undressed' (2011: 313).

In the spring of 2010, Turkey and Brazil managed to strike a deal with Iran along similar lines. By that time Iran had produced 2,500 kilograms of LEU, so a swap bringing 1200 kilograms out of the country made it less attractive in Washington. Brazil and Turkey also recognized Iran's right to enrich under the NPT. The next day, the P5+1 announced that they had reached agreement on a fourth sanctions resolution on Iran for not having stopped its enrichment programme. Hillary Clinton branded the agreement a 'transparent ploy' by Iran to avoid new sanctions (Lee 2010).

Another meeting of the P5+1 and Iran took place in Istanbul in January 2011, and then three more meetings in Istanbul, Bagdad and Moscow in April, May and June 2012. Yet another meeting was held in Almaty in February 2013, also without results.

The Game-changer

The JPA specified that the first step, lasting for 6 months, obliged Iran not to enrich uranium over 5 per cent, and to dilute or convert to oxide what had been enriched to 20 per cent. Activities at Natanz, Fordow and Arak would not be advanced; there would be no new enrichment facility and no reprocessing or construction of reprocessing capabilities; and the IAEA would get managed access to uranium mines and mills and centrifuge production facilities. In return, sanctions would be lifted and Iranian assets abroad released, to a value of an estimated USD 6 billion. The parties aimed to conclude a comprehensive, final agreement of a specified long-term duration, at the end of which Iran would be treated in the same manner as any non-nuclear weapon state party to the NPT (CNN 2013).

That agreement has no legal status. It is not even signed. This way, potential spoilers were not let into the act. The weakness was the lack of a formal mechanism for dealing with acts of non-compliance. In this respect, however, the informal approach was vindicated, because the parties did take care to comply with all their obligations.

Understanding the Role of Dialogue

Power Shifts and Bargaining Cards

Iran's nuclear programme surfaced at the peak of the US unipolar moment, and Iran was treated accordingly: in top-down fashion. For the US side, there was no need to negotiate: talks were rewards for good behaviour, not means for achieving results. Overwhelming power would do the job. The arrogance of power and the patronizing style was somewhat tempered by the vexing problems in Iraq and Afghanistan, where Iran was called upon to assist – but it was not until Barack Obama took office in the White House that the declaratory policy changed in favour of negotiations based on mutual respect.

In 2003, the Europeans had stepped in to negotiate. They saw themselves as a 'human shield' against the use of force. Still, they were under the impact of US power and disbelief in negotiations, which may explain why their August 2005 offer to Iran was so thin on substance: it was simply not deemed appropriate to offer much. Or perhaps they had in mind to negotiate bazaar-style, not putting all their carrots up front (ElBaradei 2011: 144) – the offer of June 2006, which was more forthcoming than the previous one, suggests that this may have been the case. Anyhow, the Europeans had gravely misread developments in Iran.

Deeply disappointed by the results of the negotiations, the new government of Mahmoud Ahmadinejad took corrective action. Teheran adopted a more aggressive foreign policy, raised its regional ambitions, pursued its nuclear programme with greater vigour, and turned to the East and South for political support.[12] As his chief nuclear negotiator, Ahmadinejad appointed Ali Larijani, who had stressed the importance of ties with China and Russia; further, Ahmadinejad courted the non-aligned movement; and tried to get Iran accepted as a member of the Shanghai Cooperation Organization (but in vain). In part, this was a general foreign policy re-orientation; in part, it was also a tactic for weathering the nuclear crisis.

This way, Iran raised the stakes. So did the West – first by obtaining a mandatory Security Council resolution which denied Iran the right to conduct fuel-cycle works; second, by a series of UN sanctions resolutions followed by comprehensive US and European sanctions blocking oil imports from Iran and blacklisting the Iranian central bank. Third, cyber-attacks were undertaken to delay the enrichment programme; and fourth, nuclear scientists were assassinated and covert operations undertaken to stir unrest and gather information. All the time, the military option was kept alive. For ten years, the haggling over Iran's nuclear programme was a power play. The logic was zero-sum.

---

12 Ahmadinejad and his team preferred the phrase 'expansion of capacities' instead of 'looking to the East' to describe Teheran's new foreign-policy orientation.

Why then did Russia and China go along with the other P5+1 on so many proposals and Security Council resolutions?

Russia always wanted to prevent Iran from completing the fuel cycle. In this respect, it has been attuned to the USA and the EU all the time. It undertook to finish the Bushehr reactor and would have liked to get more reactor contracts – not only for economic reasons, but also because command over parts of the Iranian nuclear programme gave good bargaining chips in negotiations with the West ('if you are more cooperative in this or that respect, we will be more cooperative on Iran'). In the face of important trade-offs with the West, Iranian concerns were expendable. Moreover, working relations with Teheran were valuable conduits for Russian influence in the Middle East, and important for regaining influence in Central Asia.

For China, too, relations with the USA clearly trumped those with Iran. In this century, China's stakes in Iranian oil production have been fast growing – up to the point when the US issued secondary sanctions. Politically, China's relations with Iran are not very comprehensive, and there are no strategic bonds. Both China and Russia have worked to modify UN resolutions; and, like the other BRICS countries, China is in favour of diplomacy and against the use of force. But as long as Russia accommodates to Western policies, China has had little reason to break out of the P5+1 consensus.

Ahmadinejad's turn to the East was, therefore, not much of a success. Iran remained solidly stuck in its confrontation with the West and its differences with the big powers – until 2013, when 'Direction West' and a solution to the nuclear problem became the unambiguous top priority in Iranian foreign affairs. Thus, when the Ukrainian crisis erupted in the winter of 2014, Rouhani did not waver, but used the occasion to reconfirm his interest in rapprochement with the West, indicating that Iran might help in diversifying Europe's natural gas supplies.

As long as the negotiations are productive and there is realism to the objective of a final solution to the nuclear problem, 'direction West' will remain the priority. Also, this is key to realization of common interests in the region. However, if this is the trajectory along which things are moving, Iran will naturally re-orient itself in a multi-centric world where China and other Asian states matter more and more, and the USA and Europe less and less.

The Strategic Perspective

Before the breakthrough of 2013, there was never a shared strategic vision of what to go for.

Neither was there a shared perspective of what the talks should cover. In 2003, Iran had proposed a grand bargain, resolving the nuclear problem in the framework of Middle East politics writ large. The US scoffed, even reprimanding the messenger for having conveyed it.[13] The negotiations with the EU3/EU covered various issues in addition to the nuclear one, and so did the P5+1 offer of June 2006. However, the United States never believed in the EU exercise. With hindsight, the P5+1 offer of June 2006 seems to have been a means to obtain Russian and Chinese support for the UNSC resolution under Chapter VII of the UN Charter, ordering Iran to stop all fuel cycle works, research and development (R&D) included. In practice, the verification requirements of the offer amounted to indefinite suspension, which Iran was certain to reject – and Iranian rejection would make P5+1 consensus easier to achieve.

Later, Iran made more proposals for a comprehensive settlement with the West and a solution to the nuclear problem in that context.[14] In the words of Mousavian, 'Iranians have always believed that reconciliation with the United States should come in the form of a broad-based policy, not with a piecemeal deal on the nuclear issue, unless a nuclear deal is comprehensive and covers Iran's full rights' (Mousavian 2012: 247). Iran therefore wanted direct contact with the United States, without which such a deal could never be struck. At one point in the fuel-swap negotiations it even proposed that Iranian LEU could be held in US custody – a clear invitation to bilateral talks with the US Government.

During his first term, Obama sent different signals. Or else he held back for lack of constructive Iranian response to his overtures. He tried – in Oman and in other ways – to engage the Iranians, knowing that on several occasions Iran, too, had wanted bilateral talks. But the breakthrough had to wait for a new government in Teheran.

Rouhani and Obama agreed to limit the negotiations to the nuclear issues, so as not to overburden the talks. Both Iran and the USA were ready to do business in a win–win perspective, for a comprehensive overlap of national interests had evolved. Rouhani had served as chief negotiator and knew the issues, and he launched a broad confidence-building campaign to alleviate ingrained US scepticism. His style, dramatically different from that of his predecessor, was conducive to this. When things began to happen, they moved quickly.

Exchange of Concessions

Both the Rafsanjani and the Khatami governments had tried to mend fences with the West, especially with the EU. When developments in 2003 called for a

---

13 This person was the Swiss caretaker of US interests in Iran, Tim Guldiman.

14 For instance, in May 2006 ElBaradei conveyed a message from Larijani to Condoleezza Rice: 'The Iranians were interested in direct talks with the United States. They were ready to discuss not only Iran's nuclear issues, but also Iraq, Afghanistan, Hezbollah, and Hamas' (ElBaradei 2011: 194).

radical change of nuclear policy, the Khatami team made sweeping concessions to get negotiations with the EU going and bring hostilities to an end. In this period, the EU3 became key economic partners for Iran.

The Iranian concessions upfront were expanded somewhat during the negotiations, and at the end the EU3/EU made a comprehensive offer. Concessions were never traded step by step.

Between 2006 and 2009 the parties exchanged proposals, but came to the table only once to discuss them. In this period, they were shadow-boxing at a distance, leaving it to the EU's Solana and Iran's Larijani/Jalili to look for openings. When supporters of diplomacy seemed to make progress, they were undermined. The spoilers had the upper hand.

In October 2009, the parties had a brief but intense give-and-take over the proposed fuel swap. The negotiators were quite innovative, but could not overcome the domestic constraints under which they were labouring.

It was not until the Istanbul meeting of April 2012 that Iran and the P5+1 agreed on a step-by-step approach based on reciprocity.[15] At that point, there were expectations of a productive continuation. However, the approach was not followed up in practice. Neither did the February 2013 meeting in Almaty lead anywhere. As so many times before, the subsequent meetings in Bagdad, Moscow and Almaty did not come to much more than exchanges of different positions and proposals. Diplomats described them as 'the dialogue of the deaf'.

Thus, it took ten years to come to a sustained exchange of give-and-take in the mutual interest. Iran and the USA paved the way for the JPA in bilateral talks. The other P5+1 basically endorsed what had been agreed, except for a French intervention to tighten the language about the Arak heavy-water reactor. In some important respects, the Iranian concessions were similar to those made by Iran in the Teheran and Paris agreements of 2003 and 2004: suspension of fuel-cycle activities and expanded access for inspectors. In 2003, Iran let the IAEA apply the AP: that was not part of the interim deal, but the Agency got access to the sites for centrifuge production and mining and milling of uranium. While the EU3 had been short and vague on offers, this time commitments from the P5+1 were more specific.

Agreed Criteria

Ashton's summary of the April 2012 talks in Istanbul had an interesting ambiguity: 'We have agreed that the non-proliferation treaty forms a key basis for what must be serious engagement to ensure that all the obligations under the treaty are met while fully respecting Iran's right to the peaceful use of nuclear

---

15 '... we will be guided by the principle of the step-by-step approach and reciprocity' (Ashton 2012).

energy' (Ashton 2012). Some wanted to read this as an opening for a solution based on the right to enrich in return for comprehensive inspections to ensure that all obligations under the treaty were met – in accordance with the principles of the NPT and the extra inspection activities needed to clarify the remnants of the past. However, the phrase 'a key basis' hinted that the NPT was not the only basis: there were also the Security Council resolutions requiring Iran to suspend all fuel-cycle works and accede to the Additional Protocol.

The treatment of Iran stands in stark contrast to Argentina and Brazil, which have more advanced enrichment programmes than Iran and which never accepted the AP, yet enjoy full fuel-cycle rights. In Iran, even R&D on nuclear enrichment has been deemed a threat to international peace and security. That shows how utterly embedded the Iranian case has been, and still remains, in politics and lack of trust.

In some respects, ambiguity has worked to the Iranians' advantage. Because of their nuclear programme they have been basking in international attention, leaving Egypt and other Arab states by the wayside. If others believe they are dealing with a would-be nuclear weapon state, they may be more inclined to accommodate to Iranian interests. For instance, when the UAE ambassador to Washington said that if Iran crosses the threshold, Gulf states may have to turn away from the USA and accommodate to Iran, ambiguity seemed to work in Iran's interest.[16] It added weight to Iran's voice in the Middle East.

The JPA seeks to remove that ambiguity. What Ashton referred to as 'a' basis is now *the* basis. The interim part of the agreement accepts continued enrichment, and the comprehensive solution would involve 'a mutually defined enrichment programme'. The preamble to the JPA states: 'the comprehensive solution would enable Iran to fully enjoy its right to nuclear energy for peaceful purposes under the relevant articles of the NPT in conformity with its obligations therein'. If the negotiations succeed, the Security Council Resolutions must, sooner or later, be replaced by a new resolution in conformity with these principles.

Confidence-building: The Functions of IAEA Inspections

The talks were conducted against the backdrop of IAEA safeguards and negotiations with Iran about the modalities of inspections. Inspections have the potential to build confidence, but from February 2006, when the Iran file

---

16 'The United Arab Emirates ambassador to the United States told Jeffrey Goldberg of the *Atlantic Magazine* in 2010 that if the United States allowed Iran to cross the nuclear threshold, the small Arab countries of the Persian Gulf region would have no choice but to leave the American orbit and align themselves with Iran out of self-protection' (Zuckermann 2012).

went to the Security Council, the Agency was no longer in a position to search for potentially undeclared facilities.

Iran withdrew its permission to apply the AP, so the Agency had to revert to the standard safeguards agreement (INFCIRC 153) which limits verification to declared activities involving nuclear materials. More and more, it lost track of ongoing activities. For instance, it could no longer follow the production of centrifuges – how many, where, and of what kind – only register what was installed at the declared facilities. The IAEA was further hampered by Iran's withdrawal from code 3.1. of the subsidiary arrangement. The scope of the unknown grew, and with it the potential for speculations.

In 2007, Iran and the IAEA agreed on a work plan to resolve the outstanding issues of the past. After a few months, only one issue remained: the alleged weaponization studies originating from a laptop that the US had received in 2004, containing information about the so-called Green Salt (uranium tetrafluoride, UF4) project, which included high explosives testing, design of a missile re-entry vehicle to accommodate a nuclear warhead, and administrative interconnections between these studies. Taken together, they pointed to a possible nuclear weapons programme. The problem was to verify the authenticity of the information. The material had no chain of custody, no clear source, no date of issue, no document markings and nothing else that could determine its authenticity (Kelley 2014).

The parties made active use of IAEA reports to influence the course of events. The Western powers shared information with the Agency selectively, at times of their choosing, to alert it to suspicious activities. On one occasion, the US President also did his best to cast doubt on his own National Intelligence Estimate (NIE), which had failed to confirm his allegations against Iran: the 2007 NIE stated that Iran had pursued weapons-oriented activities up to 2003, but that these activities were stopped that year and had not resumed since. In response, President Bush argued that Iran was dangerous nevertheless. Something similar happened in 2011, when the new NIE held on to the same conclusion, but with little impact on the perceptions of US politicians. The list of statements claiming that Iran could or would get nuclear weapons in the more or less immediate future grew steadily longer.

Sometimes, Western demands for more inspections were made in the knowledge that nobody can prove a negative and in the hope of finding incriminating evidence. Iran claimed that more access gave rise to more questions: except for the work plan, it therefore opened up only partially, in calculated moves and for specific political ends. Under these circumstances, the confidence-building effect of the inspections was questionable at best and counterproductive at worst. All the time, inspections were turned and twisted for political ends.

The breakthrough of 2013 created an atmosphere more conducive for clarification of Iran's nuclear history. The Agency and Iran agreed on a step-by-step plan, the first leg of which was clarification, by 15 May 2014, of seven unresolved issues, including Iran's work on exploding bridge wire detonators.[17] More difficult questions related to 'possible military dimensions' would be addressed on a timetable to be agreed.

If intelligence reports and independent experts are correct in saying that, until 2003, the programme had military ingredients, how would that information be handled? In part, publicity is a matter of time and circumstance to minimize the spin that spoilers might give to it and to get the proportions right. In part, the question is whether the military elements have long-term consequences for Iranian capabilities. If not, 'grandfathering' would be an option, with or without publication of the sensitive elements – without, if it is judged to jeopardize realization of the deal. The handling of such sensitive issues also depends on a deeper understanding of the extent to which the activities were politically authorized or conducted by scientific and technical experts on their own initiative. Experience from other countries shows that if experts are left on their own, they sometimes veer off in directions that may be scientifically interesting, but not in conformity with international obligations.

Such issues would be for the Joint Commission of the P5+1 and Iran, established by the JPA, to consider together with the IAEA.

Domestic Constraints

In both Teheran and Washington, the Iranian nuclear programme has been a matter of intense contention between rivalling political groups. On many occasions, the Iranians tried to get in direct contact with the Americans, but they were not uniformly in favour of it depending on the circumstances. That changed with Hassan Rouhani, who got broad and strong support for his policies.

Under Ahmadinejad, the nuclear programme became the signal expression of sovereignty and independence, which were among the hallmarks of the Iranian revolution. He pushed the programme aggressively. However, in the autumn of 2009 Ahmadinejad appeared genuinely interested in a fuel swap deal, but came under fire from his opponents in the reformist as well as in the conservative camps. His opponents wanted to deny him the success of an agreement with the West, and they succeeded. In the turbulent aftermath of the presidential elections that year, the Iranian political system became bogged down in institutional and personal rivalries. Leaders threatened to put each

---

17 These may have civilian and conventional military applications as well as being a trigger mechanism for nuclear bombs.

other before the court, and Ahmadinejad was unable to exploit the opportunity represented by the new US President.

The USA is strongly pro-Israel, and US strategy documents have repeatedly named Iran as the number one enemy. Accepting Iran as a legitimate state with legitimate national interests, and as a regional power with a political agenda of its own, is therefore hard to swallow, especially for the US Congress. For many members of Congress, regime change in Teheran remains the key objective.

This was, in short, the political context that Obama inherited in 2009. For a while, his policy was to hold the Israelis back, buy time, impose more sanctions, make probes to test the realism of serious diplomatic engagement, and wait for the Iranians to be ready for it.

Personality Factors: The Role of Leaders and Negotiators

The domestic constraints left little chance for personal initiatives and personality traits to play a role in the conduct of diplomacy. Before the breakthrough, what came closest was the Solana-Larijani relationship. The two men spent considerable time together, also behind closed doors, and probably had as good a working relationship as the dire framework conditions would allow.

Both of them were pragmatic negotiators with personal stakes in diplomatic progress. Larijani recounted a phone call with Solana immediately after UNSC Resolution 1696 of July 2006 had been adopted – which made any fuel-cycle activity including R&D a threat to international peace and security – in which Solana said, 'The spoilers have done their job' (Mousavian 2012: 252). A few months later, it appeared that Solana and Larijani had reached a two-page agreement where Iran agreed not to launch new cascades for enrichment for a period of two months as a voluntary, non-binding and temporary measure, if UN sanctions were lifted.[18] This was a variation of ElBaradei's freeze-for-freeze proposal a little earlier, where Iran would stop adding new centrifuges while the P5+1 would refrain from new sanctions resolutions. The USA turned it down, but the other powers agreed to give Solana more time before considering further sanctions. However, it ended in a second sanctions resolution, UNSC Res.1747 of March 2007.

New negotiations between Solana and Larijani started in the spring of 2007. There were indications of a possible agreement between them, and the BBC reported that Larijani had carried an unofficial proposal for limited suspension which had been turned down by the EU. It was also rejected, out of hand, by Ahmadinejad. A third round took place in the summer of 2007. Shortly thereafter, Larijani resigned amid fierce criticism from Ahmadinejad, who complained about clandestine negotiations between 'some people' and the

---

18 Published by the *Washington Post* half a year later (Mousavian 2012: 254).

European countries, meaning Larijani. The rift between them was indeed deep, Ahmadinejad being idealistic and aggressive while Larijani was more pragmatic and attuned to international conditions and global power equations.

When Larijani resigned, 'all of his efforts to find a formula for sustained negotiations with the P5+1 had been blocked' (ElBaradei 2011: 266). He was replaced by Saeed Jalili, known to be a hard-line conservative.

In one respect, the Solana-Larijani talks were similar to the 'walk in the woods' during the INF (euro-missile) negotiations of the 1980s, featuring Paul Nitze and Yuli Kvitsinski. In yet another wave of rearmament and East–West confrontation, they had conducted a bilateral on the margins of their instructions to find a way out of the stalled negotiations. Solana and Larijani seem to have done much the same.

When Rouhani took the reins, the style changed completely. He and his negotiators were not only business-like: they were good communicators as well. They displayed a new openness, and their public diplomacy built confidence. The Rouhani coalition enjoyed broad and strong support at home, so its commitment to a negotiated solution appeared unambiguous.

Bargaining With a View to a Win–Win Solution

Search for win–win outcomes requires mutual understanding to make communications effective. As a minimum, both parties must be able to present the positions of the other in their own words, yet in such a way that the other would agree (Deutsch 1957). After Rouhani was elected, frequent communications between the negotiating teams – on the phone in-between the meetings – created that understanding.

That said, negotiating positions are not the same as national interests. A fair reading of national interests requires proper understanding of the social, economic and political factors that determine the policies of 'the other'. And that, in turn, requires political space and legitimacy for efforts at comprehending. For a long while, all of that was lacking, especially on the US side.

After the Iranian revolution of 1979, Washington and Teheran exchanged condemnations, and no diplomats. US governmental expertise evaporated for lack of career prospects. The superpower was united around adversarial attitudes, took the high ground and spoke power politics. It knew what to say and do, so not only did those who could present nuances and alternative readings of Iranian affairs become superfluous: at times they were also a nuisance. Of course, Iranian understandings of the USA suffered, too, but the smaller party has to be more attentive to the behaviour of the big adversary than vice versa. By comparison, European-Iranian affairs were in a better state.

To the extent that there was a search for win–win options, it took place a step below the top decision-making level, between negotiators who had developed a personal interest in diplomatic progress. Negotiators are sometimes tempted to finesse and stretch their mandates, probing the scene to achieve results. Solana and Larijani tried their luck – as did ElBaradei. He was heavily criticised for it, and fiercely so for the work plan with the Iranians to settle the historical scores of the nuclear programme. Larijani resigned when diplomacy with the P5+1 got stuck. Typically, whenever they seemed to be making progress, another Security Council resolution blocked it. Or the rivals for political power in Teheran denied each other a diplomatic success. Or some other top-level move, such as a damaging piece of intelligence, came in the way. When the negotiators tried to find a way ahead they were quickly undermined and brought to order.

However, while the diplomatic track was blocked, overlapping national interests evolved, more and more, between Iran and the US. At the same time, it became increasingly obvious that the alternatives to a negotiated solution – sanctions and the use of force – were futile and detrimental to both sides. Therefore, when Rouhani came to power in Teheran he found a ready partner in the White House, and that allowed them to take advantage of what had become a distinctly win–win situation.

Summary and Conclusions

For ten years, there was no shared vision of what to go for or what the talks should cover. There were many exchanges of positions, but few attempts at sustained exchanges of concessions. There were no agreed criteria – the NPT being 'a key basis', and Security Council resolutions another. Subordinated to politics, international inspections became bones of contention. Iran stalled and reverted to the minimum safeguards obligations under the NPT; Western leaders asked for more inspections in the knowledge that nobody can prove a negative and in the hope of finding incriminating evidence.[19] All the time, the domestic constraints were tight and the negotiators were held on a short leash. When the most enterprising among them tried to find common ground at the margin of their instructions (Solana, Larijani) they were quickly reined in. When ElBaradei agreed with Iran on a work plan to clarify Iran's nuclear history, he was fiercely criticized for the initiative. The diplomatic process was far, far away from anything resembling integrative approaches to conflict resolution (Fisher and Ury 1991) or communicative action (Habermas 1984).

The talks were characterized as 'dialogues of the deaf': they were about little more than exchanges of positions and associated questions of clarification. There was no sustained process of give and take. When, at long last, it was

---

19 Hans Blix argues that mistakes made in Iraq are made over again in Iran (Serri 2011).

agreed in principle to go step by step on the basis of reciprocity, the parties proved unable to do so in practice.

The talks were also 'dialogues of the blind', for lack of understanding of 'the other'. In 2005, the EU3/EU either failed to grasp the turn that Iranian politics was taking, or they were held back by the United States. More likely, it was a combination of both. Washington was not in the mood to listen and understand, and power politics trumped the search for diplomatic solutions. Most of the time, also the UK and France addressed Iran top-down. More than anything else, the name of the game was power play.

Sometimes actors go to the negotiations table because it is deemed the correct thing to do, not because they believe in a diplomatic solution. For instance, if military action is contemplated, failed talks may be important to gain legitimacy for it. Sometimes talks are motivated by the opposite – resorting to diplomacy in an effort to *avoid* a military outcome. That was the main concern of the Europeans from the beginning in 2003 and for other members of the Permanent 5 when they became involved in the talks in 2006, and it was a leitmotif for ElBaradei.

At long last, in 2013 the parties reached out for realization of common interests. Iran was seeking to get out of isolation, while the USA was lowering its military profile in the region in order to concentrate on the Asian pivot: out of Iraq, out of Afghanistan, in the back-seat during much of the bombing of Libya, and refraining from military involvement in Syria. Also, Iran and the USA had overlapping interests in the stabilization of Iraq and Afghanistan and, potentially, in turning Hezbollah into a purely political organization, which would meet some of the Congressional conditions for lifting sanctions against Iran. This confluence of national interests created a unique opportunity to solve one of the most deep-seated conflicts in international affairs. The transition from diplomatic futility to realization of common interests had been waiting for the right constellation of governments: now, it occurred rapidly.

Diplomacy was reinforced also because the alternatives – sanctions and use of force – appeared increasingly counterproductive. For Iran, a US military attack could be devastating. For the USA, another major war in the Middle East could be a disastrous setback for its global strategy focusing on Asia. The sanctions did not solve the problem either. When UN sanctions were first imposed, Iran had centrifuges in the low hundreds. By 2013 the number had grown to 19,000, and more efficient centrifuges had been developed. The longer the sanctions lasted and the more comprehensive they were made, the bigger the problem became. Inflicting more pain did not yield more gain: it is the prospect of sanctions *relief* that can yield negotiating benefits. Sanctions can work only if they can be lifted.

But did the sanctions bring Rouhani to power? The question is critically important, for another outcome of the 2013 presidential elections might have meant continued stalemate.

A poll undertaken by Teheran University/University of Maryland shows that only 2 per cent of Rouhani's supporters cited the lifting of sanctions as a reason for supporting him. 96 per cent said that sanctions were worth it in order to retain the country's enrichment right (Parsi 2014). Did the sanctions account for the new, constructive Iranian approach to negotiations? Rouhani tried to clinch a deal also between 2003 and 2005, when he was chief negotiator. Ten years later, he got another chance with the USA and the P5+1 and this time, Washington was ready for business, too. In the meantime, the sanctions had become a heavy burden on the Iranian economy, so the chance of getting them lifted made Rouhani's motivation for seeking a diplomatic solution all the stronger. The sanctions gave the USA more leverage – but so did 19,000 centrifuges for Iran.

The diplomatic modalities that broke the ice were dual track. On the one hand, there were bilateral US-Iranian talks shielded by secrecy: this was necessary to get the process started.[20] Simultaneously, Iran launched a public confidence-building campaign that conveyed a sincere interest in reconciliation with the West, and in a style radically different from the past.

The parties failed to meet the self-imposed deadline of 20 July 2014, for the conclusion of a final long-term deal, and agreed to continue the talks. Both the Iranian and the American negotiators were keenly aware that they had to do their very best to satisfy their demanding domestic constituencies. On the other hand, they also knew that drawn-out negotiations would strengthen the spoilers. They therefore gave themselves another four months, until 24 November – i.e. a bit less than another six months extension of the JPA – to achieve a long-term solution.

They failed to meet that deadline, too, but noted that significant progress had been made. Believing that a diplomatic settlement remained possible, they aimed at a headline agreement by the end of March 2015, and to have all elements of a final agreement ready by the end of July.

After the JPA was adopted, the opposition to a negotiated long-term solution ceded ground to the supporters, slowly but surely, in the US and elsewhere. This is known from a variety of contexts: there is a general propensity to accommodate to new facts. Still, in the public realm, incompatible red lines were drawn. Iran emphasized that none of their facilities should be dismantled:

---

20 'I am convinced that the only way to get this particular process started was to do it quietly, and we did everything we could to bring that about, which is not an easy thing in this day and age'. Deputy Secretary of State William Burns to Al-Monitor (Rosen 2014).

what had been built at great cost should not be reversed. The USA asked for a significant reduction of Iranian enrichment capacity; specifically, that the number of operating centrifuges be reduced to allow for a warning time of the order of 6–12 months in case of breakout. While being matters of fact, none of these positions seemed entirely logical. In the case of Iran, it was hard to argue that preservation of facilities based on first generation centrifuges should be a top priority. For the USA, a maximally effective safeguards regime would seem more important than the number of centrifuges at known, safeguarded facilities, for if Iran were to use material from such facilities for weapons, the alarm bells would ring immediately. Better, then, to base a breakout on clandestine installations.

Other issues of contention were the timescale for elimination of sanctions, the credibility of US offers in that respect, and the length of the normalization process. The USA asked for more than 10 years, Iran for less than 10.

In the Middle East, the dramatic territorial gains of the islamist group ISIS; the breakdown of the US sponsored Israeli-Palestinian peace process and the summer 2014 war in Gaza; and the implications of the ongoing US strategic shift to Asia turned the national and regional political agendas away from the Iranian nuclear problem. When the first extension of the JPA was announced, no one seemed to pay much notice (Alpher 2014). The second extension did not draw much attention either. However, faced with a choice between final agreement or diplomatic breakdown, the consequences will in both cases be so far-reaching that everybody will pay notice.

References

Alpher, Y. 2014. *Iran and the P5+1: Did Anyone in the Middle East Notice the Four Month Extension?* NUPI Report.

Ashton, C. 2012. Statement by High Representative Catherine Ashton on behalf of the E3+3 following the talks with Iran, Istanbul. European Union, Brussels. 1739(12) 14 April.

Clapper, J.R. 2012. *Unclassified Statement for the Record on the Worldwide Threat Assessment of the US Intelligence Community for the Senate Select Committee on Intelligence* [Online, 31 January]. Available at: http://www.intelligence.senate.gov/120131/clapper.pdf [accessed: 7 August 2014].

CNN 2013. The Iran Nuclear Deal: Full Text. *CNN* [Online, 24 November]. Available at: http://edition.cnn.com/2013/11/24/world/meast/iran-deal-text/index.html [accessed: 7 August 2014].

Coleman, P. 2011. *The Five Percent: Finding Solutions to Seemingly Impossible Conflicts.* New York: Public Affairs.

Deutsch, K.W. 1963. *The Nerves of Government: Models of Political Communication and Control.* New York: Free Press.

ElBaradei, M. 2011. *The Age of Deception: Nuclear Diplomacy in Treacherous Times.* New York: Metropolitan Books.

Engelbrekt, K. and Hallenberg, J. 2007. *The European Union and Strategy: An Emerging Actor.* London and New York: Routledge.

Fisher, R., and Ury, W. 1991. *Getting to Yes: Negotiating Agreement Without Giving In.* New York: Penguin Books.

Framework. 2005. *Framework for a Long-term Agreement between the Islamic Republic of Iran and France, Germany and the United Kingdom, with the support of the High Representative of the European Union* [Online]. Available at: www.pricenter.org/data/resources/Iran Framework050805.pdf [accessed: 7 August 2014].

Habermas, J. 1984. *Theory of Communicative Action,* translated by T. McCarthy. Boston, MA: Beacon Press.

IAEA 2004. *Communication dated 24 November 2004 received from the Permanent Representatives of France, Germany, the Islamic republic of Iran and the United Kingdom concerning the agreement signed in Paris 15 November 2004,* INFCIRC/637, 26 November.

IAEA 2011. Implementation of the NPT Safeguards Agreement and relevant provisions of Security Council resolutions in the Islamic Republic of Iran. IAEA Board of governors. Gov/2011/65, 8. November [Online]. Available at: http://www.isisnucleariran.org/assets/pdf/IAEA_Iran_8Nov2011.pdf [accessed: 7 August 2014].

Islamic Republic of Iran 2005. *Response of the Islamic Republic of Iran to the Framework Agreement Proposed by the E-3/EU* [Online]. Available at: www.basicint.org/countries/iran/IranResponse.pdf [accessed: 7 August 2014].

Katzman 2014. *Iran Sanctions,* Congressional Research Service, 26 June.

Kelley, R. 2014. *The Agreement with Iran, NUPI report* [Online]. Available at: http://english.nupi.no/content/download/494465/1643242/file/The%20Agreement%20with%20Iran.pdf [accessed: 7 August 2014].

Lee, M. 2010. *Clinton Calls Iran Offer a Ploy to Avoid Sanctions,* Associated Press, 26 May.

Miller, S.E. 2007. Proliferation Gamesmanship: Iran and the Politics of Nuclear Confrontation, *Syracuse Law Review,* 57(3), 551–59.

Mousavian, S.H. 2012. *Iranian Nuclear Crisis.* Washington, DC: Carnegie Endowment for International Peace.

Parsi, T. 2011. *A Single Roll of the Dice.* New Haven, CT: Yale University Press.

Parsi, T. 2014. No, Sanctions Didn't Force Iran to Make a Deal. *Foreign Policy* [Online]. Available at: http://www.foreignpolicy.com/articles/2014/05/14/sanctions_did_not_force_iran_to_make_a_deal [accessed: 7 August 2014].

Pleming, S. 2006. Rice says time for talking with Iran is over, Reuters, 23 January.

Rosen, L. 2014. No illusions' about nuclear diplomacy with Iran. Al-Monitor. 16 January [Online]. Available at: http://www.al-monitor.com/pulse/originals/2014/01/iran-diplomacy-bill-burns-interview.html [accessed: 7 August 2014].

Sahimi, M. 2010. Iran's Ever Imminent Nukes: A History of Hysteria, *Anti War Com* [Online, 5 May]. Available at: http://original.antiwar.com/sahimi/2010/05/04/irans-ever-imminent-nukes [accessed: 7 August 2014].

Samore, G. 2011. The ball is very much in Teheran's court', RFE/RL. [Online, 14 April]. Available at: www.rferl.org/content/interview_samore_russia_iran_us_policy/3557326.html [accessed: 7 August 2014].

Sanger, D. 2012. Obama Ordered Wave of Cyberattacks against Iran, *The New York Times* [Online, 1 June]. Available at: http://www.nytimes.com/2012/06/01/world/middleeast/obama-ordered-wave-of-cyberattacks-against-iran.html?pagewanted=all&_r=0 [accessed: 7 August 2014].

Serri, H. 2011. Iran's Inspectors are Repeating the Iraq Mistakes. *Informed Comment* [Online, 18 November]. Available at: www.juancole.com/.../serri-irans-un-inspectors-are-repeating-the-iraq-mistakes.html [accessed: 7 August 2014].

Zuckermann, M.B. 2012. *US News and World Report*, 12 March. [Online]. Available at: http://news.yahoo.com/mort-zuckerman-obama-must-act-promptly-prevent-nuclear-162559068.html [accessed: 7 August 2014].

Chapter 7
Libya: The Promise and Pitfalls of Diplomacy

Målfrid Braut-Hegghammer and Pernille Rieker

Introduction

This chapter examines the role of diplomacy in crisis resolution between Libya and the international community from the mid-1990s until the fall of Muammar Gaddafi. After decades of radical policies and growing tensions, the Gaddafi regime found itself subject to international economic sanctions and isolation. Following repeated attempts to engage the West in dialogue, a series of secret negotiations began in the late 1990s. These talks culminated in the negotiated decommissioning of Libya's nuclear weapons programme in late 2003. As a result, Tripoli transitioned from international pariah toward a normalized status in international society. Within a decade of this breakthrough, the Gaddafi regime crumbled in the wake of a domestic revolution bolstered by a NATO-led air campaign.

These tumultuous developments give rise to questions about the possibilities and pitfalls for dialogue – and negotiated reform – with a radical and isolated authoritarian regime. What role did dialogue and diplomacy between the USA, EU member states and Libya play in this period? What can account for the substantial breakthroughs of earlier talks and negotiations – and why did diplomacy ultimately fail to resolve the conflict between the Gaddafi regime and the international community?

We examine these shifts, focusing primarily on the period between 1995 and 2011. During these years a series of secret talks and negotiations unfolded between the West and Libya. We enquire into the impact of domestic structural changes, external shocks such as the US-led War on Terror, and the roles played by force and diplomacy in shaping Libya's policies and behaviour during this period.

Isolation and Rapprochement

Colonel Muammar Gaddafi came to power after a military coup in September 1969. Under his rule, the Libyan regime adopted anti-colonial and increasingly radical foreign policies, fuelled by an oil boom in the early 1970s. Gaddafi developed an idiosyncratic ideology based on radical anti-colonial principles (manifest in his *Green Book*) and began to direct domestic and foreign policies in an increasingly radical direction. He set up Revolutionary Committees – groups of young radicals seeking to institute the principles of the Gaddafi regime in the realm of the state as well as society – to spread the principles and practices of his revolution among a sceptical population. These radical movements gained influence over the formal agencies of the state, also in the sphere of foreign policy, even (for a time) replacing professional diplomats. Gaddafi's revolutionary project was to challenge and undermine the state. The Revolutionary Committees were central agitators of the revolution, answerable solely to Gaddafi personally in his role as the Leader of the Revolution.

This shift led to controversial practices, like the declared policy of targeted assassinations of opposition figures residing abroad, through agents based in Libyan embassies. Combined with several high-level defections among Libyan ministers and diplomats, the emergence of the Revolutionary Committees undermined the Libyan diplomatic apparatus. In conversations between senior Libyan officials and their US counterparts during the late 1970s, schisms and tensions within the Libyan state were becoming evident. For example, in 1976 US Secretary of State Henry Kissinger met with Libyan UN ambassador Mansur Khikhia. During this meeting, Khikhia alluded to several difficulties on the Libyan side as regards coordination policies and internal lines of communication (National Security Archives 1976). Dealing with the Libyan regime was becoming increasingly complicated.

During the 1970s and 1980s, Gaddafi's idiosyncratic and radical ideology created frictions domestically and at the international level. Libya clashed with neighbours Egypt and (between 1978 and 1987) Chad. More broadly, Libya offered support for anti-colonial movements that employed terrorist and guerrilla tactics, providing financial support and training facilities. This support was given to radical movements across North Africa, the Middle East and Europe. These activities (particularly sponsoring movements that carried out terrorist attacks) caused increasing strains in Libya's relations with states in the Middle East and, Europe, and with the USA.

During the 1980s Libya's radical policies led to clashes with Western states and alienated their former ally, the Soviet Union. In 1981, US jets shot down two Libyan planes in the Gulf of Sidra. Two years earlier, attacks on the US embassy had led to the closure of the embassy. Over the next few years, US President Ronald Reagan characterized Gaddafi as the 'Mad Dog' of the Middle East, and defined Libyan regime change as a policy objective. In 1984, diplomatic relations between Libya and the UK were broken off after the shooting of a British police officer outside the Libyan embassy in London. During this time, Libyan agents were involved in a series of attacks on foreign soil targeting Western individuals. The 1986 attack on the La Belle discothèque in Berlin, the 1988 bombing of Pan Am flight 103 over Lockerbie, and the bombing of the French plane UTA 772 over Niger in 1989 caused hundreds of casualties. The international community's response to these actions – ranging from bombing raids in 1986 and US economic sanctions – made the Gaddafi regime increasingly isolated and vulnerable.

Coming in From the Cold

The early 1990s brought tremendous international pressure and heightened domestic discontent, with several direct challenges to Gaddafi's leadership. When two Libyan agents were accused of responsibility for the Lockerbie bombing, Tripoli initially refused to extradite them. Suspicions that Libya was culpable led to the imposition of international economic sanctions through UN Security Council Resolution 748 (1992). These sanctions, combined with the US sanctions targeting the Libyan oil industry, weakened the already embattled Libyan economy.

The Libyan regime struggled in the face of these mounting challenges. On the one hand, regime elements tried to develop a more constructive engagement with the outside world. Initial attempts to reach out to the West and resolve issues by diplomatic means were rolled back after the imposition of UN sanctions. Tripoli sought to build broader support against these sanctions in the international community, trying to signal their respect for international law through other avenues. Notably, Libya accepted the 1994 ruling of the International Court of Justice that the contested territory along the Libya–Chad border, which had caused several wars between the two states, rightfully belonged to Chad.

While Libya's cooperative attitude was noted, growing domestic challenges undercut these limited attempts to improve the regime's international standing. Specifically, dissatisfaction with the state of the economy and the excesses of the Revolutionary Committees created a deepening sense of crisis. The converging domestic and foreign pressures were a towering challenge for the Gaddafi regime, which had been divided on the question of rapprochement versus continued radical foreign policy practices for several years. Assassination attempts and crumbling support of key tribes posed a serious home-grown challenge to the regime's long-term survival. In the mid-1990s the regime faced its greatest challenge so far: an Islamist uprising in Benghazi that lasted from 1995 to 1998. This made clear the shortcomings of the Libyan security services and military, and highlighted Islamist elements as a key challenge to the long-term survival of the Gaddafi regime.

During this turmoil the Gaddafi regime became disillusioned with its radical policy experiments. As Libya had provided ample financial support and assistance to terrorist groups, their struggles in coping with an insurgency at home was of grave concern to the regime. Following mounting domestic discontent and strained foreign relations, Gaddafi and his closest advisors concluded that it would be necessary to adopt a more conciliatory approach to international relations, to secure long-term survival (Braut-Hegghammer 2008). To improve the domestic economy, and thus maintain the *rentier* state practices shoring up domestic support for the Gaddafi regime, tackling the international sanctions became a top priority.

Faced with both international and domestic pressure, reformist elements in the Libyan regime persuaded Gaddafi of the need to improve the country's international standing. In the early 1990s, prior to the imposition of sanctions, a group of Libyan regime officials had assembled an informal team of senior diplomats and scholars. This group attempted to find a way out of Libya's isolation. They were motivated by a desire to rehabilitate the Libyan economy by reintegrating the country in international society. Libyan officials reportedly reached out to US officials as early as 1992, offering to strike a deal on the Lockerbie issue, but this initiative was rebuffed (Jentleson and Whytock 2005/06; St John 2004b). When such efforts failed, Libya sought to find ways of getting the sanctions regime lifted or at least lessened, through a series of diplomatic overtures to Western powers.

The Gaddafi regime began to call into question the legitimacy of the sanctions regime, seeking to erode international support for these measures. Initially there was little sympathy to be found, as the regime's radical policies had alienated potential allies throughout the Middle East. Recognizing the lack of support in this region, Gaddafi then reached out to African states to create new allies through economic support.

Throughout this period, the regime sought to mobilize liberal institutionalist symbols and multilateral institutions. For example, Gaddafi argued that the sanctions regime actually violated the norms of procedural justice recognized in international law and the domestic legal systems of most states; that supporting the sanctions constituted disrespect for the wishes of the international community rather than respect for them; and, finally, that such disrespect was itself a threat to international peace and security (Hurd 2005: 504). Furthermore, the regime cited its willingness to accept the ICJ ruling on the Libya–Chad border dispute as an example of its own respect for international law. Through such arguments, Libya managed to secure support from several African countries, while representatives from the West – in particular the USA and UK – increasingly found themselves having to discuss and defend the legitimacy of the sanctions.

'The Libyan Model': Negotiated Reform Through Secret Talks

Two sets of talks recast Libya's relations with the international community between the mid-1990s and 2003. The first was the Lockerbie negotiations concerning the handover of the two suspects for trial. The second was the secret trilateral negotiations to end Libya's longstanding efforts to acquire nuclear weapons and other weapons of mass destruction (WMDs). While these differ in format, both processes can be considered as a Track I (back-channel) type of dialogue, as these initiatives were taken by political leaders and high-level diplomats. Through a series of secret meetings, high-level representatives from both states developed a *quid pro quo* programme for addressing difficult issues that impeded the development of a bilateral relationship. In this process, delegates managed to build trust, which was sorely lacking after years of broken diplomatic relations.

Through this incremental approach the negotiators were able to demonstrate to their political leaders that each delegation could deliver on its promises. This incremental approach (combined with secrecy) strengthened the standing of these delegations, notably the Libyan representatives, against domestic factions that opposed rapprochement.

Lockerbie Talks

In the late 1990s, Libya became engaged in talks that explicitly held the promise of lifting sanctions as a reward for a series of Libyan policy decisions to end longstanding controversial practices. First, in April 1999 Libya decided to hand over the two suspects of the Lockerbie attack for trial in The Hague, in return for the suspension of UN sanctions. According to former US Secretary of State Martin Indyk, who opened the new round of talks in May 1999, these were predicated on two explicit conditions: Libya would keep the negotiations secret, and would no longer seek support for getting the UN sanctions lifted (St John 2004a: 3). In return, the objective of the talks was to work toward lifting these sanctions. The issue of WMDs was set aside at this stage in order to resolve the Lockerbie issue first (ibid.). Third, once the Lockerbie issue was settled, talks to address the WMD issue similarly took a *quid pro quo* approach, stating explicitly what Libya had to do (and what the USA and the UK were prepared to respond with) to achieve the lifting of US sanctions. The parties to these talks agreed to change their public postures to accommodate dialogue, including agreement to 'tone down the rhetoric and begin a meaningful dialogue in pursuit of a step-by-step process' (St John 2004a: 3).

As Libyan diplomats were working out these issues over the negotiating table, they also faced the challenge of securing Gaddafi's approval for a series of decisions and announcements that constituted several of radical (and astounding) policy reversals. When the UN sanctions and the US oil embargo began to take their toll on the Libyan economy, Gaddafi was persuaded by senior officials that improving the country's economic situation should to be a key priority. This followed an extensive debate within the senior echelons of the Libyan regime, where a more moderate wing had advocated economic reform and normalizing relations with the international community (Braut-Hegghammer 2008). This sense of urgency was not matched by the international community.

The Libyan regime also approached US and European oil companies that had been in Libya before the oil embargo to generate additional support for their efforts to get the sanctions regime lifted. When European oil companies began making visits to Libya, US oil companies started to put pressure on Washington. Tony Blair, the new British Prime Minister, also tried to persuade Clinton to approach Gaddafi in order to find a solution. In 1998, Washington accepted a compromise solution: Gaddafi would hand over the two suspects of the Lockerbie terrorist act to a court in The Hague, the Netherlands, to be judged under US rules by British judges. In addition, the Libyan regime provided compensation to the victims' families. Following the trial, which ended in January 2001, the UN sanctions were lifted, but not the unilateral US sanctions.

The Clinton administration seized this opportunity to initiate a new round of talks. This time the aim was to open a subset of issues linked to the Middle East Peace Process, in which the US President was heavily involved at the time, as part of the dialogue with Libya. The US administration attempted to persuade the Libyan leader to end his support for Palestinian organizations, offering the lifting of sanctions as an incentive for closer relations. The Gaddafi regime was ready to turn a new page.

Secret Talks and a Breakthrough

After George W. Bush assumed the US presidency in January 2001, the Bush administration's preoccupation with the threat from 'rogue states' made the Libyan regime feel increasingly vulnerable. The sense of urgency about resolving Libya's conflict with the United States intensified after the 9/11 terrorist attacks that year, and the Gaddafi regime now sought to re-brand itself as a potential partner in the US-led War on Terror. Libya offered to share intelligence information with the USA. This offer was not solely an opportunistic move on the part of the Libyans, as the Gaddafi regime also saw radical Islamist terrorism in Libya as a key threat to its survival.

The ensuing war on terror – and growing pressure on Iraq, with allegations of residual WMD threats – intensified the Gaddafi regime's desire to resolve the remaining issues that stood in the way of fully normalized relations with the USA. Gaddafi's son, Saif al-Islam, who was a PhD student at LSE in London, contacted officials at the British Secret Intelligence Service MI6, and passed on the message that his father was ready to consider abandoning Libya's WMD programmes. The sensitivity of these negotiations required strict secrecy and compartmentalization on all sides (Tucker 2009: 364).

Between March and September 2003, US, British and Libyan officials held a series of secret meetings in London, Geneva and Tripoli. While the Libyans were forthcoming, repeatedly stating their readiness to abandon the pursuit of WMDs, a key concern was that Gaddafi would not verifiably give up the entire programme. A turning point came on 3 October, when the USA, Britain, German and Italy arranged the at-sea diversion of a German-owned container ship, the *BBC China*, en route from Dubai to Libya. Containers on board were found to hold thousands of parts for centrifuges used to enrich uranium. Subsequently, the Libyan side invited inspectors from the USA and Britain to visit the sites associated with its WMD programmes and collect the sensitive nuclear technology intended for the weapons programme. On 19 December, the Libyan regime publicly announced its decision to abandon the pursuit of WMDs and their means of delivery. The announcement came only a few days after Saddam Hussein had been captured and killed in Iraq.

In this process, the Libyan regime was a flexible and committed negotiating partner, offering a much-needed public diplomatic success for US President Bush and British Prime Minister Tony Blair in the wake of the 2003 Iraq War debacle. In fact, this outcome has been cited as the most successful case of coercive diplomacy since the 1962 Cuban Missile Crisis (Jentleson and Whytock 2005/06). For the Libyan side, it was clear that the United States was keen to present the agreement as a crucial success following a series of disasters that had culminated in the failure to find WMDs in Iraq). Tripoli wanted to close the nuclear file after the *BBC China* interception, and collaborated with US British inspectors who travelled to Libya to examine the proscribed weapons programmes before international organizations like the International Atomic Energy Agency became involved. However, it later emerged that the Libyans retained some chemical weapons capabilities, even after the inspections that had been intended to account for complete nuclear disarmament on the part of Libya.

The negotiations that led to Libya's WMD disarmament benefitted from the experience and trust established during the Lockerbie negotiations. Some of the US and British negotiators later expressed surprise at how quickly the

Libyan side acted to facilitate inspection visits and the removal of centrifuge technology. Once the Libyan dictator had made a strategic decision, and committed himself to it, the notoriously inefficient state apparatus was able to implement his decision within days. Later in the process, when inspectors from international agencies arrived, the Libyans were still cooperative but clearly less forthcoming.

After the 2003 announcement of Libya's negotiated nuclear *volte-face*, this deal was cited as a model that could be applied in getting other isolated states to move toward normalized relations with the international community. Libyan leaders and their counterparts in Europe and the USA quickly presented this 'Libyan model' – negotiated normalization – as a fruitful approach for other states.

Role of Dialogue in this Period

As we have seen, a combination of domestic and external factors contributed to facilitate dialogue during this period. At the domestic level, mounting challenges following popular dissatisfaction combined with the emergence of an intensified external threat to the regime after the 9/11 terrorist attacks in the USA and the announcement of the Bush Doctrine. During the 1990s, the Western side had not perceived any urgency about opening negotiations. The Libyans had to work hard, and through various channels, to convince Washington that it was also in the US interest to negotiate. The lack of trust (especially on the part of the West) was a challenge, but through skilful secret negotiations, this challenge was overcome – at least temporarily.

Various interpretations have been offered of Gaddafi's decisions to facilitate the Lockerbie trial in the Netherlands, and dismantle the proscribed WMDs under international verification. Some argue that this is a successful case of multilateral sanctions against Libya in the 1990s, others see it as part of a broader shift within the Gaddafi regime towards *Realpolitik* and a desire to improve Libya's international standing (Blakely 2010; Braut-Hegghammer 2008; Pargeter 2013). The 2003 negotiations that ended with the Libyan nuclear turnabout were influenced by a combination of these two factors, but were also by the war on international terrorism. Ultimately these decisions indicate that the Gaddafi regime rationally considered pros and cons in this process, finding that the long-term benefits outweighed the short-term costs – which included payments to the families of the Lockerbie victims and the political costs of showing that the regime had given in to Western pressures.

In this case, both sides chose to negotiate for two sets of reasons: 1) to resolve a series of distinct problems in secret, and 2) achieve a breakthrough agreement that could transform their bilateral relationship. This eventual transformation was held to bring benefits to both parties: the 'Libyan model' was politically advantageous for both sides in the talks, ensuring a case of negotiated counterproliferation whose causes could be presented according to the preferences of each side (the Libyans underlining the voluntary and negotiated nature of this agreement while the US side emphasized the role of its own recent use of force against Iraq as a key factor); and the opening of Libya's economy and oil sector would bring economic benefits to all.

In this series of negotiations, the focus on a win–win solution appears quite similar to Fisher and Ury (1991) 'integrative approach', presented in the introduction. However, it is also important to note that without the external and internal factors that favoured dialogue, the result would probably have been very different. The need to restore the Libyan economy and to fight regime-threatening terrorism was a crucial factor in shaping Gaddafi's willingness to negotiate in this period. This was a rational decision, based careful weighing of interests (primarily economic and political) on both sides. The main obstacles facing these talks were not cultural, they were political – as each delegation faced considerable political obstacles at home (including the Lockerbie families, in the US case; and radical regime elements, in the Libyan case).

Disappointments, Crises and New Negotiations

Within a year, the Libyan leader began to express disappointment at what had been achieved through the 2003 deal. In December 2004, Gaddafi stated:

> Actually we were somewhat disappointed by the response from Europe, the United States, and Japan. They did not really repay Libya for its contribution to international peace. And we are still waiting. If we are not repaid, other countries will not follow our example and dismantle their programmes in turn. When we spoke with North Korea and Iran, which are suspected of having nuclear programmes, they said: 'But what was the recompense in your case? What did you obtain from the international community? So why do you want us to dismantle our programme? (Rome RAI Television Network 2004).

Gaddafi's disappointment reflected the lengthy process in the US Congress involved in getting all US sanctions lifted, and resentment that Libya had (in his view) been promised further concessions and benefits that were not forthcoming. Over the following years, Libyan officials grew increasingly frustrated at seeing how their country had not become a more respected member of the international community, had not received more assistance and cooperation in technical fields as well as in the military realm, and was excluded from events like the 2010 Nuclear Security Summit held in Washington, DC. Gaddafi criticized this decision, pointing out that this would make the Libyan model less attractive to states like North Korea and Iran (Lee 2010).

At the domestic level, the Libyan regime moved away from the 'post-revolutionary' emphasis on rapprochement toward a hardliner position. The officials who had been personally involved in negotiating agreements with the USA and the UK found themselves outweighed by more hardline regime elements. The regime faced a tricky balancing act, unable to agree on a way forward to revitalize the economy and strengthen the regime's domestic standing. A key obstacle was the reluctance of regime members to loosen their personal grip on power: that meant they could not deliver on expectations in the population and in the international community that Libya would reform its domestic economy and become more integrated in the global economy.

There were three turning points or crises in relations between Libya and the West after the 2003 breakthrough: (1) the crisis linked to the Bulgarian nurses sentenced to death following an HIV outbreak in a Libyan hospital; (2) the return of hardliners and more anti-Western officials in the Libyan administration; (3) the 'cartoon crisis' after some Danish and Norwegian newspapers published drawings seen as dishonouring the Prophet. A particularly challenging aspect of the crises facing the regime between 2003 and 2011 was that they had domestic ramifications – in the form of clashes between civilians and security forces, grieving families, and the Libyan economy. As the regime sought to cope with these crises, concerns for domestic legitimacy seemed to come increasingly into conflict with the objectives of strengthening the country's international standing.

The Bulgarian Nurses

Following the 2003 diplomatic breakthrough, Libya entered into a new round of negotiations with the West in 2007. These negotiations concerned five Bulgarian nurses and one Palestinian doctor who had been charged with deliberately infecting 426 children with HIV in 1998 at the El-Fatih hospital in Benghazi. These six individuals received death sentences that were upheld in Libya's highest court in 2007. As the evidence strongly suggested the infections had been caused by general malpractice and not intentional acts on the part of the accused, the international community heavily condemned both the court ruling and the use of torture to extract confessions from the defendants. The epidemic triggered powerful emotions in Libya, consistent with the scale of the outbreak – it was, according to some, the largest hospital-induced HIV epidemic to date. Although initial Libyan reports had noted the poor sanitary conditions at the hospital, the Bulgarian nurses and Palestinian doctor were rapidly pointed out as the main suspects in an alleged conspiracy involving the CIA and Mossad. The fact that this took place in eastern Libya, an area with a long history of resistance to the Gaddafi regime, may have bolstered the regime's desire to seek a negotiated solution without losing face in Libyan public opinion.

The European Union entered into negotiations with the Libyan regime to find a solution to the crisis. Gaddafi was adamant that the court system in Libya was independent of political pressure, and emphasized that the judicial system could not be overruled. A key issue that delayed a negotiated settlement was disagreement within the Libyan regime concerning the type of agreement that could lay the foundations for a negotiated solution. Hardliners insisted on financial compensation to the 426 families, and proposed an exchange of the medical personnel in return for the Libyan national convicted of the Lockerbie attack, who was imprisoned in Scotland. Moderates, led by Saif al-Islam Gaddafi and senior diplomat Abdellati al-Obeidi, were prepared to admit to Libyan responsibility for the HIV epidemic. They took a more conciliatory approach, which ultimately found favour with Gaddafi (Der Spiegel Online International 2007). In these negotiations, the Libyan regime insisted on reaching an agreement that would include financial compensation – such as Libyan compensation to the Lockerbie families – and not overturning the guilty verdict imposed by the Libyan judicial system.

Following lengthy negotiations, in 2007 a deal was struck between Libya and the EU. The Libyan High Judicial Council overturned the death sentences, and extradition to Bulgaria was negotiated for all six. In July 2007, Libya announced that a settlement had been reached including the establishment of a fund of €9.5 million to improve conditions at the hospital in Benghazi where the HIV epidemic had broken out (Reuters (CNN) 2007). France played a key role in late stage of these deliberations. Shortly after the six were released, it emerged that President Nicolas Sarkozy had offered the prospect of an arms trade agreement and opened for potential civilian nuclear cooperation between the two countries.

The Libyans wanted a fund to be established to aid the families of the 425 children, and asked for USD 1 million per child. Bulgaria provided the first USD 44 million in debt relief, the Libyan government contributed USD 74 million, while the EU promised only €9.5 million to the Benghazi hospital (Spiegel Online International 2007). The Libyan government had to cover the outstanding amount. As a result, Gaddafi could claim that the EU would compensate the victims, whereas the EU counterparts could point to the sizeable Libyan portion, to refute allegations that this was a reparations fund.

Resolution of this conflict cleared the way for further cooperation between Libya and the European Union. This was clearly beneficial to both sides, due to Libya's geostrategic location and role as oil exporter to major European countries. The settlement also demonstrated that Libya had learned from prior experience, and sought an incremental *quid pro quo* approach that included tangible benefits and avoided interference with key domestic institutions like the judiciary.

Cartoon Crisis

The Libyan balancing act proved fragile. The regime continued to be concerned about its weak domestic political standing, seemingly upheld mainly by the lack of feasible alternatives, while remaining unwilling – or unable – to bring about reform. In early 2006, Benghazi was shaken by protests following the publication of cartoons in Denmark and Norway depicting the Prophet Muhammad. The protests followed the TV appearance of an Italian minister, Roberto Calderoli, wearing a T-shirt with an offensive depiction of the Prophet on 15 February. A protest in Benghazi led to an attack on the Italian consulate: eleven protesters were killed by security forces and dozens were injured. The subsequent reaction of the regime – reportedly offering the victims burial as martyrs – reflected concerns that such demonstrations might also bring about intensified criticism of domestic issues. In stark contrast to Syrian attacks on Norwegian and Danish embassies, the regime in Libya opted to repress the demonstration on this occasion, apparently valuing its relationship with Western allies over frustrations expressed by the people.

Role of Dialogue

The 2003 agreement and recognition of Gaddafi as a partner in the war against terrorism led to Libya's reintegration into the international community. However, it soon became clear that this integration had its limits. Libyan disillusionment, and lessons learned from tough negotiations with Western counterparts, informed the objectives and tactics of subsequent dialogues and interactions. During the two key crises following the 2003 'Libyan model', the behaviour of the Gaddafi regime was evidently influenced by concerns about its domestic standing. Thus we see that domestic factors and domestic support were important in an authoritarian state like Gaddafi's Libya. Emotions, and in this case humiliation, as referred to in *Geopolitics of Emotions* (Moïsi 2009) may well have influenced the character of the negotiations between the West and Libya in this period.

As we have seen, the negotiations on the issue of the Bulgarian nurses were still geared towards a win–win solution. Meanwhile, Gaddafi had become reluctant to back down, due to concerns about his domestic standing. He also preferred the institutionalized dimension of the legal apparatus, to distance himself from the deal in an issue so sensitive in domestic public opinion. There was also a domestic struggle over the direction of negotiations – a bargaining position (the hardliners) or a more conciliatory one (the moderates, including Gaddafi's son Saif Al-Islam).

The negotiations concerning the Bulgarian nurses and the Palestinian doctor and the cartoon crisis demonstrated the difficult balancing act of seeking to ensure domestic legitimacy, on the one hand, while also being perceived as a moderate, stable ally of the Western powers, on the other. The diminishing benefits of appeasing the West are likely to have informed the Libyan shift. At the same time, having learned from how the United States negotiated, the Libyans emulated certain elements, like payments to the families of the HIV-infected children, in subsequent talks.

Thus far, officials of the Libyan regime officials and other states had been able to get around their differences (such as democracy and human rights) on the basis of mutual interests. By 2011, when popular revolts and demonstrations in several Arab countries put the spotlight on democratic aspirations and power abuses by Western-supported regimes, the normative basis of the Libyan regime became a major concern. Soon, the regime's response made it impossible to continue the bilateral relationship that had emerged between Libya and the West. In the next section, focusing on the period after the Arab Spring, we will see how the West moved away from the negotiations option.

Libya and the Arab Spring

In 2011, the improved relationship between the Gaddafi regime and Western allies quickly came to an end. After popular movements overturned the rulers of Tunisia and Egypt, Libya's immediate neighbours to the west and the east, Libya itself was shook by a national revolt that began in February 2011. This uprising emerged from a series of protests in Benghazi criticizing the Gaddafi regime's treatment of political opponents. Although united in its determination to overthrow the Gaddafi regime, the opposition was in practice a fragmented collection of local militia groups and political associations from across the country. The Gaddafi regime responded in a far more brutal and uncompromising manner than the Egyptian and Tunisian authoritarian regimes had done. This response drove a wedge between the Libyan regime and its former Western allies. Gaddafi and his regime soon found themselves isolated and under mounting international pressure.

Within days, the revolt had spread across the country, and loyalist forces had lost control of key cities, notably Benghazi. Faced with a rapidly spreading revolt, the long-divided Gaddafi regime stood firm against the opposition coalition and refused to commit to substantial reform or meaningful concessions. Muammar Gaddafi, who at that time had ruled Libya for more than 41 years, characterized the protestors as drug-fuelled foreign agents with connections to al-Qaeda. His son Saif-al-Islam, who had previously stood out as an apparent champion of reform and liberalization, also maintained that the regime would strike back firmly against the protests until the rebellion had been fully stamped out. By late February, a counteroffensive had begun, and government forces succeeded in pushing the opposition forces back to Benghazi. Reports soon emerged of brutal repression of the civilian protestors, further tarnishing the reputation of the Gaddafi regime.

Faced with the violent repression of the protests by Libyan security forces and mercenaries, Western leaders voiced support for the opposition movement and denounced the response of the Gaddafi regime. Within weeks, British and US leaders declared that the Gaddafi regime was no longer considered the legitimate ruler of Libya. A National Transitional Council was established in Benghazi to serve as an opposition governmental agency. On 10 March 2011, France became the first state to officially recognize the Council as the legitimate representative of the Libyan people. Gaddafi's military attacks against the revolts were condemned by the UN, several countries imposed economic sanctions against Libya, and the UN Security Council voted to refer Gaddafi and other government officials to the International Criminal Court for investigation (UNSC Resolution 1970). The decision to refer Gaddafi to the ICC appears to have been 'a red line' for the Libyan leader, who in previous crises had insisted on avoiding personal culpability for acts such as the Lockerbie bombing.

Regional actors responded to the Libyan conflict with various preferences for a negotiated solution versus military intervention to protect civilian protestors from Gaddafi's promised revenge. The African Union sought to facilitate a negotiated settlement that would essentially enable Gaddafi to maintain his position, while also facilitating some reform. The Arab League, on the other hand, voiced strong criticism of the Gaddafi regime's harsh response. Support for the Libyan opposition movement stood in contrast to the more gradual support accorded by Western states to the opposition movements in Tunisia and Egypt. In particular, the French response to the Libyan conflict may have been driven by perceptions that France had been too slow in supporting the anti-regime protesters in Tunisia. As key European states, notably the UK and France, pressed for action to shield the Libyan opposition from the violent response Gaddafi had publicly pledged to deliver, the USA remained reluctant to signal commitment to support the uprising in the form of military intervention.

Despite initial reluctance to support the Libyan opposition movement actively, the international community was united in its strong criticism of the Gaddafi regime's harsh response to the protesters. While principles of non-intervention and fears of setting a precedent that could come to haunt the international community in the case of Syria contributed to this initial restraint, the characteristics of the Libyan regime also influenced the response of the outside world. Despite the country's geostrategic importance and oil exports, the idiosyncratic regime had rendered Libya a marginal actor in international relations and Middle Eastern politics. Following Gaddafi's continued interference in other Middle Eastern states, including alleged support for an assassination plot targeting the Saudi Arabian royal family, there was little backing for the Gaddafi regime to be found among these states. While the opposition movement was at best a loose coalition, lacking a political programme and internal coordination, the brutal response of the Gaddafi regime soon led Middle Eastern and Western states to treat the opposition as legitimate representatives of the Libyan people and to seek to curb the Gaddafi regime's campaign to end the protests.

On 17 March 2011, the UN Security Council passed Resolution 1973, sanctioning the establishment of a no-fly zone and the use of 'all means necessary' to protect civilians in Libya. Subsequently, NATO provided aerial protection to shield the opposition forces from the government forces. This move was welcomed by key regional actors, as evidenced in the Arab League's call for the imposition of a no-fly zone prior to the adoption of Resolution 1973.

The NATO campaign nullified the military superiority of the Gaddafi loyalist forces, and the bombing campaigns targeting the regime's strongholds further weakened their capability to withstand the pressure. This campaign provided the rebels with time and space to make gradual advances toward the capital. As the Gaddafi regime was targeted with military and economic sanctions, it was soon clear that the regime would eventually crumble. The question was how long it would be able to hold out.

In the late spring of 2011, the Gaddafi regime appeared to be beyond saving. The violent campaign to defeat the uprising led by former apparently liberal figures such as Saif-al-Islam Gaddafi indicated that the regime could not be engaged in a meaningful dialogue or negotiations. As the rebellion continued, moderate elements in the Gaddafi regime joined the uprising. Already in late February 2011 the Libyan UN ambassador, a former childhood friend of Muammar Gaddafi and a fellow revolutionary, had criticized the brutal repression in the country and called for foreign intervention to curb Gaddafi's offensive.

No Willingness to Negotiate

Attempts made by the African Union to mediate between the two sides faltered due to the insistence of the opposition on regime change and the refusal of the Gaddafi regime to commit to meaningful change. The mutually exclusive objectives of the contenders rendered negotiations futile. The lack of trust between the two sides, and their contradictory objectives, made the success of any attempt at dialogue or negotiated settlement highly unlikely. Both sides displayed a lack of will to negotiate a solution. The objective of the opposition movement was to topple the Gaddafi regime and instate a democratic form of government. As such, the Gaddafi regime was not considered a legitimate actor, so there was little room for negotiation apart from an orderly transition to democratic rule. The Gaddafi regime, for its part, refused to have direct contact with the opposition movement, although reports indicated some attempts by the regime to communicate proposals to the opposition movement to end the conflict. Furthermore, the African states seeking to facilitate such a dialogue appeared to enjoy scant support among Middle Eastern and Western states. With two intransigent parties in a civil war, Libya did not offer fertile grounds for dialogue or a negotiated solution to the conflict.

Conclusions

This chapter has presented an analysis of the role that diplomacy and secret talks have played in different phases in relations between Libya and the West from the 1990s and up until 2011. A series of secret talks played an important role in the conflict and crisis resolution between the two parties. The agreements between Libya and the West concerning Lockerbie and the lifting of sanctions, abandoning Libya's WMD programme and the release of six foreign health workers were clearly the results of willingness on both sides to reach a settlement and a delicate process of securing domestic support legitimacy and being perceived as a stable ally of the West.

The dialogues between Libya and the West in the period prior to 2011 were clearly of a Track I type (undertaken by diplomats) and were outcome-oriented, aimed at transforming bilateral relations for shared political and economic benefits. The talks were undertaken in secret (back channel) and can therefore be characterized as informal processes rather than regular diplomatic negotiations. Further, the fact that there were clear interests on both sides made it possible to find solutions. The talks had a 'win–win' character and were largely consistent with the 'integrative' approaches of dialogue and negotiation.

The challenge for the West in this period was how to handle Gaddafi's rather original and unconventional personality and approach. Interestingly, the process of secret talks seemed constructive in that regard, since it resulted in some kind of trust between the parties – trust that had been lacking for many years. The talks were therefore also a test in handling different emotions on both sides.

However, the fact that the Gaddafi regime was overthrown with the support of its former negotiating partners only a few years after the last negotiated agreement also points up the uncertainties associated with negotiating with authoritarian regimes. Recent research on 'audience costs' has cast doubts on the long-standing assumption that authoritarian regimes are less influenced by domestic pressure with regard to upholding agreements and commitments (Snyder and Borghard 2011). Any leader – even a dictator – needs domestic support if a negotiated agreement is to be respected in the long term.

In the case of Libya, the level of domestic support as well as the unique character of the regime was of great importance in shaping interactions and dialogue. While the conflicts between Libya and the West cannot be interpreted as what Peter Coleman refers to as a '5 per cent' conflict, they may be an example of the perspective presented in Robert Mnookin (2011) *Bargaining with the Devil*. In his view, engaging in a dialogue with hostile regimes must have a chance of succeeding and it must be legitimate and morally justifiable. In earlier periods, the context seemed to be in favour of negotiations. However, this was clearly no longer so by the time of the 2011 crisis. External factors like the Arab Spring and internal factors in Libya (the uprising, human rights abuses) now made a military option preferable instead. As the Libyan case demonstrates, dialogue has real potential, but also some clear limitations, when dealing with authoritarian regimes.

References

Blakely, K.R. 2010. The Libyan Conversion in Three Acts: Why Quadhafi Gave Up His Weapons of Mass Destruction Program, Thesis. Monterey: Naval Postgraduate School.

Braut-Hegghammer, M. 2008. Libya's Nuclear Turnaround: Perspectives from Tripoli, *The Middle East Journal*, 62(1), Winter, 55–72.

Bush, G.W. 2002 *State of the Union Address*, Washington [Online, January 29]. Available at: http://www.washingtonpost.com/wp-srv/onpolitics/transcripts/sou012902.htm [accessed: 1 July 2014].

Fisher, R. and Ury, W. 1991. *Getting to Yes: Negotiation Agreement Without Giving In*. New York: Penguin Books.

Gaddafi. 1976. Green Book [Online]. Available at: http://openanthropology.org/libya/gaddafi-green-book.pdf [accessed 1 July 2014].

Hurd, I. 2005. The Strategic Use of Liberal Internationalism: Libya and the UN Sanctions, 1992–2003. *International Organization*, 59 (Summer), 495–526.

International Crisis Group (2011) Holding Libya together: Security challenges after Qadhafi. *Middle East/North Africa Report* N°115 [Online, 14 December]. Available at: http://www.crisisgroup.org/en/regions/middle-east-north-africa/north-africa/libya/115-holding-libya-together-security-challenges-after-qadhafi.aspx [Accessed: 1 July 2014].

Jentleson, B.W. and Whytock, C.A. 2005/06. Who 'won' Libya? The Force Diplomacy Debate and Its Implications for Theory and Policy, *International Security*, 30 (Winter), 47–86.

Lexis-Nexis 2004. Libyan Leader Laments No "Concrete" Reward for Giving up WMD, Rome RAI Television Network (in Italian), 17 December.

Matthew, L. 2010. Gadhafi: US Nuclear Snub of Libya Hurts Peace, *Associated Press*, 26 April.

Moïsi, D. 2009. *Geopolitics of Emotions: How Cultures of Fear, Humiliation and Hope Reshape the World*. New York: Anchor Books.

Pargeter, A. 2012. *Libya: The Rise and Fall of Qaddafi*. New Haven, CT: Yale University Press.

Reuters (CNN) 2007. Libya Commutes Medics' Sentences [Online]. Available at: http://www.cnn.com/2007/WORLD/africa/07/17/libya.medics.reut/index.html [Accessed: 1 July 2014].

Snyder, J and Borghard, E.D. 2011. The Cost of Empty Threats: A Penny, Not a Pound, *American Political Science Review* 105 (August), 437–56.

Spiegel Online. 2007. Quiet Pressure from Berlin: How EU and German Diplomacy Helped Save Bulgarian Nurses', *Aus dem Spiegel: Der Spiegel Online International* [Online]. Available at: http://www.spiegel.de/international/world/0,1518,495974,00.html [Accessed: 1 July 2014].

Spiegel Online International. 2007. French Posturing over Bulgarian Nurses: Why Did Cecilia Sarkozy Go to Tripoli? *Spiegel Online International* [Online]. Available at: http://www.spiegel.de/international/europe/0,1518,496269,00.html [Accessed: 1 July 2014].

St John, R.B. 2004a. Apply "Libya Model" to Iran and Syria", *Foreign Policy in Focus*, 21 October.

St John, R.B. 2004b. Libya Is Not Iraq: Preemptive Strikes, WMD and Diplomacy. *The Middle East Journal*, 58(3), 386–402.

Tucker, J.B. 2009. The Roll-back of Libya's Chemical Weapons Program. *The Non-Proliferation Review*, 16(3), 363–84.

UN Security Council Resolution 748 (1992) Libyan Arab Jamahiriya [Online] Available at: http://www.un.org/en/ga/search/view_doc.asp?symbol=S/RES/748(1992) [Accessed: 1 July 2014].

Vitkine, A. 2011. *Gaddafi: Our Best Villain*. Documentary: NRK nettv.

Chapter 8
Peace Dialogue, the Afghan Case 2001–2014

Michael Semple

Introduction to the Afghan Conflict

This chapter describes efforts undertaken since 2001, by the Afghan government and international political actors, to engage the Taliban movement in a dialogue about peace. The protagonists in this dialogue process understood that engagement with an armed opposition faction was unlikely to deliver progress unless it could be nested within a broader and more comprehensive peace process. Nevertheless, in the chapter the focus is exclusively on the Taliban dialogue – because of the movement's central role in violence during the period, and because so many key actors concentrated their efforts on this Taliban track.

The account below of Taliban peace dialogue experiences is selective, focusing on the most significant processes. Some dialogue processes were intended to be confidential. Others have been only partly documented, with few details available in the public domain. Some of the observations below, particularly with regard to Taliban responses to the dialogue experience, are based on the author's own experience as a practitioner. The intention is not to document every round of dialogue which occurred, but to identify the main challenges and lessons learnt from peace dialogue during the period.[1]

The conflict in Afghanistan from December 2001 through 2014 pitted the Afghan Taliban against the US-led intervention force and the Afghan government that had been installed through the 2001 Bonn Accords. Afghanistan had already been at war for 23 years at the time of the US intervention. The Taliban insurgency subsumed multiple conflicts that had remained unsettled from previous phases of the war. The post-2001 conflict rapidly developed a distinctive geography. Most of the Taliban leadership moved to Pakistan, to re-organize their movement and its national structures there. After a brief hiatus in

---

1   This chapter is based upon the author's interviews with Taliban and other conflict actors conducted during the period 2001–2014, supplemented by documentation of dialogue processes and published commentaries on dialogue, reconciliation and the Taliban Movement.

2002, the Taliban launched armed resistance against the new authorities across the border in Afghanistan.

The Bonn Accords of December 2001 re-established government, with a road map for constitution-making and elections. The process was based on the assumption that the Taliban were no longer a force in politics, so no serious effort was made to involve them. However, after 2004 it became clear that the re-organized Taliban posed a significant security threat to the new order. Alongside its armed campaign, the movement developed an effective propaganda operation and projected a narrative of resistance against foreign occupation. Although the leadership had a narrow social base, the Taliban used the resistance narrative to project themselves as a national movement.

The Taliban movement was founded in 1994 on a platform of ending factional violence and introducing a Shariat-based system headed by the Taliban's *Emir*, Mullah Omar. The distinctive feature of the movement has been its cohesiveness, which proved critical in sustaining a protracted armed struggle against a militarily more powerful enemy. The robustness of the Taliban insurgency provided a rationale for the ratcheting up of the international military presence after 2004. It also inspired the idea in Kabul that peace and security were attainable only if the Taliban could be persuaded, through dialogue, to end the armed campaign. However, Taliban cohesiveness and the movement's broader organizational culture have helped to condition responses to that dialogue.

The Evolving Conflict and Changing Character of Dialogue

An incident at the climax of the US invasion illustrated a form of dialogue across the frontlines which was to prove elusive in future years. In December 2001, as the Taliban were about to evacuate their stronghold Kandahar, the movement's deputy chief of staff, Mullah Abdul Ghani Baradar, travelled incognito to rendezvous with Hamid Karzai and his column of anti-Taliban fighters at Shahwalikot. The parleys resulted in a decision that Baradar would summon much of the Taliban cabinet from Kandahar to agree on terms for integrating the movement into the new Afghanistan which Karzai was to head. The Taliban agreed to relinquish Kandahar without a fight. Karzai guaranteed the security and dignity of Taliban leaders, who would be free to return to their homes. The Shahwalikot parleys were one of those tantalizing moments that had the potential to transform the conflict, but in the event achieved little. Karzai soon abandoned the agreement, unable either to persuade his US allies to honour it or to rein in Afghan allies who had scores to settle. The few Taliban leaders who tried to reintegrate peacefully in their home areas were soon targeted by the new authorities or US forces. The USA tried to detain

Taliban leaders in Afghanistan and encouraged the Pakistan authorities to do likewise on their side of the border – exactly the opposite of what had been decided in Shahwalikot. The episode provided a timely lesson of the perils of dialogue in the complex Afghan conflict. It was not hard for the Taliban top military commander to establish contact with his Afghan foe. But the inability of either side to speak for their allies rendered the agreement between the two Afghan parties basically irrelevant. What could be achieved through dialogue was conditioned by many aspects of a complex conflict environment and did not depend solely on the aptitude of the interlocutors.

In terms of intensity and the configuration of actors, the conflict passed through four stages after the initial US intervention. From 2002 to 2004 there was a *hiatus*. The Taliban insurgency had not emerged as a major security challenge, and violence was low (average 63 Western troops killed per year; civilian deaths were not systematically recorded). In the *early insurgency* 2005–2007, the Taliban generated rising violence by attacking the limited NATO deployment in their southern heartland and activating sufficient fronts elsewhere to give the appearance of a national campaign (average 184 Western troops killed and 1820 civilian deaths annually, after systematic monitoring started in 2006). The period of '*surge*' was 2009–2011, when the USA doubled its troop numbers and entered into direct confrontation with the Taliban (Western troops killed peaked at 599 and civilian deaths rose to 2,774 annually). Finally, 2012–2014 was the period of '*transition*', with a phased withdrawal of Western troops, while Taliban sustained their insurgency against both the Afghan government and the residual NATO forces. The annual number of Western troops killed fell sharply to 281 in 2012 and 2013, whereas annual civilian deaths rose further to 2,863. Thus the conflict moved from low intensity to relatively high intensity, and from Taliban directly fighting Western forces to Taliban fighting Afghan forces supported by the USA and allies.

The policy of state actors engaging with the Taliban developed in parallel to this evolution of the conflict. In the early period 2002–2004, the Afghan government's National Security Council was sympathetic to the idea of reaching out to the Taliban. The first published framework legitimizing dealings with the Taliban came in 2005, when the government announced a combatant reintegration initiative, the 'Strengthening Peace Programme'. Serious efforts to develop policy on engagement with the Taliban, with buy-in from the main state actors, came only from January 2010 onwards. As part of preparations for the London Conference on Afghanistan in that month, the Afghan National Security Council adopted a document proposing a new framework for understanding and dealing with the Taliban. Arguing that the majority of those active in the Taliban insurgency were potentially reconcilable, it proposed programmes to reintegrate low-ranking Taliban, as well as political outreach to woo senior figures. The London conference endorsed the idea of large-scale reintegration. During 2010 the Afghan government followed up by developing a new institutional infrastructure for peacemaking. The Obama administration also adopted a strategy of encouraging an understanding between the Taliban and the Afghan government, alongside the military surge which the US president had ordered from July 2009. Special envoy Richard Holbrooke helped develop the new engagement strategy. After Holbrooke's death, it was left to Secretary of State Hillary Clinton, in February 2011, to spell out the new US willingness to deal with the Taliban.

The policies of engagement with the Taliban that were developed in the decade up to 2014 did not focus specifically on 'dialogue'. They advocated the pursuit of 'reintegration' and 'reconciliation'– the latter in the sense of an envisaged political agreement that would allow the Taliban to end their conflict with the Kabul government. However, dialogue rapidly emerged as a key tool that all comers used in pursuing an understanding with the Taliban and eventual reintegration or reconciliation. Dialogue with the Taliban had become an established part of peacemaking practice in Afghanistan before 2009, but it was low on the Afghan government agenda and absent from the US agenda. Then, parallel to the military surge, as US and Afghan policies converged in favour of 'reconciliation' after January 2010, there came a new drive towards peace dialogue with the Taliban.

Multiple actors were involved in facilitating dialogue with the Taliban. The Kabul government was involved throughout, gradually becoming increasingly insistent on its prerogative to monopolize political outreach to the Taliban, justified by the mantra of 'Afghan-led process'. Washington became involved in dialogue during the second half of the conflict, the phases of *surge* and *transition*. The range of actors involved in dialogue peaked in the third phase of the conflict, as did the Western troop presence. International civil society bodies organized dialogue events; the USA started to get involved, and the Afghan government raised the profile of its efforts.

Dialogue and Reintegration in the Early Years – Talking with Taliban 2002–2007

The new Afghan National Security Council (NSC) reached out to members of the Taliban, in Pakistan and in Afghanistan. The NSC and other Kabul-based actors sought dialogue with known members of the Taliban, many of whom had sought refuge in Pakistan, to discuss how they could reintegrate peacefully in the new set-up. Much of the dialogue in this period involved documenting Taliban grievances regarding arbitrary detentions, and harassment of their members by power-brokers allied to the new authorities. The earliest contacts pre-dated and attempted to pre-empt the insurgency. Field commanders, former Taliban officials and even some senior leaders were more open to dialogue in this period than at later stages in the conflict – in part because it took time to re-establish leadership structures, and in part because Taliban harboured a residual hope that the international community might observe some neutrality between them and their Afghan rivals. This early dialogue produced some tangible results, like the decision by the senior Taliban figure from northern Helmand, Abdul Wahid alias Rais Baghran, to reintegrate. Dialogue commenced with a low-profile, informal format. Then, in 2005, the National Security Council launched a formal reintegration process, the Strengthening Peace Programme, headed by former President Mojadedi. This allowed the establishment of an infrastructure to screen and support Taliban personnel who opted out of the insurgency. The dialogue in this period helped improve understanding of the drivers of the nascent insurgency. However, the reintegration deal on offer was of scant interest to the movement as a whole, which saw it as tantamount to surrender. Neither was there political will in Kabul to address Taliban grievances, nor was the Taliban leadership willing to hold back from escalating its military campaign.

The Flourishing of NGO and Third-country Dialogue Initiatives 2008–2011

For approximately four years after 2007 there was a proliferation of initiatives to engage the Taliban in dialogue – several launched by international NGOs; others headed by individual political figures and hosted by Muslim countries in the region. The spreading Taliban insurgency persuaded many that a political settlement with the movement would be necessary to bring peace: simple reintegration deals would not be enough. In addition 2009 brought a new US administration, intent on focusing on the Afghan war and less averse to dealing with the Taliban than its predecessor had been. And well before the USA embraced the idea, President Karzai became an enthusiastic advocate of accommodation with the Taliban. By 2010 *The Guardian* noted twelve different channels of dialogue trying to engage the Taliban. Initiatives in this period included Qayyum Karzai's meetings in Saudi Arabia, the East West Institute's 'Abu Dhabi Process', a meeting in Maldives convened by Afghan political entrepreneur, Humayun Jarir, the son-in-law of Gulbadin Hekmatyar, forums in Peshawar and Dubai held by the Pugwash Conferences and attempts by Humanitarian Dialogue to develop a negotiation channel with the Taliban leadership. The post-2007 initiatives tried to explore ideas of a political settlement involving the Taliban and to consider what sort of peace process might bring it about. The processes were convened in part or entirely in third countries – outside Pakistan and Afghanistan. However, the organizers struggled to find a format in which currently serving Taliban could participate. Unconvincingly, it was frequently suggested that Taliban must be let off UN sanctions lists so that representatives could be able to travel to such events. Perhaps the high point of NGO efforts to use dialogue to catalyse a peace process with the Taliban was the Century Foundation Afghanistan–Pakistan task force. This was led by Lakhdar Brahimi and Thomas Pickering and eventually delivered a proposal for an international mediator.

Kabul's New Peace Infrastructure, 2010–2014

In line with the new NSC strategy and the decisions of the London Conference, during 2010 the government of Afghanistan launched a new institutional infrastructure for peacemaking. It convened over a thousand delegates in Kabul in June, as the National Consultative Peace Jirga. The gathering supported the idea of a new peace initiative and mandated the establishment of a 'High Peace Council' (HPC). Like the 2005 Strengthening Peace Programme, the HPC was to preside over another reintegration scheme. It also hoped to pursue the broader idea of 'reconciliation'. In fact, President Karzai preferred to task his closest aides, rather than the full HPC, with establishing direct contact with the Taliban. He confined the HPC to a more symbolic role, but through its existence was able to insist on exclusive Afghan (government) control over possible peacemaking. Although the HPC made little overall progress, it was charged with one interesting dialogue track – that with high-profile Taliban prisoners. In particular, Karzai prioritized attempts to access and dialogue with Mullah Baradar, who by then had been detained in Pakistan. The idea was that a senior member of the Taliban leadership, with a track record of engagement with Karzai, might carry sufficient influence with the rest of the movement to persuade them to negotiate and end the insurgency. The Pakistan authorities allowed an HPC delegation to meet with Mullah Baradar but he was unwilling or unable to talk on behalf of the Taliban, and the process was aborted.

State-facilitated Track II Dialogue in 2012 – the Taliban in Chantilly and Kyoto

Two state-sponsored Track II events in 2012 seemed to break the mould of previous dialogues, because senior serving Taliban officials participated in these publicly acknowledged events and even met with an aide to President Karzai. In June the Taliban sent former Planning Minister Qari Din Mohammad to participate in a colloquium in Kyoto. In December they sent a member of the Political Commission, Shahbuddin Dilawar, to a gathering in Chantilly which was also attended by political figures representing a range of Afghan interest groups and constituencies. The gatherings hinted that the Taliban had dropped their refusal to meet directly with the Afghan government. To their own constituency, the Taliban justified participation by saying they were simply explaining the policies of their Islamic Emirate. Din Mohammad read a prepared statement, and both he and Dilawar essentially reiterated the movement's rejection of the existing Afghan set-up, while remaining open to the possibility of letting other Afghans into a Taliban-led inclusive government after the departure of foreign troops. However, the Afghan government reacted negatively to the Kyoto–Chantilly experience: the Taliban delegations had become the main focus of attention, and the format deprived the government of its ability to speak authoritatively on behalf of Afghanistan. Instead of opening up the space for dialogue, these two events closed it down. The Afghan government made clear its objection to any further events other than those it might organize itself, and prevailed upon the UN to cancel a forum in Turkmenistan which would have been a follow-up to Chantilly.

Dialogue to Set the Scene for Negotiations – Doha 2011–2014

The most sustained dialogue process which for a while seemed to offer hope of paving the way to negotiations was that associated with the Emirate of Qatar. The willingness of the Taliban to send delegations to the 2012 events was a result of this 'Qatar Process'. In the early stages, German diplomats brokered dialogue between Taliban representatives and US officials. This resulted in Washington encouraging Qatar to host a Taliban delegation. This delegation was staffed by members of the Taliban Political Commission – in effect, the movement's 'foreign ministry'. The Taliban announced that they were in contact with the USA, which marked a major departure for the movement. However, initial attempts to get agreement on a prisoner exchange, portrayed as a confidence-building measure, broke down, and the Taliban entered a period when they declined direct contacts with the USA. The presence of the Taliban delegation in Qatar meant that there was an ongoing opportunity for discreet dialogue, and the Qataris and non-US diplomats continued to engage with the delegation. The US side made a significant political investment in the process through 2013, culminating in June in the announcement of the opening of a formal Taliban office, and a carefully scripted Taliban declaration of intention to dialogue with Afghan and international parties. The publicly acknowledged process collapsed within a day, because the Kabul government objected to the profiling of the delegation as a quasi-embassy. However, the delegation from the Taliban's Political Commission was able to stay on in Doha and continue its activities, without the platform of an office. After June 2013, members of the Political Commission met with Western diplomats and UN delegations, both in Doha and in the United Arab Emirates. The Taliban announced a break in talks with the USA, but continued to work to realize the originally envisaged prisoner release deal. Eventually in May 2014 the prisoner exchange, which had been on the agenda from the earliest stages of the Qatar Process, went ahead, but without any formal linkage to the anticipated broader political process.

Evolving Understanding of the Taliban

The modest progress on dialogue came only after international actors had started to absorb an enhanced understanding of the Taliban Movement. At every stage along the way, gaps in the understanding by non-Taliban of the movement they were dealing with had hindered efforts to launch dialogue. Especially significant misconceptions of the Taliban included the belief in 2002 that the movement would no longer be a factor in Afghan politics, the ignorance of the centralized nature of the Taliban organizational structure, underestimation of the importance of ideological motivation and loyalty to the movement, and the assumption that the Afghan Taliban and al-Qaeda were inextricably linked. Another aspect of the Taliban which architects of dialogue struggled with concerned the nature of linkages between the Taliban and the Pakistani security establishment – were Taliban really proxies, or did they enjoy a degree of autonomy? And, ultimately, could Pakistan, as President Karzai seemed to believe, 'deliver' the Taliban? The assumption that the Taliban were no longer relevant delayed the start of serious efforts to engage them. The failure to appreciate the cohesiveness of the movement and the importance of its ideology led to initial excessive reliance on individual reintegration programmes unsupported by any political dialogue. The assumption that the Taliban and al-Qaeda were 'joined at the hip' provided a deterrent to US support for dialogue, until Hillary Clinton and Joe Biden took a clear stance, recognizing the divergence of interest between the two movements and offering to engage with the Taliban if they made a clean break with their internationalist allies.

Poor understanding of the Taliban meant that those who wanted to promote dialogue underestimated the extent to which Taliban internal authoritarianism limited what could be achieved through conventional approaches. In consequence, it took a decade of experiments before internationally sponsored dialogue found a way of accommodating Taliban authoritarianism, by engaging with the movement's Political Commission. Less progress was made on the alternative approach of circumventing this authoritarianism. That the early enthusiasts for engagement underestimated the extent to which the movement leadership was able to control external engagement is evidenced from the expectations they expressed about their dealings with the Taliban. As debate in Kabul moved towards the more political formulation of 'reconciliation' with the Taliban, supporters of this idea routinely expressed the hope that the Taliban would agree to talk on the precondition of accepting the 2004 Afghan constitution. Once the Afghan government committed itself to pursuing 'reconciliation', in 2010, in the run-up to each event with reconciliation on the agenda, there was speculation whether a Taliban delegation would participate. The idea that senior Taliban, individually or as delegations, would consent to participate in processes choreographed by the powers they were fighting, or that they would give prior commitments which contradicted the movement's declared stands, flew in the face of well-established Taliban practice. Serving members of the movement were under central authority and would face severe consequences for unauthorized contact with the Afghan government or for contradicting the stance of the leadership.

The USA was able to make progress on dialogue when it appreciated, firstly, that the Taliban had a well-defined command structure, including specialized departments such as the political commission; and, secondly, that the good offices of a mutually trusted Muslim ruler could help access this structure. The sustained investment by the USA and Qatar in developing an official channel for engagement with the Taliban paid off, by providing a unique address for engagement with the Taliban leadership and allowing the US side to recover its prisoners of war. However, the structure of a single official channel reinforced the Taliban's authoritarian approach to controlling dialogue. The leadership gave their Political Commission in Qatar a restricted mandate, which meant that there were long periods in which dialogue was suspended. When meetings did take place, Taliban participants were largely in listening mode and simply promised to refer the issues to the leadership for consideration. The implicit recognition which the Qatar Process offered the Taliban did not cause them to rethink their armed struggle. But the necessity of protecting what they had started meant that as soon as the USA was engaged in Qatar it became reluctant to engage with other dialogue tracks. Those inside the Taliban movement who were critical of a hardliner leadership which controlled participation in the Qatar Process interpreted Washington's exclusive focus on Qatar as evidence that the hardliners had successfully co-opted the US side. The implication is that developing an official channel is worthwhile, but there is a case for complementing it by retaining additional non-official dialogue channels.

Dissident Dialogue – Mohtasim in Turkey and Dubai, 2014

Those inside the Taliban Movement who were privately critical of open-ended armed struggle but who were reluctant to break with the leadership remained marginal to the dialogue process. More effort would have been required in the choreography of dialogue to afford participation opportunities to movement loyalists who favoured a more conciliatory approach than the leadership was prepared to contemplate. In the absence of any such effort, Taliban pragmatists remained on the sidelines; any dialogue that took place after the launch of the Qatar Process was dominated by the hardliners or those obliged to speak on their behalf. The Century Foundation's task force provided an example of a format which was somewhat supportive of Taliban participation free from official restrictions. This process was based on consultations rather than a set-piece roundtable format. This meant that those leading the dialogue were able to have multiple points of contact with the Taliban rather than a single authorized channel. The format could also offer a degree of anonymity to interlocutors, who did not have to interact with each other.

On a more profound level, some Taliban pragmatists have argued that they can legitimize their participation in dialogue by obtaining a mandate from their peers and supporters. The rationale for this is that a collective which decides to send a representative to talk is less vulnerable to accusations of breaking ranks than an individual. However, a dialogue process that could provide scope for informal collectives to mandate participants would require significantly more preparation than one based on simply extending invitations to known individuals.

The one track based around Taliban pragmatists involved Mohtasim Agha Jan. Mohtasim was a senior Taliban leader who had served as Finance Minister in their government and after the reorganization of the movement had chaired the Political Commission. He was first associated with dialogue when reported to have met the brother of the Afghan President, through Saudi good offices, in 2009. Mohtasim survived an assassination attempt in Karachi 2010 and ended up being offered refuge in Ankara. He then established a media profile for himself with a series of interviews in which he called on the Taliban to agree a political settlement and an end to the armed campaign. He profiled himself as a serving leader and loyalist of Mullah Omar, while condemning the violence conducted in Mullah Omar's name. In February 2014 the Afghan government briefed the media that an aide to the President, acting on behalf of the High Peace Council, had travelled to Dubai to meet with Taliban figures convened by Mohtasim. This was the high point of Mohtasim's dissident dialogue. He wanted to demonstrate to the rest of the movement that there was a viable alternative to armed struggle, an alternative which enjoyed some support among the Taliban. The Afghan government chose to publicize this. Soon, however, the dissident dialogue faltered, when Mohtasim was reported detained and deported. The UAE authorities considered that this now public and controversial dialogue initiative went beyond anything they had authorized or were prepared to tolerate on their territory. Although Taliban hardliners were clearly relieved at Mohtasim's predicament, his message that there was an alternative to armed struggle continued to challenge their narrative of the war.

The experience of engagement with a pragmatist demonstrated the potential of a 'dissident peace dialogue' complementary to the official track. Despite Mohtasim's claims to be a *bona fide* member of the leadership and a confidant of the supreme leader, he approached dialogue with the status of a dissident. He thus challenged the sole authority of his peers to talk on behalf of the movement and articulated ideas which they were reluctant to embrace but which had potential resonance with the base. Predictably, the official leadership responded to this element of subversion by refusing to share a platform with Mohtasim. Thus they only allowed their delegates to participate in the Chantilly platform on condition that Mohtasim not attend. They also tried to impose a social boycott, penalizing Taliban who had contact with Mohtasim. In a tough warning from the leadership to its cadre to avoid flirting with the dissidents, a former Taliban minister with links to Mohtasim, Haji Raqeeb, was assassinated in Peshawar. However, arguably, this dissident dialogue challenged Taliban thinking about approaches to the armed struggle and peacemaking in a way that encounters stage-managed by the official leadership could not. Through his presence in the media, with a series of interviews, Mohtasim articulated the idea that the NATO commitment to troop withdrawal meant that the Taliban movement should make the transition to non-violent struggle for Islamist reform and participation in a pluralist Afghanistan. Therefore, when the media reported the dialogue between Mohasim's Taliban and the Afghan government, the official leadership could be in little doubt regarding Mohtasim's line in the dialogue – he had already spelled it out publicly. However, from January 2013 onwards, Washington remained single-mindedly focused on developing and protecting its official dialogue track with the Taliban through Qatar. So as to avoid jeopardizing this track, the USA avoided encouraging Mohtasim's dissident peace dialogue. As President Karzai had already been largely successful in killing off civil society or UN-led dialogue, the result of the US focus on the official track was that there were few opportunities in which Mohtasim or other pragmatic Taliban members could articulate their pro-peace ideas. Nevertheless, the limited experience of dissident peace dialogue suggests that it can provide one way of building support for the idea of accommodation and escaping the controls on debate imposed by an authoritarian organization. But such dialogue requires platforms and sponsors, separate from the official track, whose participants may find the dissident dialogue challenging.

Sustaining Dialogue

The Afghan experience illustrates the challenge of the long and elastic timetable. The current phase of the Afghan conflict went on for eight years before there was top-level national and international political will to invest in dialogue. There was some continuity on the Afghan side during this period, as key figures within both the Afghan government and the Taliban movement remained engaged throughout. However, turnover was rapid in all senior international positions – UN mission chiefs, International Security Assistance Force (ISAF) commanders and US Special Representatives. It was not even obvious who within the international community had lead responsibility for dialogue or for sustaining the relationships with Taliban figures in periods when high-level dialogue was not on the agenda. None of the actors who at various times tried to promote peace dialogue managed to make the kind of investment in relationships of trust with Taliban interlocutors that might have sensitized the process to Taliban concerns or increased the Taliban's confidence in participating. That task was well beyond the reach of conventional diplomacy.

Assessing Dialogue Outcomes

The overriding strategic objective for the various parties who launched dialogue with the Taliban was to end the violent conflict by persuading the movement to halt its insurgency on the basis of an accommodation with the government in Kabul. Instead, the Taliban sustained their insurgency throughout the decade of international intervention in Afghanistan, until 2014. Both the Afghan government and Western proponents of dialogue hoped for a political process within the lifetime of the intervention up to 2014. However, dialogue did not bring about peace within this timeframe, and thus can be judged a strategic failure.

On the other hand, dialogue with the Taliban can be credited with more modest success, contributing to the foundations of a longer-term peace process and mitigating some of the effects of the ongoing conflict. Engagement with the Taliban through Doha at least provided an address for the movement's official leadership. This address was available for future initiatives to engage with those running the insurgency, and marked an advance from the earlier situation when there had been considerable uncertainty regarding the standing of various interlocutors who claimed to talk on behalf of the Taliban. The Doha channel also built Taliban confidence in the utility of engagement, by virtue of the June 2014 prisoner release.

Dialogue contributed to a tentative sense that there was scope for accommodation between the Taliban and the order in Kabul. But sense of possibility did not lead to any groundswell on either side to realize the hope. Proponents of the armed struggle on the Taliban side and those opposed to accommodation on the government side may actually have been alarmed by the prospect of progress. Direct encounters between senior serving Taliban and Kabul political figures, as in Chantilly, provided opportunities for them to be exposed to each other's perspectives. However, there was little evidence of the emergence of any common understanding as to a mutually agreeable political roadmap. In this sense, dialogue symbolized the possibility of cooperation – without contributing much to the evolution of ideas about what a resolution might look like.

The activities of Taliban pragmatists, most notably Mohtasim Agha Jan, made a different contribution by showcasing what can be characterized as a Taliban rhetoric of peace – a set of arguments that affirm the previous struggles of the Taliban but call for an early end to the armed struggle. This peace rhetoric challenged the orthodox Taliban view that the armed struggle was the only way to achieve the ideal of a more Islamic Afghanistan. On the other hand, the publicity given to dialogue between Taliban allies of Mohtasim and the Afghan government symbolized for the official Taliban leadership the risk of the movement splitting, or ultimately of pragmatists negotiating some kind of peace deal without them. In the absence of substantive progress towards defining a settlement this at least generated pressure for deal-making.

The modest gains achieved in mitigating the effects of conflict include sensitizing the Taliban to issues concerning civilian casualties. Although the UN continued to report a high proportion of civilian deaths caused by the Taliban, the movement did eventually establish a commission to monitor civilian casualties. Over time, the movement seemed to show greater awareness of the adverse consequences of civilian casualties and of the need to exercise restraint over its fighting forces.

As to the negative consequences of dialogue, international actors, the Afghan government and the Taliban all harboured fears about the risks associated with participating in dialogue. All those fears proved exaggerated, however, and none of the actors faced serious adverse consequences arising from dialogue. Reservations held by the main international actors about venturing into peace dialogue were that this would compromise their stance against terrorism, or could undermine the authority of their ally, the Afghan government. The Afghan government shared the fear that dialogue with the Taliban would undermine its authority. It worried that the arrival of the Afghan Taliban at talks could lower the status of the government to a *primus inter pares*, and felt that its international allies did not take this risk seriously enough. The Taliban were concerned that participation in talks would be taken as recognition of the Afghan government, and that this would expose the movement's leadership to accusations of capitulation, delegitimizing it within pro-jihad constituencies and undermining its capacity to sustain the armed struggle. The fact that the Afghan government presided over a decade of dialogue efforts and then completed its term in May 2014 with no evidence of loss of authority or of conceding legitimacy to the Taliban suggests that international and Kabul fears were overblown. The only episode in which the legitimacy issue came to a head was during the controversy surrounding the Taliban's move to raise a flag in their representative office in Qatar in June 2013. However, a pragmatic solution ultimately allowed a Taliban delegation to operate in Qatar, without a publicly visible office. Meanwhile, in the three years after acknowledging a move towards participating in dialogue, the Taliban leadership retained its grip on the movement, sustained its armed struggle and did not face any significant defections or splits. The only indication that the leadership faced adverse consequences from the move to dialogue came in 2014 when a maverick commander and his grouping, the Fidai Mahaz, said they objected to the Taliban's engagement in the Qatar Process. However, the leadership's ability to claim credit for securing the release of Taliban leaders from Guantanamo Bay helped them maintain support for engagement, despite the opportunistic threats from these anti-dialogue extremists. Indeed, the paucity of adverse consequences from dialogue indicates that the protagonists could have safely embraced dialogue earlier and gone further.

Factors Determining Dialogue Outcomes

How the Nature of the Taliban Movement Constrained Dialogue Outcomes

The Afghan Taliban Movement has a strong authoritarian tradition, and this affected the nature of dialogue with the movement and its members throughout the 2001–2014 period. The Taliban's organizational practices have severely limited the scope for informal dialogue to engage its decisionmakers in any meaningful way. The movement operates with a highly centralized model in which all authority flows from the Amir or supreme leader. Notionally, all significant appointments are made by the Amir. But Mullah Omar's inaccessibility since 2001 means that appointments have been centralized in the hands of his *naib*, or deputy. The leadership has insisted that it must authorize any political contact with non-Taliban entities – particularly the Afghan government and foreign powers or NGOs linked to foreign powers. The leadership has only rarely authorized envoys to engage in contacts, and has periodically taken the trouble to issue public denials of reported Taliban participation in dialogue processes.

The Taliban restriction of external contacts goes far beyond the kind of conservatism that other media-shy organizations practise. The authoritarian tradition has allowed almost no scope for internal debate on political issues or questioning of the leadership's conduct of the armed struggle. Speaking privately, Taliban members frequently mention how they fear persecution or at least loss of privileges if they question the leadership's strategy. There is almost no scope even for internal dialogue on sensitive issues such as alternatives to armed struggle. Furthermore, several issues relevant to peacemaking are virtually taboo: these include the sacred status of armed *jihad*, the treachery inherent in any Taliban member having contact with foreigners or government officials, and the status of Mullah Omar as a rightly guided leader. Unless in the company of close and trusted friends, few Taliban dare address these taboos, although any dialogue intended to explore ways for the Taliban to exit armed conflict could legitimately touch on all of them. In any case, few members active within the movement dare to defy the official bar on external contacts, irrespective of the subject for discussion.

The key doctrine underpinning Taliban cliquish authoritarianism is 'obedience to the Amir', according to which members of the movement means unquestioningly accepting the orders of the supreme leader and the officials under him. In the context of the post-2001 armed struggle, the implicit contract facing members of the Taliban has involved the obligation to defer to the leadership on all issues and maintain secrecy, in return for which they receive status and resources. This contract has limited the choices for anyone seeking to organize a dialogue with the Taliban. If you opt for an officially authorized Taliban participant, you will probably end up with an empty seat, as the leadership accepts few invitations. If you opt for someone thought to be close to the movement but not currently holding an official position, this raises questions of the extent of his access and influence – can he authoritatively speak to Taliban positions, or relay results of the dialogue back to serving members of the movement? The hyper-centralization of decisionmaking is designed to insulate the movement from the kind of informal influences through which Track II dialogue can sometimes impact official positions. Some serving officials of the movement choose to conduct unauthorized external contacts anonymously, simply by hiding such participation from the leadership. However, the steps required to preserve confidentiality create numerous other problems in the dialogue process, including the difficulty of holding plenary sessions.

While the movement's authoritarian approach to internal organization has limited who might participate in dialogue, the leadership's war strategy has dictated what the Taliban can say. The spirit of the Shahwalikot moment – an openness to dealing with the new order in Afghanistan – seems to have lasted through 2002 at most, allowing even senior figures such as Taliban Foreign Minister Mutawakil to try to initiate dialogue. Thereafter the leadership opted for re-organization and armed struggle to assert the legitimacy of the Taliban's Islamic Emirate. Consistent with this, they disavowed contact with Kabul, which they dubbed a puppet government, and became highly restrictive in their approach to dialogue with anyone else. When, after almost a decade of armed struggle, the Taliban acknowledged that they had opened dialogue with the United States, the leadership announced to members that a 'political front' was required, to complement the military front. Members were told that the Taliban could gain international recognition through participation in dialogue, commensurate with what they had achieved on the battlefield. Parallel to the strategic goal of achieving recognition for their Islamic Emirate, Taliban leaders have remained focused on more tactical objectives, in particular the release of prisoners and fund-raising. They have been prepared to contemplate participation in dialogue if there were prospects of achieving these objectives. During the early stages of the Qatar Process, the Taliban successfully put prisoner releases on the agenda. Indeed a principal way in which the Taliban have gauged the utility of any potential dialogue track has been the prospect of achieving releases through it.

Throughout the post-2001 insurgency the Taliban leadership has been based in Pakistan. This has been an added complicating factor for any dialogue process. The Taliban's continued access to this 'safe haven' has been critical to the success of their armed struggle, so they have been reluctant to do anything that might jeopardize their presence in Pakistan. They live and operate 'semi-covertly', avoiding public exposure like media appearances or official meetings. The Pakistan authorities have tried to maintain a degree of deniability regarding the Taliban presence. The attitudes of the Taliban and the host country alike have essentially ruled out Pakistan as a venue for dialogue. Even participants in a process which enjoyed Pakistani official sanction and participation, the Afghanistan–Pakistan Regional Peace Jirga in 2007 and 2008, found themselves unable to access any Taliban leaders in Pakistan. The politics of the safe haven combined with the Taliban antipathy to appearing to deal with the Kabul government have shaped the geography of dialogue and forced facilitators to look to third-country venues.

'Quality control' in participant selection has proven a recurrent challenge in Taliban dialogue. This factor has been greatly exacerbated by the Taliban official reticence, the requirements of anonymity or confidentiality and the Taliban inaccessibility in Pakistan. Attempts at dialogue have been plagued by impostors, charlatans and minor figures who simply exaggerate their importance. The two most famous examples of dialogue impostors were the 'fake Mansoor', a man posing as Mullah Omar's deputy, whom NATO reportedly helped to meet President Karzai in 2010; and the suicide bomber who killed High Peace Council chairman, Burhanuddin Rabbani, in 2011. In both cases, the impostors exploited the scarcity value of Taliban interlocutors (the government side was so keen to find senior Taliban willing to talk that they did not conduct due diligence checks) and the willingness of the government to maintain initial confidentiality. More generally, in a dialogue process involving people associated with the Taliban who do not actually claim to be current officials, it is difficult to assess the extent of their authoritativeness and influence. This ambiguity even applies to well-known and respected figures who held high office in the Taliban administration up to 2001, such as former Foreign Minister Mutawakil and former ambassador to Pakistan, Salaam Zaeef. After their release from periods of incarceration they have been based in Kabul and have therefore not had any formal association with the movement during the period of the insurgency. Although these figures have contributed important ideas to previous rounds of dialogue, they are at pains to clarify that they cannot speak on behalf of the current leadership. The Taliban's cultivated inaccessibility and imperviousness to external influence create a moral hazard problem. The easier it is for a Taliban-related figure to participate in dialogue, then the less likely it is that he is connected to current Taliban leadership thinking.

The Taliban's authoritarian practices do not only restrict direct participation in dialogue, they severely restrict the flow of ideas and help keep the leadership insulated from attempts to influence them. Although veterans of the movement occasionally participate in dialogue, they are highly circumspect in feeding ideas from the dialogue back into the movement. They tend to avoid acknowledging having participated in dialogue, and in movement circles they are reluctant to challenge taboos or question the leadership. The leadership has predominantly developed its strategy without reference to the base. This lack of consultation is reinforced by the device of the inaccessible but unchallengeable Amir. The 'visible' leadership attributes key decisions, such as that of launching the Doha process, to this personage. But even fairly senior members of the movement wishing to question decisions or strategy cannot approach him, and they dare say little in front of his lieutenants. The movement has two national-level organs which ostensibly deal in ideas – the Cultural Commission and the Council of Religious Scholars. However neither of these is able to influence leadership strategy or initiate debate. They are politically subordinate to the Amir and his lieutenants, and function as propagandists and legitimizing tools, supporting the strategy of armed struggle ordained by the leadership. This imperviousness means that although Taliban dialogue participants may offer useful insights into thinking within the movement and even suggest helpful actions by the other parties, they have limited opportunities for sharing with their leadership any insights they may have gained in the dialogue. The authoritarian organization and insulation of the leadership also enable the movement to sustain hypocrisy beyond the level possible for an organization subject to more internal or external accountability. During the insurgency the Taliban have excelled at exaggerating military achievements and downplaying their forces' role in civilian casualties, while representing their fight as being against foreign forces and barely acknowledging that Taliban fighters mainly fought against Afghans. Getting past Taliban official and counterfactual descriptions of the situation on the ground is a major dialogue challenge.

Alongside the structural and organizational barriers, the leadership's commitment to sustained armed struggle constitutes the most fundamental Taliban barrier to dialogue. The leadership has prioritized the armed struggle over any form of political activity, generally holding back from authorizing dialogue for fear of undermining the armed struggle.

Afghan Government Stance and its Impact on Dialogue Outcomes

A rather different set of challenges arose from the attitude of the government of Afghanistan to dialogue. From an early stage in the conflict, Kabul showed itself prepared to engage in dialogue with members of the Taliban, and the government's 2010 reconciliation policy provided a formal endorsement of engagement with the movement. In practice, however, government support for dialogue was both conditional and opportunistic. Meanwhile, government actions directly undermined some of the dialogue initiatives.

The Afghan government repeatedly publicized claims of contacts with Taliban intermediaries, indicating that this heralded progress towards political agreement. The publicity covered *bona fide* contacts, as when government sources leaked news of the early stages of the US dialogue with the Taliban in the Qatar Process, as well as contacts of doubtful significance with figures who lacked a mandate to talk for the Taliban. The government pursued two objectives in this drive to publicize erstwhile discreet dialogue. Firstly the government sought to legitimize itself by demonstrating that the Taliban were prepared to deal with it, despite their public assertion to the contrary, and indicating that the government had the capacity to preside over a peace deal. Secondly the government sought to assert a monopoly over dialogue with the Taliban. It publicized dialogue knowing fully that this would embarrass those involved, principally the Taliban, who sought to achieve progress in discrete talks before preparing their constituencies to accept that dialogue was necessary. The government proved unwilling to concede the space to other actors for peace dialogue with the Taliban, irrespective of whether those pursuing the dialogue were state or non-state actors and whether the dialogue was formal or informal.

In addition to essentially spoiling those efforts at dialogue which it did not directly control, the Afghan government also invested in high-profile events and structures, which it portrayed as a peace process, but which did not include contacts with influential Taliban or substantive dialogue. Confronted with slow progress towards dialogue with the leaders of the Taliban movement, the government was content to pursue the theatre of a peace process. It publicized claims that groups of Taliban fighters had reintegrated peacefully and accepted government authority. It accorded much fanfare to the deliberations of the 2010 'national consultative peace *jirga*' and then of the 'High Peace Council' – which resolved to pursue peace but consisted entirely of figures who were already stakeholders in the Kabul-based political order.

In the process the government created tactical and strategic obstacles to any peace dialogue that might have included the Taliban. Potential Taliban participants feared that confidentiality would be compromised; dialogue facilitators feared government sanctions. More strategically, the spectacle of government sponsorship of what they considered to be fake peace processes led pro-peace Taliban to question whether the Kabul government could ever be trusted as an interlocutor.

International Actors and Dialogue Outcome

As to international actors, their investment in dialogue in the period 2001–2014 was minuscule in comparison to their investment in the military campaign. Despite the eventual US decision to embrace dialogue, within the overall scheme of the decade plus intervention, dialogue with the Taliban was a low priority in which Washington and its allies were little involved.

The position of the USA and allies with regard to peace dialogue was also coloured by their role as protagonists in the post-2001 conflict. In the first place, the original ideas of the 'war on terror', with the Taliban cast as terrorists even if not unambiguously listed as a terrorist organization, made Western governments cautious about engaging with them. This also added a slightly exotic quality to the idea of 'talking with the Taliban' when dialogue finally found its way onto the agenda. The position of the US allies as protagonists also meant that they were committed to supporting the government in Kabul: they could not engage the Taliban as neutral parties. Furthermore the USA and allies committed to the idea of an Afghan-led approach to peacemaking, which meant that they were reluctant to pursue independent contacts or dialogue without the blessing of Kabul. Finally, the status of the USA as a protagonist and the chief financier of the government in Kabul acted as a barrier to it accepting a role as international mediator. A striking feature of the dialogue experience between 2001 and 2014 is the lack of international mediation.

The inability of the international community and the Afghan President to come up with a common approach to peace dialogue constrained progress almost as much as did Taliban authoritarianism. The collapse of UN efforts to convene a forum in Turkmenistan, the paucity of civil society organized dialogue events after Chantilly and the hiatus in the Qatar Process after June 2013 all show how the sensitivities of the Afghan government severely restricted the scope for dialogue. Once the Afghan President had decided that engagement with the Taliban which his government did not control risked undermining government authority, it is not clear that there was any formula available which could have won Kabul's blessing for continued dialogue. This shows how protagonists to a conflict are apt to politicize and seek to control the dialogue process. Therefore the United Nations Mission in Afghanistan (UNAMA), dependent as it was on maintaining a working relationship with the Kabul government for the rest of its business, found itself at a disadvantage in trying to facilitate a peace dialogue. Cooperation with the Kabul government would have been the best basis for facilitating dialogue. But in the absence of cooperation, autonomy would have sufficed. Unable to muster cooperation or autonomy, UNAMA had to lower the profile of its dialogue efforts.

How Approaches to Facilitation Affected Outcomes

The Afghanistan dialogue experience also highlighted the importance of location. Those wishing to pursue dialogue never had access to an ideal location, and this compounded the challenges inherent in the nature of the conflict and of the conflict actors. An ideal location would have been one that was secure, accessible, supportive and reputation-enhancing for all participants. The latter point was particularly important for Taliban participants in dialogue. Rather than being concerned solely about the practicalities of whether they could safely reach a dialogue venue, they repeatedly expressed concern about how travelling to different venues could affect their reputation among peers. In simplest terms, travel to Western countries would open Taliban to accusations of selling out, whereas their reputation would be enhanced by visiting Saudi Arabia and other conservative Sunni Muslim countries. Qatar provided a brilliant illustration of what it meant to have a supportive host, as the Emir, in consultation with officials in Washington, made support to the Taliban delegation in Qatar a foreign policy priority. This meant that the Qatar Process and the Taliban based there had the blessing of the ruler, with access to visas, protocol, accommodation, meeting venues, publicity where appropriate, confidentiality when appropriate – and all this for an open-ended duration in a secure, stable environment. The fact of being hosted and patronized by a respected Muslim leader, plus all the trappings which came with this process, legitimized the Taliban's participation in the Qatar Process and enabled the leadership to overcome any residual misgivings about the risk of sell-out or compromising the *jihad*. What Qatar provided to the official Taliban delegation can offer a template for the ideal location for Afghan peace dialogue. However, US concerns about protecting its official channel with the Taliban meant that once the Qatar Process got going there was little prospect of Qatar hosting a broader peace dialogue accessible to anyone but representatives of the official Taliban leadership. Unofficial processes, by operating low-profile, were able to find alternative venues in the Gulf. However, the security and legal sensitivities arising from the 'war on terror' meant that any host government could quite reasonably expect to exercise a veto on dialogue with Islamist militants on its territory. If the international community or the Afghan government had taken a strategic decision to pursue dialogue with Taliban, they would have had to make the diplomatic investment of preparing a long-term venue for that dialogue in a friendly Muslim state. The aim would have been to encourage and facilitate participants from different parts of the Taliban movement and their non-Taliban interlocutors at least as well as the Emirate of Qatar facilitated its guests.

There was a continuing tension between participants' desire for confidentiality while engaging across the frontlines and the desire of Afghan officials either to achieve propaganda gains or sabotage the process by publicizing dialogue processes. With the exception of a handful of showcase events, confidentiality remained key to Taliban participation, both official and unofficial. Although the Qatar Process reached a point (briefly) where Taliban participants were prepared to face the media and issue statements and interviews, in both the earlier stages and when talks resumed after the debacle of the office-opening, the Taliban side expected confidentiality. This concern for confidentiality around engagement, even when contacts were properly authorized by the leadership, was partly motivated by the latter's need to manage expectations within the movement, but also because the leadership expected opposition to its role in dialogue, from Kabul as well as from the Pakistan authorities. The concerns for confidentiality of Taliban figures who contemplated participating in dialogue in an unofficial capacity or without the blessing of the leadership went far beyond the concerns of Taliban-authorized interlocutors. They believed that their personal security would be compromised if their participation was made public, so Taliban participation in events was frequently conditioned upon the hosts agreeing to maintain confidentiality.

The contribution of civil society to the strategic-level peace dialogue process was modest and short-lived. The hostility of the Afghan government, the impenetrability of the Taliban, and security concerns around engagement with militant Islamists all acted as deterrents to engagement on the part of civil society. For a period, civil-society organizations like the Pugwash Conferences circumvented the challenges by organizing peace dialogues with Afghans drawn from many interest groups but not serving the Taliban. Former Taliban leaders who were resident in Kabul, most prominently Mullahs Zaeef and Mutawakil, received invitations to roundtables because they were assumed to be authoritative voices regarding Taliban perspectives and were also able to travel relatively freely. Mediation organizations such as Humanitarian Dialogue did try to develop dialogue channels which involved currently serving Taliban and accessed those actually running the insurgency. However, the notable developments in dialogue up to 2014 – Qatar, Chantilly and Kyoto – all involved significant state backing and no autonomous civil-society action. That part of Afghan peace dialogue that involved real Taliban proved a difficult environment for civil society to operate in.

Conclusions

Set against the overall massive costs of the war, the (admittedly modest) achievements from a decade of Afghan peace dialogue efforts suggest that pursuing engagement was justified. However, the Afghan experience also indicates numerous lessons learnt and ways in which the dialogue process could have been strengthened. Those who promoted dialogue failed to take adequate account of the nature of the Taliban as an organization. They were also slow to reconcile the competing imperatives of the main parties to the conflict – the desire of the Afghan government to control dialogue processes versus the desire of the Taliban movement to keep its distance from the government. Similarly, no actor succeeded in using relationships cultivated during the low-key dialogue of the early years to enhance the dialogue when it became a higher political priority in the later phases of the conflict.

References

Afgan Mission. 2010. The Resolution Adopted at the Conclusion of the National Consultative Peace Jirga, Islamic Republic of Afghanistan Permanent Mission of Afghanistan to the United Nations in New York [Online]. Available at: http://www.afghanistan-un.org/2010/06/the-resolution-adopted-at-the-conclusion-of-the-national-consultative-peace-jirga [accessed: 11 August 2014].

Brahimi, L. and Pickering, T. 2011. Afghan people's dialogue on peace, laying the foundations for an inclusive peace process, Afghanistan Negotiating Peace – The Report of The Century Foundation International Task Force on Afghanistan, The Century Foundation, New York [Online]. Availible at http://www.aihrc.org.af/media/files/People's%20Dialogue%20FINAL%20report.pdf ? [accessed: 11 July 2014].

Bew, J., Evans, R, Frampton, M., Neumann, P. and Porges, M. 2013. Talking to the Taliban, Hope over History? ICSR [The International Centre for the Study of Radicalisation and Political Violence], London [Online]. Available at: http://www.aihrc.org.af/media/files/People's%20Dialogue%20FINAL%20report.pdf [accessed: 11 July 2014].

Borger, J. 2010. Who can broker a deal with the Taliban?, *The Guardian* [Online, 24 October]. Available at: http://www.theguardian.com/world/2010/oct/24/who-can-broker-deal-taliban [accessed: 1 July 2014].

EastWest Institute (EWI). 2010. Seeking solutions for Afghanistan – second report on the Abu Dhabi Process', EWI, New York, October [Online]. Available at: http://www.google.no/url?sa=t&rct=j&q=&esrc=s&source=web&cd=3&ved=0CC0QFjAC&url=http%3A%2F%2Fmercury.ethz.ch%2Fserviceengine%2FFiles%2FISN%2F127331%2Fipublicationdocument_singledocument%2Faa3aae9e-b8e4-493e-81f4-07ab7043e6ee%2Fen%2FAbuDhabiReport2.pdf&ei=5t7oU4DCCMXmyQOo-ICwCQ&usg=AFQjCNHYwCYEmySGIMpq4nbKbP7K3fSgsA&sig2=vQW-eEQ48G56VckDf8gPTw&bvm=bv.72676100,d.bGQ [accessed: 11 August 2014].

FCO [Federal and Commonwealth Office] 2014. Afghanistan: The London Conference – Communiqué, FCO, London, January 2010APDP, Kabul, June.

Grenier, R. 2010. Making room for the Taliban, *Al Jazeera* [Online 31 January]. Available at: http://www.aljazeera.com/ focus/2010/01/20101288945976804.html [accessed: 11 August 2014].

Grossman, M. 2013. Lessons From Negotiating With the Taliban, YaleGlobal [Online, 8 October]. Available at: http://yaleglobal.yale.edu/content/ lessons-negotiating-taliban [accessed: 11 August 2014].

Hadley, S. and Podesta, J. 2012. The Right Way Out of Afghanistan – Leaving Behind a State That Can Govern, *Foreign Affairs*, July/August [Online]. Available at: http://www.cfr.org/afghanistan/right-way-out-afghanistan/ p28604 [accessed: 11 August 2014].

Imtiaz, S. 2013. The Outcomes of the 'Taliban/Paris Meeting on Afghanistan', *Al Jazeera Studies*, January [Online]. Available at: http://studies.aljazeera.net/en/ reports/2013/01/2013124111354190395.htm [accessed: 11 August 2014].

Inderfurth, K. 2012. A Taliban 'Rope-a-Dope' Strategy?, *Foreign Policy*, January [Online]. Available at: http://afpak.foreignpolicy.com/posts/2012/01/25/a_ taliban_rope_a_dope_strategy [accessed: 11 August 2014].

Islamic Republic of Afghanistan Office of National Security Council 2009. Policy for National Reconciliation and Reintegration of Armed Opposition Groups', Kabul, December. (A detailed commentary on the policy is available online at: https://www.afghanistan-analysts.org/a-goa-reconciliation-policy-in-the-making/) [accessed: 14 August 2014].

Kuehn, F. and van Linschoten, S. 2013. Missed opportunities – lessons from the west's talks with the Taliban pre-2001, unclassified research paper, Foreign and Commonwealth Office, London, August.

Maldives Process 2010. Details of Maldives Meetings between HIG and Government representative on 30/01/2010 (in Male), unpublished memo. Commentary available from the *Free Library. S.v. Maldives Moot to Talk Peace with HIA, Taliban* [Online]. Available at: http://www.thefreelibrary.com/ Maldives+moot+to+talk+peace+with+HIA%2c+Taliban.-a0217924542 [accessed: 12 August 2014].

Masadykov, T., Giustozzi, A. and Page, J.M. 2010. Negotiating with the Taliban: Toward a solution for the Afghan conflict, Crisis States Working Papers Series 2, LSE, London [Online]. Available at: http://www.lse.ac.uk/ internationalDevelopment/research/crisisStates/Publications/wpPhase2/ wp66.aspx [accessed: 12 August 2014].

Muhtasim, A.J. 2013. About current peaceful efforts for solution of Afghan conflict, March [Online]. Available at: http://www.larawbar.net/35835.html [accessed: 11 August 2014].

Political Office of the Islamic Emirate of Afghanistan 2012. Position of the Islamic Emirate of Afghanistan on the foreign troops pull out, the Afghan issue and reconciliation in the country', Kyoto, June .

Porter, G. 2011. Evidence of 2002 Taliban Offer Damages Myth of al-Qaeda Ties, IPS, February [Online]. Available at: http://ipsnews.net/news.asp?idnews=54384 [accessed: 11 August 2014].

Pugwash Conferences 2013. Summary of the Pugwash meeting on Afghan reconciliation, Dubai 15–17 January, Pugwash, Rome [Online]. Available at: http://pugwash.org/2013/01/17/summary-of-the-pugwash-meeting-on-afghan-reconciliation-dubai-15-17-january-2013 [accessed: 11 August 2014].

Shinn, J. and Dobbins, J. 2011. *Afghan Pace Talks – A Primer.* Santa Monica, CA: Rand Corporation,

Van Linschoten, S., Kuehn, F. and Kuehn, A. 2012. *An Enemy We Created: The Myth of the Taliban/Al-Qaeda Merger in Afghanistan, 1970–2010.* London: Hurst: .

Chapter 9
The Attempts of Dialogue in Sudan[1]

John Ashworth

Introduction

This chapter offers some reflections on informal dialogue processes during the Sudanese civil war of 1983–2005 and in the new Republic of South Sudan following its independence in 2011. It is written by a practitioner, rather than an academic, an eyewitness who was there and was part of the processes described there. For that reason there are fewer references cited than might be expected in an academic tome. The author is a primary source. The chapter does not pretend to offer a comprehensive overview of every aspect of dialogue in Sudan: it is rather a case study of certain processes involving dialogue, and highlighting the role of the churches in spearheading dialogue.

The main emphasis is on Track III dialogue, led by civil society actors, in this case the church.[2] However, there is some overlap with Track II, as in some cases leading individuals from within the church played a personal role. There is also some overlap with Track I, as the Track II and III processes often resulted in the same actors playing a role which led to negotiations and conflict-prevention outcomes. This demonstrates the shortcomings of any attempt to impose models onto what is by its nature an organic process.

During more than two decades of war in southern Sudan, the church was the only institution to remain present on the ground with the people during an era when there was no government, no civil society, no NGOs and no UN presence, and even the influence of traditional chiefs and elders had been eroded by the young comrades with guns. The church thus gained tremendous

---

1   In 2005 Sudan split into two countries, the new Republic of South Sudan (formerly southern Sudan) and the rump Republic of Sudan (the old northern Sudan).

2   Note that in Sudan and South Sudan generally the church is seen as a separate entity which is related to civil society but does not come under the heading 'civil society'. In part this is because the term 'civil society' has come to refer to a particular group of modern local NGOs and civil society organizations (CSOs) created in the image and likeness of the international NGOs which fund them.

credibility and moral authority, and the southern Sudanese people and their liberation movements recognized its leadership and guidance towards peace and reconciliation through dialogue. Even the Islamist regime in Khartoum could recall the key role that the World Council of Churches and All-Africa Conference of Churches played in resolving through dialogue the previous civil war, which ended with the signing of the Addis Ababa Agreement in 1972, where the church was trusted by both sides (Scherf 1971). 'The church' here refers to the ecumenical body of various Christian denominations working together, which was one of the characteristics of the church in Sudan during the conflict (as in South Africa during the anti-apartheid struggle), and not to any single church or denomination.

Even before independence from the Anglo-Egyptian Condominium in 1956, southern Sudanese felt that they were second-class citizens in a country and culture dominated by northerners. Various options for autonomy and federalism were mooted, and some were tried briefly and unsuccessfully. Two civil wars were fought as successive regimes in Khartoum escalated their policies of Arabization and Islamization.

The root causes of the conflicts in Sudan are generally held to be identity and the centre–periphery dynamic.[3] Sudan was (and still is) a multi-ethnic, multi-cultural, multi-religious, multi-lingual country. In practice, however, the Sudanese identity was defined by the ruling elite as Islamic and Arabic. Groups which did not conform to this identity became second-class citizens, at various times marginalized, harassed, oppressed, disenfranchised, assimilated or exterminated. Political and economic power, access to resources and development, and most other facets of life were concentrated in the geographic centre of Sudan, around Khartoum and the Nile valley, in the hands of a small number of ethnic groups. All other groups on the periphery were marginalized and neglected. At its core, Sudanese citizenship depended not on being born in Sudan of a Sudanese family, but on where in Sudan one was born, and the specifics of one's ethnic and religious background. Southerners failed both tests – they were neither Arabized nor Islamized, and they were on the periphery – which is why the southern conflict broke out first and lasted for so long. However various northern groups also gradually came into conflict with the centre – Darfur, the Nuba Mountains, southern Blue Nile, the Eastern Front failed one or both of the identity and centre–periphery tests to some degree.

The second war was deadlier than the first, but by the early 1990s much of the fighting was a proxy war in which southerners fought southerners. It was in this context that the churches began the dialogue-based reconciliation work that became known as the People-to-People Peace Process.

---

3 See Deng 1994 and Johnson 2003.

This chapter examines several examples of dialogue in Sudan, beginning with the People-to-People Peace Process which led to the Entebbe Process, and the accompanying international dialogue. It then looks at three more recent dialogue processes in the new state of South Sudan: the Jonglei Peace Process, the negotiations between rebel David Yau Yau and the Government of South Sudan, and the Committee for National Healing, Peace and Reconciliation; followed by some reflections on the new conflict which broke out in South Sudan on 15 December 2013. It then considers the model used by the People-to-People and similar dialogue processes, and ends with a few comments on how these examples shed light on the three interrelated questions introduced in the Introduction to this book: (1) What was the character of the dialogue between the actors prior to, during, and after the 'peak' of the conflict/crisis? (2) To what extent has the dialogue been successful? (3) What determines whether a dialogue can succeed or not in the different cases?

The People-to-People Peace Process[4]

In 1991 the Sudan People's Liberation Army (SPLA) split. Dr Riek Machar Teny Durgeon staged an unsuccessful coup d'état against Dr John Garang de Mabior, but the bulk of the army remained loyal to Garang, leaving Machar with a relatively small group of his own followers. The split proved disastrous for the liberation struggle. Before long, the new offshoot had joined with the Khartoum government to fight against the mainstream SPLA, and the SPLA lost most of the territory that it had previously controlled. Although ethnicity was only one of the reasons for the split,[5] it became a major issue which led to massacres of thousands of civilians in the two main ethnic groups, the Dinka of Dr Garang and the Nuer of Dr Machar. From an early stage the church attempted to mediate between the two leaders. At times it appeared that they were very close to reconciliation, but ultimately the attempts failed. The two leaders were not prepared to reconcile.

In 1994, partly as a result of the split, the mainstream SPLA convened the Chukudum Convention, which brought together several hundred people from all over South Sudan. This marked the beginning of changes within the SPLA, aimed at making it more democratic and accountable, improving its

---

4   See Ashworth 2014: Chapter 6.

5   The original split was between SPLA mainstream and SPLA-Nasir. The reasons for the split included a power struggle between individuals; ethnicity; the poor human rights record and lack of democracy within the movement; and disagreement over whether the main aim of the liberation struggle was independence for southern Sudan or a new, democratic, secular dispensation for the whole of a united Sudan.

human rights record, creating a political wing – the Sudan People's Liberation Movement (SPLM) – and instituting a civil administration in the 'liberated areas' which it controlled.

This was followed in July 1997 by a meeting in Kajiko, near Yei, for dialogue to iron out differences that had developed between the churches and the movement. It was a fiery meeting, but ended well, helped by a prominent Kenyan cleric who had served in the army before becoming a pastor, and who could thus speak in language understandable to both parties. The SPLM/A mandated the church to handle peace and reconciliation matters,[6] as well as other issues such as the provision of chaplains to the armed forces.

At that time the ecumenical church coordinating body in the 'liberated' (rebel-controlled) parts of Sudan was the New Sudan Council of Churches (NSCC), led by Dr Haruun Lual Ruun. After much deliberation, the NSCC decided that, having failed to bring together the two principles, Dr Garang and Dr Machar, it would now start at the other extreme, from the grassroots. Consequently, in June 1998, a meeting was held in Lokichoggio, northern Kenya, attended by influential chiefs and elders from the two communities, the Dinka and Nuer from the west bank of the Nile, along with church leaders from the area.[7]

This was the first time in almost ten years that the chiefs had been able to meet together, and was a first step in building trust, which was to become one of the key elements of the People-to-People Peace Process. The chiefs achieved this through telling their stories – the second key element. At the Lokichoggio meeting, 'the leaders began to recall how they and their ancestors had historically dealt with conflicts and restored peace'.[8] Thus emerged the third key element: the use of traditional peacebuilding techniques. The fourth element followed quickly: 'We are capable of making reconciliation even if Garang and Riek are not present. Don't blame them – we are capable of making peace. We are responsible'. This statement reflects the principle that the community is the primary actor in peacebuilding. It must take responsibility; it must be ready and willing to make peace. At one point the elderly and arthritic Episcopal (Anglican) Bishop Nathaniel Garang, a co-founder of the NSCC, held a heavy wooden chair above his head, clearly suffering from the effort to do so, and cried, 'Who will help me with this burden?' A chief rushed forwards to help him – and the fifth element, symbolism and imagery, came into play.

---

6 Some would argue that the church does not need to be 'mandated' to do this, as it already has its own mandate from God. Nevertheless, it is useful to have a clear go-ahead from the *de facto* authority on the ground.

7 Both communities are also found elsewhere in South Sudan, but the process began on the west bank.

8 This and following quotes are from NSCC, 2002, unless otherwise stated.

A great deal of practical preparation then ensued. Not only the local people but also the military factions controlling the area had to be mobilized. Perhaps the most important, and emotionally powerful, preparations were the exchange visits in which five chiefs and a women's representative from each community, accompanied by church leaders, visited the other community. Again traditional rituals were performed. There was great fear, but also great courage, joy, hospitality and reciprocity. At one point, chiefs from one community offered to act as hostages to guarantee the safety of the others; the offer strengthened the resolve of the others and was graciously declined. 'Ancestors took risks for peace, and so must we; being a chief means being ready to lead, even to die … so let us go in pursuit of peace, this is required of us' … 'The commitment, and the words and deeds of honour among the chiefs spread rapidly throughout all the communities'. People were now convinced that a real peace process was under way.

A site was chosen for the first main peace conference in February/March 1999, in a relatively obscure Dinka area called Wunlit. There were major logistical problems to be resolved. A whole new village of 150 mud and thatch houses, plus a conference hall, had to be built from scratch, boreholes drilled, latrines dug, the dirt road repaired, an airstrip created, kitchens prepared, and much more. Hundreds of delegates (one third of them women) and hundreds more support staff congregated there – a total community of up to 2,000 people, all in the centre of an active war zone, with security guaranteed by the SPLA. This was truly a community effort.

It is difficult to capture the atmosphere of such a meeting. One of the high spots was the slaughter of a white bull (*mabior* in the local language). 'Mabior is the Bull of Peace that will be sacrificed for reconciliation and peace … Anyone who breaks this commitment to peace will follow the way of Mabior … The elders are making a peace and are taking an oath not to repeat atrocities previously committed. A curse is placed on any who partake of the Mabior sacrifice and later break the oath … It is a very serious curse; it is a curse of death'. The sacrificial bull was a strong animal which did not die easily. 'This bull was anxious and angry, pulling at his tether, trying to charge the priests of the fishing spear as they danced around him chanting and taunting him with spears. Finally he gave in. His throat was cut and the blood held up for blessing and oblation' (Ashworth 2014: 156). Its struggles impressed the participants and gave added weight to the ritual. The fighting spirit of Mabior made a powerful impression on everyone. One Chief spoke, 'You, Dinka and Nuer, I caution you to be very careful of what you have observed in Mabior. It was very wild. I have never seen a bull as wild as that bull. Mabior will take revenge on anyone who revives these conflicts. Mabior died for our reconciliation'.

Most of the meeting was concerned with the sixth element: *truth*. In the Nilotic tradition, peace can be achieved only when everyone knows fully what wrongs were committed. The two communities each have a chance to tell their story, to 'vomit out' all the suffering and bitterness. It is a painful time for all. There is also an opportunity for rebuttal, but often there is no rebuttal. Both sides acknowledge the truth of the accusations, but also recognize that they have both suffered in a similar way at the hands of the other. This leads to agreements including practical actions for peace, followed by the signing of a covenant.

Finally, the peace has to be taken home and acted upon. Peace committees were formed to follow up – and to date there has been no major breach of the peace accord on the west bank.

The process then moved to the east bank of the Nile. Meetings were held in Waat (October 1999) and Liliir (May 2000), again after much groundwork. The situation on the east bank was complicated by various factors, including the number of different ethnic groups involved and various political considerations, so there was not such a clearcut resolution as in Wunlit. Nevertheless, progress was made. As is often the case elsewhere as well, peacebuilding in southern Sudan is not based on one-off peace conferences which are a 'success' or otherwise, but on a long process of dialogue which has its ups and downs but constantly chips away at the conflict. This included several smaller conferences and meetings with sub-sections of the main ethnic groups.

By November 2000 it was time to take stock and evaluate the process. A meeting called 'Strategic Linkages' was held in the small village of Wulu, on the west bank, bringing together representatives from all the other conferences. Their basic message was: 'We have made peace, but it is our sons who continue to encourage conflict' (referring here of course to Garang and Machar). It highlighted a dynamic which the church had always been aware of: that where an ethnic conflict often has its own roots, it is manipulated and exacerbated by political and military interests. This led to 'Strategic Linkages 2', held in the Kenyan city of Kisumu in June 2001. This meeting brought traditional leaders, elders and women from the grassroots together with civil society, politicians, intellectuals, diaspora and representatives of the various factions of the liberation movements.

The failure of the SPLM to fully endorse the Kisumu conference made church leaders aware of a final important element of the process: *empowerment*. Churches had originally set out to make peace through dialogue, not to empower people, but the latter was an inevitable result of the process. The SPLM may have felt challenged by this dynamic, which was not what they had expected when they gave the church a mandate to bring peace and reconciliation through dialogue. Nevertheless, several important SPLM figures attended 'unofficially'. The clear message from the conference to both Garang and Machar was, 'We fully support the liberation struggle and Dr John's leadership of it, but it is unacceptable that you continue the conflict between yourselves and your factions; you must unite'. While it is impossible to know exactly what caused the two 'doctors' to reconcile soon afterwards, the Kisumu conference was clearly a major factor. The reunion of the two main factions as a result of the years of patient dialogue led by the church significantly reduced the suffering of the people on the ground and hastened the end of the civil war.

The Entebbe Process[9]

Negotiations sponsored by the African regional grouping IGAD resulted in the January 2005 Comprehensive Peace Agreement (CPA), which ultimately led to the referendum in January 2011 and independence for South Sudan in July 2011. The IGAD negotiations, first in Machakos and then in Naivasha, Kenya, were strictly between the two warring parties, the Government of Sudan and the SPLM/A, and excluded all other political and military factions as well as civil society and the churches.

However, refusing to be completely sidelined, the church initiated its own process with civil society, known as the Entebbe Process, to shadow the Naivasha process. This was the logical next step following the Strategic Linkages conferences, which themselves were part of the grassroots People- to- People Peace Process.

The first meeting in Entebbe, Uganda, held at the end of July 2002 just a few days after the warring parties had signed the Machakos Protocol, brought together 35 church leaders from all over Sudan. It was necessary for the church to reflect on its own position and for all its leaders to be singing from the same hymn sheet before they tried to assist the broader community. The church leaders 'fully supported the commitment of parties to the negotiated, peaceful, and comprehensive resolution of the conflict based on the IGAD Declarations of Principles for the benefit of all people of the Sudan and welcomed the Machakos Protocol as a framework for the ongoing peace negotiations' (*Communique*, 2 August 2002) and called for 'a wider and inclusive meeting that will bring together civil society of both the north and the south ... as a follow up to this consultation to discuss issues of reconciliation and good governance during the interim period'.[10]

The second Entebbe conference, the 'Sudan Civil Society Forum on Good Governance and Reconciliation', took place in October 2002. As the 14-page advisory statement noted:

---

9 See Ashworth 2014: Chapter 8.

10 Recommendations of the church leaders' consultation on the right to self-determination and good governance, 02 August 2002.

Over one hundred representatives of various southern and several northern Sudanese civil society organizations, church leaders, other Sudanese organizations and Sudanese diaspora attended this forum. The participants consulted together, many for the first time, on important matters of good governance, reconciliation, the role of civil society and other matters affecting the future of Sudan. Participants viewed this forum as an important step in building the civil society in Sudan and in gaining confidence for promoting people-oriented issues of justice, peace, reconciliation, good governance, representation, human rights, democratic forms of participation, and essential services for the peoples of Sudan.[11]

Detailed recommendations were given. Dr Riek Machar participated, as did elder statesman and former Vice President Abel Alier and several southern Sudanese elders from Khartoum. This was the first time representatives from northern and southern civil society had come together for dialogue – indeed, it was the first time many of the northern groups had even been able to meet each other, as they did not enjoy freedom of expression or association in the north, which was a police state. The Entebbe conference was much appreciated by ordinary people in both south and north.

One senior Ugandan diplomat who came for the opening ended up staying for the whole meeting. He said, 'I came with doubt, but after listening to and speaking with the church leaders, I've decided to stay. There are pieces missing, and the church leaders have them!'[12]

The third Entebbe conference, held in December 2002, was essentially a South–South dialogue, bringing together leaders of militias and other armed groups (including those allied with Khartoum) as well as SPLA officers.

The overall purposes of this Forum were (i) to seek understanding of the importance, nature and realisaization of reconciliation and good governance from now through an interim period envisioned by the Machakos peace talks and (ii) to begin the process of dialogue and reconciliation between different parties, groups and people of South Sudan.[13]

---

11 *Advisory Statement in the Context of Machakos Protocol from the Civil Society Forum on Good Governance and Reconciliation*, 11 October 2002.

12 Several years later in a different context, this same sentiment was expressed when a Sudanese church delegation led by Archbishop Daniel Deng Bul visited Washington DC in 2010 to advocate for the South Sudan independence referendum. White House officials were surprised to learn new information which they had never heard from their own sources, and to hear a different analysis from that presented to them by their own experts

13 *Consultative Statements of the Civil Society Forum (III) for South—South Dialogue*, 13 December 2002.

Once again there were detailed recommendations (16 pages this time) not only to the SPLM/A, but to other political and military factions in South Sudan as well.

It was the forerunner of the later South—South dialogues organized by SPLM/A that eventually united the south after the signing of the CPA. It was also the meeting at which the term 'Other Armed Groups' (OAG) was coined. The military leaders of various factions refused to be called 'rebels' or 'militia' and eventually agreed on the term OAG, which later became enshrined in the CPA.

The first conference was mainly one of preparation, but the second and third produced detailed, practical and thoughtful recommendations which were fed back to the SPLM/A negotiators. In this way the church and civil society were able to influence the IGAD process despite not having a place at the table. According to Lt General Sumbeiywo, the IGAD Special Envoy and lead negotiator:

> The church was not involved in the negotiations since the teams were drawn from commanders of the armies of both government and SPLA. But the church interpreted the protocol to the people and encouraged them not to lose hope … The church was playing the back-channel role. It was not involved in direct negotiations. The church mobilised and continued educating the people.[14]

The International Dimension

Southern Sudanese had often spoken of their war as a 'forgotten war', and the SPLM/A (in contrast, for example, to the ANC in South Africa) had made very little impact on world opinion. It was left to the churches to do this. During this period they pursued dialogue at an the international level through their Sudan Ecumenical Forum (SEF) (Ashworth 2014: 206), which brought together the Sudanese churches with their international partners under the auspices of the World Council of Churches to carry out advocacy for peace. Informal dialogue, advocacy and lobbying with those who could exert influence on the warring parties in Sudan took place all over the world, along with the sharing of information and analysis. The SEF focused on issues such as the bombing of civilians, the escalation of the conflict caused by oil exploration and exploitation, and the right of self-determination for the people of southern Sudan and other marginalized areas of the country. Generally the international community was not favourable to self-determination, but informal dialogue by SEF contributed to a change in the international climate in 2002 following a

---

14 Interview with Gachora Ngunjiri 2013.

meeting in London and the publication of a substantial paper, 'Let My People Choose'. Just a few months later, self-determination was enshrined in the Machakos Protocol agreed by the warring parties.

Independent South Sudan

Fast forward a few years to independent South Sudan: churches are still being asked to spearhead dialogue aimed at peace and reconciliation between communities in conflicts which are largely unfinished business from the last civil war. Three recent processes are worth mentioning here.

Jonglei is the largest and probably least developed of the ten states of South Sudan. There has always been cattle raiding between the six pastoralist communities in the state (Dinka, Nuer, Murle, Anuak, Kajipo and Jie), but since 2009 it has escalated to new levels of brutality, with women, children and the elderly being killed and mutilated, and villages and administrative centres burned, and with a death toll in the thousands. Many factors contributed to this escalation: the trauma of decades of war, made worse by the legacy of the 1991 split in the SPLA; failure to adapt to the new situation of peace; weak governance and policing; lack of development coupled with perceptions of unequal development across the state; an abundance of modern weapons; political interests in the run-up to the 2010 elections; and efforts from Khartoum to destabilize the new nation of South Sudan using tried and tested 'divide and rule' methods. A botched attempt at disarmament of civilians in 2006 only led to more violence and distrust. The Sudan Council of Churches (SCC) began to address the issue in 2011, following earlier personal efforts by Episcopal (Anglican) Archbishop Daniel Deng Bul, himself a native of Jonglei State. An SCC peace committee was formed under the chairmanship of the archbishop, and a series of fact-finding missions and consultations began across the state.

As the main conflict appeared to be between the Lou section of the Nuer and the Murle, peace between these two communities was seen as the necessary first step, to be followed by a broader dialogue that would include other communities. A limited ceasefire was negotiated, and simultaneous conferences were held in Waat for the Lou Nuer and Pibor for the Murle.

While the results of the conferences seemed to bode well for a joint conference scheduled to be held in December 2011, and facilitators from both communities were trained together by the church, the situation on the ground deteriorated rapidly. Small-scale attacks had continued despite the ceasefire; some local politicians may have had reservations about the peace process; and chiefs were finding it difficult to hold back their armed youth. The Lou Nuer mobilized a force of around 6,000 heavily armed and well organized youth and began moving against the Murle. The archbishop and other church leaders made several visits to both areas to try to calm the situation but eventually accepted the inevitable and withdrew, calling on the government and the UN peacekeeping force (UNMISS) to provide security. Fighting ensued over Christmas and New Year, and several hundred people were killed.

Assessing the situation in January 2012, the SCC concluded that in this case it could not bring about peace without the assistance of the government. There is no military solution to conflict – but sometimes the military are needed to provide a window of opportunity for peace by creating a buffer zone and providing a level of protection and deterrence. The SCC called for a two-track peace process, with the government taking responsibility for Track I, the higher-level process, and the church concentrating on Track II, the grassroots process.

The government responded by committing itself to a new comprehensive disarmament process in Jonglei State, by increasing its troop presence to provide security, and by setting up a Presidential Committee for Peace, Reconciliation and Tolerance in Jonglei State under the chairmanship of Archbishop Deng. Under pressure from the international community the government also set up a committee to investigate the violence, but that had no real local traction and never got off the ground. Meanwhile, the SCC developed its own 'Peace from the Roots' grassroots process.

Teams from the Presidential Committee were sent to four areas of Jonglei State for fact-finding and mobilization, consulting the people on the ground; this was followed by four simultaneous conferences, one covering each part of the state. The preliminary work done by the SCC in 2011 proved invaluable here. Finally, there was a large conference in Bor, the state capital, in May 2012. A major part of the conference was devoted to allowing delegates to tell their stories. Most of the resolutions and recommendations had already emerged in earlier conferences. An agreement was signed by the paramount chiefs of the six communities, in the presence of President Salva Kiir Mayardiit. Members of the committee then travelled to all eleven counties and all six communities to disseminate the peace agreement.

Meanwhile the SCC had been identifying and training grassroots peace mobilizers from each of the communities. They returned to their homes to spread the message of peace, encourage local dialogue, monitor events on the ground, provide early warning of potential problems, network with each other, and identify new mobilizers for training later. Crucially, they gained access to the armed cattle- camp youth, who are key protagonists in any such conflict, and held local dialogue meetings with them. The plan was then for these youths to be taken for an exposure visit to Holy Trinity Peace Village, Kuron, in neighbouring Eastern Equatoria State. The peace village is the brainchild of retired Catholic Bishop Paride Taban, an iconic figure in South Sudan and, a co-founder of the NSCC, whose personal history of struggle, suffering and leadership has made him a champion of dialogue, peace and reconciliation. He created a peace village in the midst of warring tribes, not dissimilar to the warring communities in Jonglei State, offering them a model for living together in peace and harmony and demonstrating how development can come if there is peace through dialogue. Kuron now has a school, a clinic, an agricultural project, a youth centre, a guinea worm eradication project, a bridge across the seasonal river, an internet cafe, a vocational training centre and much more (Kuron Village 2014).

Unfortunately, after several months of relative peace, the Jonglei peace process was disrupted by the re-emergence of a rebel leader, David Yau Yau, supported by Khartoum. This new insurgency, which escalated early in 2013, made it impossible to hold the dialogue meeting for the cattle-camp youth at Kuron. All communities had identified the lack of development, including roads as well as schools, clinics, water, food security and employment opportunities, as a major factor in the conflict; the failure of the government and the international aid community to provide a peace dividend may have contributed to the support which Yau Yau received from some within his Murle community.

In response to Yau Yau's insurgency, and at the request of local communities, a small group of bishops (Paride Taban, Paul Yugusuk and Arkangelo Wani) sought dialogue between Yau Yau and the government of South Sudan. The process was low-key, deliberately avoiding publicity. For several months the bishops shuttled between Yau Yau in the bush and President Salva Kiir in Juba using UNMISS helicopters. There were no press releases, and even supporters and back-donors found it difficult to pry information from the bishops. Eventually the government appointed a team of negotiators to continue the dialogue under the mediatorship of the bishops. Only when they were very close to agreement did the negotiations move to Addis Ababa for the final public signing of an agreement early in 2014. And here we may note that Bishop Taban has always been suspicious of dialogue held in five-star hotels at someone else's expense.

The third dialogue process worth mentioning is the Committee for National Healing, Peace and Reconciliation (CNHPR), formed by presidential decree in April 2013 to address the need for long-term reconciliation and healing after decades of conflict. The President mandated religious leaders, Christian and Muslim, to lead this independent committee, which also includes representatives of all ten states as well as women, youth, civil society and disabled groups.

In a retreat at Kuron Peace Village in December 2013, the CNHPR ascertained that nobody can impose reconciliation: only the people themselves can reconcile. The best that the Committee could do would be to create a space where reconciliation could be facilitated. Thus the Committee proposed a process of two to three years of dialogue throughout the nation. Several hundred 'peace mobilizers' will be trained to go to the grassroots level to raise awareness and begin the dialogue process. This is to be followed by conferences in each of South Sudan's 79 counties, and then in each of the ten states. Meanwhile dialogue will also be going on at the national level, with various interest groups, including government, political parties, organized armed forces, faith communities, civil society, women, youth, media, business, diaspora, academia, etc. The dialogue must be vertical as well as horizontal. All of this will culminate in a national conference which is to design a national agenda for reconciliation. All stakeholders, both individual and institutional, will then be invited to situate their programmes and activities within this national agenda.

Sadly, the new conflict in South Sudan that began on 15 December 2013 has interrupted preparations to launch this programme of dialogue. The CNHPR is now trying to find out how to contribute to resolving the current conflict without losing track of the need for dialogue aimed at long-term reconciliation, the lack of which is one of the root causes of the current conflict. One of the strategies of the Committee has been to widen the dialogue base by forming a National Platform for Peace and Reconciliation (NPPR) with two government bodies, the South Sudan Peace and Reconciliation Commission and the Specialized Parliamentary Committee on Peace and Reconciliation. All three will maintain their individual mandates and programmes; crucially, the CNHPR will maintain its independence from government, but will seek to speak with one voice, to cooperate where appropriate, and to act as a focus for dialogue.

The Republic of Sudan also has on going conflicts in Darfur, in the Nuba Mountains and in Blue Nile, and tensions in other areas. The current regime destroyed what was a very robust civil society when it came to power through a military coup d'état in 1989, and now Sudan lacks a cohesive and credible independent actor to facilitate dialogue in the way in which the church can in South Sudan.

Current Conflict in South Sudan

In a burst of optimism in July 2011 many people believed that South Sudan's troubles were over. The main problem – oppression by the Islamist dictatorship in Khartoum – had apparently been resolved when South Sudan gained its independence from Sudan. However, no attempt was made to resolve, or even to recognize, the internal problems of South Sudan. A mere two and a half years later, civil war broke out in the world's newest country.

What are these internal South Sudanese problems? The nation and its people are suffering multi-generational trauma from decades of war and oppression. Much of the fighting during the previous civil war had been southerners fighting each other, but no attempt had been made at reconciliation across the nation as a whole. The governing SPLM was slow (and reluctant) to begin the transition from an authoritarian liberation movement to a democratic political party. The national army was a hodgepodge of former militia, often former enemies, each loyal to its own leader (now with the rank of Major General). Although they were assimilated into the army after the war ended in 2005 as a result of peace negotiations in which they were not allowed to play a part, no serious attempts were made to integrate them. More were added in the pre- and post-independence era, as various small rebellions were dealt with by offering amnesty and a niche in the armed forces. Corruption and nepotism were rife throughout the government. Above all, no serious effort was made at building a single national identity and fostering unity amongst the 64 or more ethnic groups in South Sudan. State-building was pursued enthusiastically (albeit ineffectually) by the international community, but there was no nation-building. Dialogue was lacking at every level.

In some ways, then, the outbreak of a new civil war is hardly surprising. In the great sweep of history it is not even unusual. The Irish began their civil war even more quickly; Pakistan had a civil war less than 25 years after independence. The USA had a civil war 85 years after independence, albeit in a country which had changed significantly during that period. Internal problems cannot be ignored. If not dealt with, they fester and undermine the new nation. In South Sudan, after decades of violence, the protagonists responded to problems in the way they know best – by fighting. If there is a silver lining to the current conflict, it is that the problems are now out in the open and it will be difficult to sweep them back under the carpet.

Fighting broke out in several military installations in the capital city, Juba, on 15 December 2013. We will probably never be sure exactly how it started, but within hours forces loyal to the government gained the upper hand and apparently carried out targeted killings of soldiers and civilians of the Nuer ethnic group. Word spread rapidly via cell phones and social media, and revenge killings against Dinka began almost immediately in other parts of the country, initially in a spontaneous and uncoordinated manner – as in Akobo, where Nuer youths overran the UN camp, killing two UN peacekeepers and a number of Dinka who were sheltering there. Several army units defected and a full-scale civil war began, with former Vice President Riek Machar calling for the overthrow of the President. A Nuer civilian militia known as the White Army joined the fray and were responsible for much of the killing and looting. Rebels attempting to overrun Juba were beaten back largely by Ugandan forces, but the towns of Bor, Malakal and Bentiu changed hands several times. They were basically razed to the ground, with great loss of civilian life. In these towns rebels also deliberately targeted Shilluk and Sudanese as well as Dinka, killed civilians in hospitals, mosques and churches, and in Bentiu reportedly used the local FM radio station to broadcast ethnic hate messages, including calls to rape women. They are also said to have killed Nuer civilians who were judged not to be celebrating their victory enthusiastically enough. The UN peacekeeping force, UNMISS, was unable to protect civilians outside their own UN camps, where tens of thousands of people fled for shelter.

Weak government structures and the failure to reform the ruling party had resulted in a power struggle between several key individuals, among them President Salva Kiir Mayardiit, former Vice President Riek Machar, and the Secretary General of the SPLM, Pagan Amum. A small number of delegates, including Machar and Amum, walked out of a key party leadership meeting on 15 December 2013, and within hours the fighting started. Once the ethnic killing in Juba and the revenge attacks elsewhere began, this became an ethnic conflict, although it should be stressed that it had not begun as a tribal war. People follow their leaders, and in South Sudan the followers are of the same ethnic group as the leaders. It should also be noted that not all Nuer followed Machar, nor did all Dinka follow Kiir.

Today there are at least two urgent priorities. The first is a meaningful, permanent, monitored ceasefire. The second is a humanitarian response (with the necessary access to implement that response) to the disaster, in which hundreds of thousands of people have been displaced from their homes. Both of these are difficult to implement, but they are simple to understand.

The third priority is more controversial: What is the *long-term solution* to the crisis? There is no 'quick fix'. Obviously, the ceasefire and the humanitarian response must be pushed through as quickly as possible – but it would be a mistake to push too quickly for a political solution. The current international insistence on reaching an interim solution against artificially-imposed deadlines risks exacerbating the instability as leaders and factions jockey for power. Most importantly, it would be unacceptable for a handful of political and military leaders to stitch up a deal which might meet their needs, but does not meet the long-term needs of the people. The 'third bloc' (unarmed opposition leaders like Amum, who had been detained and then released by the government) is no different from the Kiir and Machar camps in this regard. Rushing into a power-sharing interim government will probably not help. What is needed is a long-term process in which the people of the nation are consulted, a process that is really owned by the people. However, this vital long-term process must be distinguished from the urgent negotiations over a ceasefire and humanitarian access. Bringing too many stakeholders in too quickly is already allowing the principals to hide behind these numbers and to procrastinate over procedural issues.

Some form of interim government is widely discussed. There is no doubt that the current government is unpopular with many in South Sudan: nevertheless, it also has many supporters. It is a democratically-elected government and its term does not expire until 2015. Many believe that it would not give a good signal to disband it at this point. More productive would probably be to concentrate on a ceasefire and a humanitarian response aimed at returning the situation to a degree of stability in 2014, and to begin preparing for an interim government during 2015 when the terms of the current president, government and parliament end. Politicians with relatively clean hands from a variety of parties and constituencies should be sought, as well as technocrats. Some argue that Kiir and Machar should have no role in it all; others that Kiir could still head the government and Machar could play a role, but that nobody in the interim government would be allowed to stand in elections at the end of its term. Given the realities of the political landscape, it would probably be necessary to have some established politicians from the old guard, representing certain constituencies. This interim government would be given a fixed term, say three years, to carry out the day-to-day business of governance – ensure that basic services continue, get the oil flowing again, run the civil service and ministries, collect taxes, concentrate on development, etc.

At the same time, the citizens of the country must be represented in an ongoing dialogue about their long-term future. One model could be an ongoing dialogue conference representing all strands of society. The faith communities would play a leading role, as would the traditional leadership of chiefs and elders, plus representatives of civil society, women, youth, academia, business, media, the diaspora, etc. All political parties would be represented, all ethnic groups, as well as those who bear arms, whether in uniform or as civilian militias. The task of this conference would be to develop, through dialogue, the long-term resolution to the problems of South Sudan. The conference would consider issues of nation-building, national identity, the constitution, the census, reform of the armed forces, reconciliation, and other issues to be identified, as well as preparing for elections at the end of the interim government's term. The conference would be sovereign: the interim government would have no power to disband the conference, control its agenda or veto its decisions. During this interim period a robust peacekeeping force would be needed, far more pro-active and combat-capable than the current UNMISS.

A number of international campaign organizations as well as some within South Sudanese civil society have been insisting that justice and accountability must be prerequisites for the peace process. While justice and accountability are obviously crucial, it is not helpful to set up such preconditions in what is to be a people-driven peace process. These issues will certainly come up during the dialogue, but they must be allowed to develop organically as an integral part of the process, not imposed from the outset. *Trust the people!* Dialogue would also be needed about the meaning of the words 'justice' and 'accountability' in the context of South Sudan; they should be explored by the stakeholders rather than defined by outsiders. Justice will almost certainly be viewed in terms of restorative and transitional justice, perhaps with hybrid courts, rather than as being purely retributive.

And what about civil society? Apart from the faith communities, there is no well-developed civil society in South Sudan. International NGOs and donors have funded the formation of Civil Society Organizations (CSOs). These are generally made up of small groups of elite, educated South Sudanese, and do not represent the ordinary people nor have much connection with them. Since the current conflict began in December 2013, a US government subcontractor has sponsored a series of civil society meetings with selected participants in Kampala, Nairobi and Addis Ababa, and this external process (external in both its organization and its geographical location) has come to represent the voice of 'civil society' in the eyes of many in the international community. However, it is deficient in at least two ways. Firstly, the groups chosen do not necessarily represent the views of ordinary South Sudanese. Secondly, by holding meetings outside the country, the sense of what is actually happening inside the country risks getting lost, or at least becoming unbalanced. This is further exacerbated by the fact that few from the diplomatic and donor community have been present in Juba. After they evacuated in December 2013 soon after the conflict started, many principals (such as ambassadors) eventually returned in January or February 2014, but most of their staff remained outside for several months. The international community thus still has a very limited grasp of the real situation. Many international staff were temporarily posted to Addis Ababa, where IGAD has been spearheading negotiations between the two warring parties. This had the advantage of keeping them in the region – but again, there is the risk that they may get caught up in how South Sudan is viewed from Addis Ababa and not within the country. Obviously some meetings need to be held outside South Sudan so that the rebels can feel comfortable, but it is dangerous to move the whole process outside. Part of the ceasefire process should include protection for rebels to move within South Sudan. The elite, the diaspora and the CSOs are obviously stakeholders and their voice is important: but it should not be assumed that they alone constitute civil society. The dialogue must be broad, and a dialogue hijacked by relatively small and unrepresentative voices can be as dangerous as no dialogue at all.

The solution to the crisis in South Sudan must come from within the country – and from the people, not simply the leaders. It must be homegrown. The international community and regional bodies like IGAD and the African Union should support the process, but they must not impose their own solutions or timelines. While the ceasefire and humanitarian access are urgent priorities, the eventual settlement, dealing with the root causes of the conflict and deciding the very future of the nation, through dialogue, will be long, slow and painful. There can be no quick fix.

The People-to-People Model

The People-to-People Peace Process has been recognized as a model of grassroots peacemaking, and many of its elements have been incorporated into later dialogue processes in Jonglei and elsewhere in South Sudan. Many international NGOs in South Sudan have tried to copy it, usually without much success. To begin with, they lack the credibility and moral authority of the church. In addition, they usually focus on highly visible conferences, forgetting all the years of patient preparation and trust-building that must take place before real dialogue can be held. They neglect the key elements which underpinned the People-to-People process: the need to foster trust, telling of stories, the use of traditional reconciliation methods, acknowledgement that the community is the primary actor and must be ready to take responsibility for making peace, the importance of symbolism and imagery, a commitment to truth, a peace agreement that includes practical measures for implementation and follow-up, and empowerment.

Perhaps 'patient preparation' should be underscored as well. It must also be recognized that a conference of several hundred people who need to tell their stories and acknowledge the 'truth' that is accepted by both sides (in other words: a meaningful dialogue) cannot be tightly time-tabled, finished and agreed within some artificial deadline. The dialogue must be allowed to continue for weeks or even months; the process itself, for years if necessary. Decades of conflict and trauma cannot be overcome in a few months; indeed it may take as many decades.[15] Quick fixes do not work. While there is of course a concern to stop immediate violence, nevertheless it must be recognized that peace is not merely the absence of war. 'Stopping the war is essential, but not sufficient for the establishment of a just and lasting peace'.[16] In contrast to most NGOs and indeed most of the international community, the church, civil society and people of South Sudan are it for the long haul.

It should be noted that the NSCC did not have access to modern 'peace studies' when planning and implementing the People-to-People Peace Process. At that time very little literature on peacebuilding was available, at least in Sudan. The call for peace and reconciliation emerged slowly, reinforced by the Kajiko meeting in 1997 where the liberation movement specifically asked the church to shoulder this task. Much of the work was reactive; there was no long-term strategy or plan. The team sat together after each step and planned the next step, but hardly knew where the process would go beyond that; it was very much "a story that grew in the telling", as Tolkien expressed it, in a different

---

15 Conversation with John Paul Lederach, Kroc Institute, University of Notre Dame, March 2013.

16 An Appeal by the Bishops of the Catholic and Episcopal Churches of Sudan, 2001.

connection. It was (and still is) an 'emergent' process.[17] As well as the formal governing body of the NSCC, a think tank was set up, comprising the Executive Secretary of NSCC and a small number of resource people from the churches and church-related agencies. And indeed, 'the passion for peace began to grow across Southern Sudan and began to take root in churches, at community levels and among common long-suffering Sudanese people' (NSCC 2002: 47).

During those early forays into peace work, the church in Sudan was unaware of the sterling work of John Paul Lederach on peace studies, and his pyramid model in which he identifies grassroots, mid-level and high-level components of peacebuilding (Lederach 1997: 39). NSCC first attempted (and failed) to reconcile the leaders (high level), then went back to the grassroots. From the grassroots, the wisdom of the elders expressed at the first Strategic Linkages conference led NSSCC to the mid-level ('We have made peace; it is our sons who are the problem now'). From there, pressure was exerted on the principals

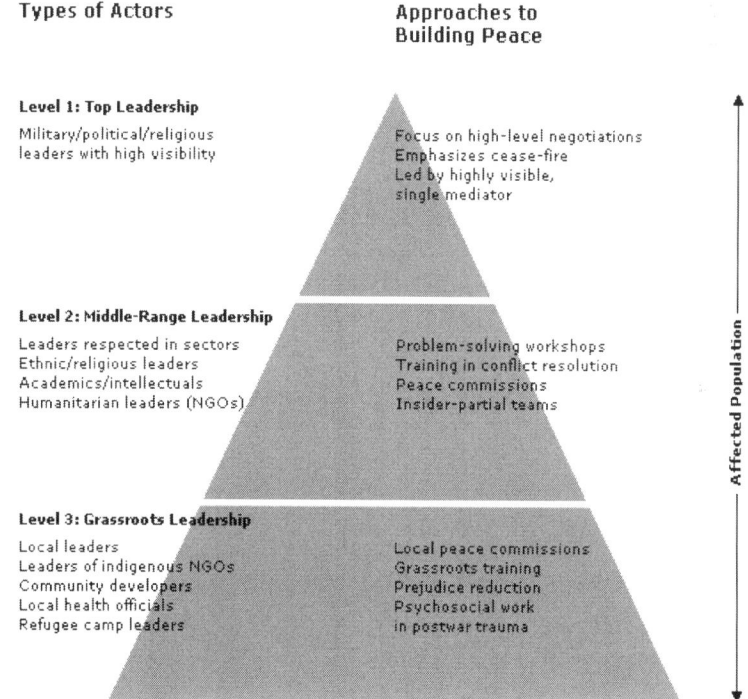

Figure 9.1   John Paul Lederach's Pyramid Model of Peacebuilding

Source: Derived from John Paul Lederach, *Building Peace: Sustainable Reconciliation in Divided Societies* (Washington, D.C.: United States Institute of Peace Press, 1997), 39.

---

17 Conversation with John Paul Lederach, Kroc Institute, University of Notre Dame, March 2013.

to make peace at the high level, and at the same time the church and civil society entered the high-level national peace process via the Entebbe conferences and the SEF. Peace-building mobilizes both horizontal and vertical dialogues.

> 'I am uneasy with the growing technique-oriented view of change in settings of violence that seems to dominate much of professional conflict resolution approaches' (Lederach 2005: 52). [He speaks of] 'invoking the moral imagination ... which is not found in perfecting or applying the techniques or the skills of a process ... My feeling is that we have overemphasized the technical aspects and political content to the detriment of the art of giving birth to and keeping a process creatively alive' of leaving space for serendipity, intuition, art and the web of relationships (ibid.: 70).

All this would be familiar to those who work for peace in Sudan and South Sudan. Indeed, it could be said that rather than designing a process, People-to-People opened up a space whereby the people themselves could pursue peace and reconciliation through dialogue; the process was designed as a result of what emerged within that space (Conversation with Fanie du Toit, 2013).

After the Liliir meeting, People-to-People Peacebuilding had caught the attention of donors, and the US government offered a multi-million dollar grant to continue the process. This grant was won by a large US NGO, which concentrated on highly visible conferences rather than the years of patient preparation and trust-building. It did not have the relationships on the ground and the legitimacy which the church had, and it relied on 'professional' techniques and skills. The People-to-People Peace Process effectively came to an end at that point: the 'moral imagination' was lacking.

Sudan has become 'a laboratory for those who study peace',[18] particularly within the Church. The dialogue experience of the peace pioneers of Sudan is now helping to inform international thinking.

Conclusions

This chapter has asked:

1. What was the character of the dialogue between the actors prior to, during, and

---

18 Conversation with Gerard Powers, Kroc Institute, University of Notre Dame, April 2013.

after the 'peak' of the conflict/crisis?
2. To what extent has the dialogue been successful?
3. What determines whether a dialogue can succeed or not in the different cases?

Perhaps the first lesson learned is how interrelated these the questions actually are. There is a great deal of overlap and cross-fertilization between them. It should also be noted that any case study of Sudan and South Sudan highlights its complexity, with conflicts pitting different actors against each other at different times and in different circumstances. Conflict is not static – nor is the dialogue needed to resolve it.

In the dialogue between the two rival leaders and their liberation movements in southern Sudan, there was no meaningful interaction between the protagonists before the People-to- People dialogue began. The same can be said of David Yau Yau and the government of South Sudan. In the Jonglei Peace Process and the Committee for National Healing, Peace and Reconciliation, which seek to reconcile communities, there has been dialogue, often at the local level between communities who are neighbours, who intermarry, who graze their animals on each other's lands, but it has been seriously degraded by the war and by local conflicts. In the main civil war between the government of Sudan and the SPLM/A, there was ongoing political dialogue of sorts encouraged by the international community, but with little progress until around 2002 – which is the point where the churches also became involved in the informal dialogue. In the currently ongoing civil war in South Sudan, there has as yet been no meaningful dialogue, despite efforts by IGAD.

After the different dialogue processes, again the results were varied. David Yau Yau was still on good terms with the government of South Sudan more than a year after the dialogue began and six months after signing his peace agreement. Dialogue has not brought the governments of Sudan and South Sudan any closer; it merely helped them to end their armed conflict and to divorce fairly peacefully. Due largely to external factors, Jonglei State descended back into conflict less than a year after the dialogue ended. The original People-to-People Peace Process brought the protagonists together in an uneasy alliance for more than a decade, until massive violence re-erupted in December 2013.

Thus one can debate whether the dialogues have been successful, although the question remains as to whether 'success' is the right paradigm for such dialogue processes. They are processes, they are ongoing, they are long-term, and they are part of the life of the nation which has its ups and downs for all sorts of historical reasons. Maybe their success should be judged on whether they can keep going in new incarnations, to keep people talking despite the new conflicts and other challenges which emerge. History may judge them many decades later, but it is too soon to judge them now.

What determines whether a dialogue can succeed? Dialogue should ultimately bring in as broad a range as possible of actors and stakeholders (although the timing and manner of their entry into the process is important, as bringing them in at the wrong stage can be detrimental), but peace can still be disturbed by external factors. In large part it is down to the commitment of the people who engage in it – and that has to include *the people*, not just the politicians. That said, the people and the dialogue are often powerless, at least in the short term, in the face of armed actors.

Dialogue must be homegrown and long-term. It may not appear to be successful at any specific stage, but ultimately it is the only real alternative to violence.

References

Ashworth, J. 2014. *The Voice of the Voiceless: The Role of the Church in the Sudanese Civil War 1983–2005*. Paulines Publications Africa: Nairobi.

Deng, F. 2014. *War of Visions: Conflicts of Identities in the Sudan*. Washington, DC: Brookings Institute.

Johnson, D. 2003. *The Root Causes of Sudan's Civil Wars*. Bloomington, IN: Indiana University Press.

Kuron Village, 2014. Kuron Village [Online]. Available at: http://www. kuronvillage.net [accessed: 1 July 2014].

Lederach, J.P 1997. *Building Peace: Sustainable Reconciliation in Divided Societies*, Washington, DC: United States Institute of Peace.

Lederach, J.P. 2005. *The Moral Imagination.*Oxford: University Press.

NSCC 2002. *The Story of People-to-People Peacemaking in Southern Sudan*. Nairobi: NSCC.

Scherf, T. 1971. *The Sudan Conflict: Its History and Development*. Geneva: World Council of Churches.

An Appeal by the Bishops of the Catholic and Episcopal Churches of Sudan 2001. *Let There Be A Just and Durable Peace in the Sudan*, United States Conference of Catholic Bishop, Nairobi, 17 [Online]. Available at: http:// www.usccb.org/issues-and-action/human-life-and-dignity/global-issues/ africa/sudan/let-there-be-a-just-and-durable-peace-in-sudan.cfm [accessed: 11 August 2014].

Chapter 10

Dialogue as Tool for Addressing Religious Tensions: Containing the Violence, or True Conflict Resolution?

Georges Fahmi

This chapter investigates the role of informal dialogue processes in dealing with religious tensions between Christians and Muslims in Egypt during the first three years after the Revolution of 25 January 2011. Because international actors have lacked the legitimacy to mediate between the two religious communities, the focus here is on domestic dialogue initiatives. The case of religious tensions in Egypt offers a chance to compare different patterns of dialogue, both outcome-oriented and process-oriented, and to gain insight into the challenges facing each type.

Under the Mubarak regime, the security forces often dealt with religious tensions between Muslims and Christians. They frequently put pressure on the various parties in both religious communities to contain these tensions and impose calm. Then, with the collapse of the Mubarak regime in February 2011, the security apparatus broke down and ceased to play that role, creating a vacuum as regards dealing with religious tensions. Initially, religious tensions escalated into violence with no attempts at containing it – as in the village of Sol in March 2011, when a Christian church was burned. Later on, various actors have sought to fill this gap and play a role in controlling tensions. These actors include religious actors themselves, both Christian and Muslim, as well as the military and the revolutionary youth movements.

This chapter focuses on three types of dialogue between Christians and Muslims aimed at containing religious tensions after 25 January 2011: informal reconciliation sessions, the National Justice Committee, and the House of the Egyptian Family. The first two represent outcome-oriented dialogue processes, whereas the third is an example of a confidence-building process. The chapter investigates three main questions: what initiatives, mainly based on dialogue, have been undertaken to control religious tensions? Were these initiatives successful? What determines whether a dialogue can succeed or not? Following an historical overview of religious tensions in Egypt, the chapter analyses the various dialogue initiatives that have sought to contain these tensions, before and after 25 January 2011. The final section explores five factors central to the success of these dialogue initiatives.

Background: Religious Tensions between Muslims and Christians in Egypt

The increase of religious tensions between Muslims and Christians in Egypt dates back to the 1970s and the rise to power of Anwar Sadat. Tensions persisted under the rule of Hosni Mubarak, and the regime delegated this file to the security forces. While many Egyptians had hoped that the removal of Mubarak in February 2011 would put an end to the problem, religious tensions have continued with even greater violence during the transitional period.

The Rule of Sadat (1970–1981)

Sadat wanted to change the alliance that his predecessor, Gamal Abdel Nasser, had established during the Cold War, from the Eastern and towards the Western Bloc. However, he feared resistance from the socialist forces loyal to Nasser's policies. Thus, he decided to support the Islamic groups in order to balance the influence of the socialist forces, mainly among the student population. He released Islamic militants imprisoned under Nasser and allowed them to work freely in the public sphere. Sadat's policies strengthened the Islamic movements and allowed them to gain influence over large sections of Egyptian society. While his strategy succeeded in containing the influence of the socialist groups, it increased the salience of religion in the public sphere, alienatinged the Christians and heightening religious tensions.

During 1971–1972, Egypt witnessed eleven religion-related incidents (Brownlee 2013: 6). The most violent clashes took place in the area of al-Khanka, in the governorate of Qalyubia, in November 1972. They erupted after a group of Muslims accused local Christians of using a building as a church without official permission. Muslim protesters destroyed the building. The recently-chosen Coptic Pope, Patriarch Shenouda III, reacted by sending a group of priests to visit the ruined building and hold prayers there. This move increased the level of tension between the two communities and led to further clashes. The Egyptian parliament set up a committee to investigate the reasons behind the religious tensions. The committee's final report noted that the rules governing the construction of churches were among the main causes of Muslim–Christian tensions, and called upon the state institutions to amend these regulations. However, the report and its recommendations were ignored by the Sadat regime.

The al-Khanka incident is seen as 'the start of the worst period for Christian–Muslim relations in modern Egyptian history' (Iskander 2012: 79). It also shifted the cooperative relation between the Coptic Church and the political regime under Nasser. Sadat perceived Patriarch Shenouda as a challenge to his own authority, and accused the Coptic prelate of trying to act like a political authority. From his side, Shenouda rejected Sadat's religious discourse and considered it a threat to the rights of the Christians.

Sadat's discourse on the application of Shari´a law raised the level of tension between Muslims and Christians. The Coptic Church repudiated Shari´a, considering it a violation of the citizenship rights of the Christian population. Islamist groups accused the Christians of working to prevent the Egyptian state from applying Islamic rules. Sadat himself adopted the same discourse, and accused the Coptic Church of using its international connections to put pressure on the Egyptian government to abandon the Islamic character of the state. In a public speech in the parliament, Sadat reminded the Christians that he was a Muslim ruler of an Islamic country.

The turning point in the relation between the regime and the Islamic movements was Sadat's visit to Jerusalem in November 1977. Throughout 1978, the Islamic communities fiercely criticized the regime new policies towards Israel. Sadat himself was criticized harshly in Islamists' mosques and through their publications. From his side, Sadat shifted his discourse and began harshly criticizing the Islamic movement, whom he accused of hijacking Islam. Sadat thought that the Islamic militants should be grateful to him, as he allowed them to work freely after years of prohibition under Nasser. From their side, the Islamic groups pressured Sadat to fulfill his promise of establishing an Islamic state and to halt the rapprochement with the west and Israel, which they considered to be enemies of Islam.

In 1978, under pressure from all Islamic actors and in an effort to weaken resistance to peace negotiations with Israel, the Egyptian parliament established a special committee to study procedures whereby existing laws could be revised to conform to Shari´a principles. Moreover, Sadat proposed a constitutional amendment stipulating that Shari´a principles would be the primary source of legislation. The amendment was endorsed in a public referendum in May 1980, together with another amendment allowing for unlimited presidential mandates.

In this tense environment, violent clashes erupted in June 1981 between Muslims and Christians in El Zawya el Hamra, a working-class neighbourhood of Cairo. The clashes were sparked by a rumour that a church was to be constructed there. The confrontation lasted for three days; the number of deaths has been contested between the Christians and the state authorities. Sadat's response against those whom he considered to be the planners behind the sectarian rifts came in September 1981, when large numbers of politicians, journalists and Islamist militants were arrested. He also placed the Coptic Pope under house arrest in a monastery 100 kms from Cairo. Weeks later, on 6 October 1981, Sadat himself was assassinated by Islamic militants, and his vice-president Hosni Mubarak assumed the presidency.

The Rule of Mubarak (1981–2011)

After Sadat's assassination, it became clear to the new Egyptian regime that its greatest threat came not from leftist groups, but from Islamic radical groups that had killed the president and tried to stage a coup. Hence, the Mubarak regime started a new phase in relations with the Coptic Church, based on cooperation rather than conflict. The Church saw its interest in supporting the regime in its war against the Jihadist groups that were also threatening the Christian population. For its part, the regime reinforced a permanent channel of communication with the leadership of the Church in order to solve problems before they might turn into crises.

However, while the Jihadist groups lost their military battle against the security forces, and had to declare a ceasefire by the end of the 1990s, attacks against Christian churches and properties continued. Especially dangerous were the two crisis in the village of al-Kosheh in the governorate of Sohag in Upper Egypt. The first incident took place in 1998, when security forces tortured hundreds of Christians when investigating the murder of two other Christians, to put pressure on them to admit committing the crime. The second came in 2000, when 20 Christians were killed in clashes that started as a commercial dispute, before turning into a confrontation between the two communities in the village.

The two incidents at al-Kosheh led some Christians to believe the regime itself, not only Jihadist groups, was discriminating against them. Although the leadership of the church and the regime cooperated, state institutions discriminated against the Christians particluary in Upper Egypt. While the Coptic Church had worked to maintain its pact with the Mubarak regime, it started to lose control over its young people, who blamed the regime and its security forces for their problems. The pact between the Church and the regime had proven efficient only in cases related to families of Coptic priests. In 2004, the wife of a priest disappeared. While some Christians claimed she had been kidnapped, Muslims said that she had converted to Islam and had left her husband. After the Church asked the regime to intervene and bring her back, the security forces located the Christian woman and delivered her to the Church. Again, in 2010 a similar crisis erupted after the wife of a Coptic priest left her home and allegedly converted to Islam. The security forces found and delivered her to the Church. However, in other cases, state institutions were unable to act, or were even part of the problem, as in al-Kosheh in 1998.

From January 2008 to January 2010, The Egyptian Intiative for Personal Rights (EIPR) documented 53 incidents of sectarian violence (EIPR 2010: 5). Criticism of Christian youth grew after the attack that left at least six Christians dead on the night of 6 January 2010, Coptic Christmas Eve, in Nag Hammadi in the governorate of Qena in Upper Egypt. Some Christians accused a member of Mubarak's ruling party of being behind the attack as the Christians in Nag Hammadi refused to vote for him. Many Christians went to the Coptic Cathedral in Cairo to protest against the Mubarak regime, asking Pope Shenouda to take a strong position against the regime's practices. In December 2010, a car bomb in front of a church in Alexandria killed at least 20 Christians. This time, Christian youth took to the streets, accusing the Mubarak regime and his security apparatus of failing to protect the Christians and their churches. Opposition movements joined the Christian demonstration, insisting that the discrimination against the Christians is a part of the Mubarak regime oppressing policies against all Egyptians.

When the call to protest against the Mubarak regime on 25 January 2011 arose, the Coptic Church asked its young members not to take part in this demonstration. However, some young people refused to listen, and joined other protesters, hoping that a democratic regime would guarantee them equal rights as citizens. On 25 January, both Christians and Muslims took to the streets against the Mubarak regime, calling for a new political regime based on freedom, justice and dignity. The slogan 'Muslim, Christian: one hand', together with the symbol of the Crescent embracing the Cross, became one of the main signs in Tahrir Square, as did images of Christians protecting praying Muslims. As the tensions between the two communities were blamed on the Mubarak regime, the Tahir protesters hoped that once the regime was removed, the discrimination against Christians would end. Although one church was attacked in the border city of Rafah between Egypt and Gaza, no other attacks were reported on any other churches despite the complete withdraw of the security forces.

Post-Mubarak Era (2011–2013)

Nevertheless, less than one month after Mubarak stepped down, in March 2011, religious tensions erupted again between Christians and Muslims in the village of Sol, in the governorate of Helwan. The violence between the two communities was triggered by an affair between a Christian man and a Muslim woman. Tensions between the two families involved quickly developed into a confrontation between the local Christian and Muslim communities. Angry Muslim youth attacked the village church and destroyed it, along with other Christian properties. The military forces that tried to control the violence could only prevent the two communities from clashing, but failed in protecting the Christian properties. Angry Christian youth from all over Egypt went to protest in front of the state television building known as Maspero, to denounce the discrimination against Christians. During the sit-in, a Christian youth movement was established under the name of the Maspero Youth Union. In order to contain the Christian anger, the Supreme Council of Military Forces (SCAF) that had taken power after Mubarak stepped down now promised that the military would rebuild the destroyed church at its own expense. However, some Muslims refused this proposal, claiming that the church had been built against their will in the first place. They wanted the military to build the church outside the village, but the Christians rejected this idea. Only after the intervention of Islamic religious figures who convinced the Muslim youth to accept this agreement was the crisis contained.

Two months later, in May 2011, religious violence erupted in the poor neighbourhood of Imbaba in the governorate of Giza. Muslim protesters accused a church in Imbaba of kidnapping a Christian woman who had converted to Islam. When the Muslim protesters wanted to enter the church to search for her, the Christians refused. The Christians of Imababa went to protect their church, fearing that the Muslims protesters might destroy it – as had happened in Sol. The confrontation between the two communities turned into armed clashes. After failing to storm one church, angry Muslim protesters stormed another church in the same neighbourhood and burned it. The clashes in Imbaba left at least 12 people dead and more than 200 wounded. The Maspero Youth Union called a second sit-in in front of the state television building, demanding that the government take responsibility for protecting the rights of the Christian population. The government responded by establishing the National Justice Committee (NJC), with Christian and Muslim intellectuals and activists as members, aimed at preparing legislation to deal with the causes of problems between the two religious communities.

Nonetheless, in September 2011, another church was attacked by Muslim protesters, now in the village of al-Marinab in Edfu District, in the governorate of Aswan. The problems started when Christians in the village started building a dome on a building. Some Muslims claimed that the Christians were trying to build a church illegally, and attacked the building. The Christians argued that the building had been licensed to be a church. The NJC sent a fact-finding committee composed of Christian and Muslim members to investigate the situation in al-Marinab. The Committee blamed the governor of Aswan for failing to contain the tensions between Christians and Muslims in the village, and called for his removal. However, the government ignored the report. The Maspero Youth Union withdrew from the Committee and accused the SCAF of ignoring their grievances. They then called a demonstration in front of the Maspero building on 4 October, but the protestors were prevented from holding this sit-in. The Maspero Youth Union then called a new demonstration on 9 October. The demonstration was violently repressed by the military police, leaving 27 dead and hundreds of wounded. This marked an important turning point in relations between Egypt's Christians and the Muslim community and state institutions.

Shortly after the election of a new parliament in January 2012, clashes erupted between Muslims and Christians in al-Amariah, in the governorate of Alexandria. Like so many interreligious clashes, the crisis started with rumours of an affair between a Christian man and a Muslim woman, and developed into a confrontation between Muslims and Christians in the village. The angry Muslim crowds attacked Christian properties. The clashes left 10 people dead. The Salafis, a religiously conservative religious movement, who enjoy a strong presence in this area interfered and worked to achieve an end to this crisis.

Religious tensions continued under the rule of Mohammad Morsi. In April 2013, clashes erupted in the area of Khosoos, northern Cairo, and left five dead. A funeral was held for Christian victims at St Mark's Cathedral, the seat of the Coptic Pope in Cairo. While the families of the victims of Khosoos were mourning their loss, the cathedral was attacked by Muslim protesters. Clashes continued, and the police failed to interfere.

After the military intervention in July 2013 against the rule of Mohammad Morsi, supporters of the Muslim Brotherhood attacked many churches all over Egypt, as they perceived the Coptic Church as being supportive of the military intervention. After the violent dispersal of the Muslim Brotherhood sit-ins in Cairo on 14 August, 42 churches were attached in addition to dozens of religious institutions, mainly in Upper Egypt (HRW 2013).

To sum up, although many Egyptian Christians had hoped for better conditions after the removal of the Mubarak regime, attacks against the Christians, their churches and properties increased after February 2011. In all, 33 sectarian incidents were reported in the press in 2008, 32 in 2009, and 45 in 2010. After the 25 January uprising, this figure jumped to 70 in 2011, and 112 in 2012 (Tadros 2013). This sectarian violence is often due to two main reasons: personal disputes between Muslims and Christians that develop into full-scale confrontation between the two communities; and disputes over the construction of churches.

Dialogue Initiatives to End Sectarian Violence Before and After 25 January 2011

The dialogue between Muslims and Christians aimed at resolving sectarian tensions changed radically after the Revolution of 25 January 2011. This section investigates the dialogue processes before and after the January events, seeking to explain the reasons behind the shift in the types of dialogue, and to what extent these dialogue processes have sought to change actor's ideas about the other religious community and hence reshape its interests, or have tried only to avoid escalation of violence between the two religious communities.

Dialogue Processes Before 25 January 2011

Before 25 January 2011, the regime, through the Ministry of the Interior, dealt with sectarian tensions solely as a security problem, without understanding the social and economic roots. Given their institutional logic, the security forces viewed sectarian violence as a series of isolated events, and failed to offer a comprehensive explanation of its causes. In each case, the chief aim of the security apparatus was to impose calm, by using its soft and hard power to put pressure on the involved parties. Together with deputies of the ruling party in the area of conflict, in reconciliation meetings it tried to impose a settlement on all parties, to avoid referring cases of sectarian violence to the judiciary.

The case of Kafr Salama in 2005 is a clear example of this approach. Religious clashes broke out between Muslims and Christians in the village of Kafr Salama in al-Sharkiah governorate when a Muslim man was killed in a dispute with a Christian. Angry Muslims attacked the Christians and their properties. In order to contain the crisis, the secretary general of the governorate and the head of the police station as well as the secretary general of the National Democratic Party in the governorate met with representatives from the Muslim and Christian communities and agreed on the following: all Christian families in the village should pay the sum of 500,000 EGP to the family of the Muslim victim; and the killer and his family should leave the village. However, some Christian families refused to pay compensation for a crime they had not committed, while they received no compensation for their destroyed property. The police arrested 11 Christians in order to put pressure on their families to accept the agreement reached in the reconciliation session (Shoukry 2009: 36–7).

In June 2008 in the village of Nazla, the province of Fayoum, Muslims attacked Christian properties after a rumour that a Christian woman who had converted to Islam and married a Muslim man a few years earlier had now left her husband and their house. The security forces declared a curfew in the village and worked towards achieving reconciliation between the two communities. The Coptic Church insisted on the need to compensate the Christians for their destroyed property. Initially, the Christians refused to attend the reconciliation session, but the security forces threatened to arrest their children if they did not attend, so they had to accept (Shoukry 2009: 69).

While such reconciliation sessions may have succeeded in preventing the escalation of violence, they have deepened the rifts between Muslims and Christians, and exacerbated the feelings of humiliation among the Christian communities. The security strategy succeeded, but at a heavy social cost. Hence, when the security forces collapsed after 25 January 2011, religious tensions flared up again, more frequently and with greater violence.

Dialogue Processes after 25 January 2011

Three main types of dialogue initiatives can be identified after the events of January 2011: informal reconciliation sessions, the NJC, and the House of the Egyptian Family. These initiatives have involved different actors with often different interests: the Christian families involved in these tensions, the Maspero Youth Union, the Coptic Church, al-Azhar, Islamic forces and the regime. While the first type of dialogue has focused on preventing further escalation of sectarian violence, the second has aimed at changing the laws that lead to such violence, and the third works to promote confidence-building among Christians and Muslims.

Informal Reconciliation Sessions

Unlike the situation under Mubarak, where the security forces were often the ones to organize and put pressure on the parties to end the conflict, reconciliation sessions after 25 January 2011 have involved a range of actors: the Salafi movement, the Muslim Brotherhood, the military and the Coptic Church. In all cases of sectarian tensions between Muslims and Christians after 25 January 2011, attempts have been made to hold reconciliation sessions, with varying degrees of success.

In the case of Sol (March 2011), the military tried to play the role formerly played by the security forces, arranging a reconciliation session between Muslims and Christians in the village. However, the military needed the help of Islamic authorities to calm down local tensions, and sought the assistance of several religious figures from al-Azhar, the salafists and the Muslim Brotherhood. However, only the popular Salafi sheikh Mohammad Hassaan could calm down the angry Muslim protesters in the village. Hassaan held meetings with local Muslim youth in order to listen to their demands, and then met with representatives of the Christian community to hear their point of view as well. The Christians asked for the church to be rebuilt and for the Christian families who left the village to be allowed to return to their homes, but the Muslims refused to allow the church to be constructed inside the village. They argued that it had originally been built against their will, due to pressure from the security forces. They wanted it built outside the village itself, but Hassaan managed to convince them to cede to the Christians' demands in order to end the crisis. After reaching this compromise, Hassaan contacted a group of Muslim religious scholars to get their approval for this solution, so as to legitimize his action. A few days later, a public meeting was held in the village to announce the end of the crisis. The meeting was attended by representatives of the military, the Muslim Brotherhood, revolutionary youth, al-Azhar and secular figures. However, it was clear that it was Sheikh Hassaan who had the greatest influence over the public. The Christian youth that were protesting in front of Maspero refused the reconciliation session, seeing the intervention of religious figures as contradictory to the principles of the rule of law and citizenship. However, the Christian families of Sol asked the youth to end their sit-in, so as not to obstruct efforts to end the crisis. As some of these families argued, even if those who attacked the Christians and their properties were sentenced to jail, their families would hold the Christians responsible, and would seek revenge.

In Imbaba (May 2011), the situation was different. The reconciliation sessions came after the crisis had been contained, so the Christians were under no pressure to reach a solution. Several rounds of dialogue were held between representatives from the Christian and the Muslim communities. The sessions involved members of al-Nour Salafi Party and the Muslim Brotherhood and influential Christian figures from Imbaba. In these sessions, the Muslims asked the Coptic Church to pay compensation for the families of the victims, but the Christian representatives refused, calling instead for Christians and Muslims to collect money for the families of the victims from both sides. Even after several sessions, no agreement could be reached.

The case of al-Ameriah (January 2012) in Alexandria is an instance of a successful reconciliation session. Salafi youth, who enjoy a strong presence in this part of Alexandria, tried to calm the situation by separating the two sides. Sheikh Sherif Hawary, a Salafi leader, moderated a reconciliation session between representatives of both communities. The session was even held at the police station, with police officers present. The representatives of the two communities agreed that that the eight Christian families involved in this crisis should leave the village, and that those accused of using arms should be handed over to the police. While the reconciliation session succeeded in ending the conflict, it sparked criticism among Christian activists and human rights organizations who refused this informal way of ending the crisis, and accused state institutions and members of parliament of renouncing on the principle of the rule of law. The newly elected parliament sent a fact-finding committee to al-Ameriah and met with the involved parties, including those who took part in the reconciliation session. While the committee acknowledged the role of the informal reconciliation session in containing the crisis, it also noted the need to enforce the rule of law and the principle of citizenship.

Comparing the three cases of Sol (March 2011), Imbaba (May 2011), and al-Ameriah (January 2012) is instructive. In Sol and in al-Ameriah, the Christians accepted the efforts to achieve reconciliation through an informal session, even it led to their having to make concessions. In the case of Sol, the

Christian families even asked the Christian youth that led the sit-in in front of the building of the state television to end it. Given their weak position, the families were willing to forgive those who had attacked them, in order to end the tension and be able to return to their homes. In the case of Imbaba, the situation was different: first, because of the urban nature of the area of tension, which rendered measures like forced displacement difficult; and second because of the strong Christian presence in the area of tension. Unlike the cases of Sol and al-Ameriah, during the informal reconciliation sessions in Imbaba the Christians were the ones who insisted on the need to apply the law, and were willing to wait for a court decision, even if it might not go in their favour.

These reconciliation sessions were frequently accused of being in violation of the law, as the victims were often denied their rights. However, the reconciliation sessions as such are not the real problem. Reconciliation sessions are part of the culture in many areas in Egypt, and in many cases they might help in avoiding further escalation of the religious conflict. The problem lies in the fact that these sessions have gone beyond merely avoiding further escalation, and have tried to achieve an agreement between the parties, outside of the law.

The Case of the National Justice Committee

The Maspero Youth Union, as well as many Christian intellectuals, have often criticized the reconciliation sessions for violating the principle of the rule of the law, and have requested the state institutions to intervene by legislation in order to guarantee equal rights for Christians and Muslims alike.

The idea of creating a committee composed of Muslim and Christian activists and politicians to work on the legal measures needed to end sectarian tension was initially raised during the first Maspero sit-in, in March 2011. While Prime Minster Essam Sharaf promised to establish such a committee, nothing happened . After the sectarian clashes in Imbaba in May 2011, the issue was raised again. Essam Sharaf decided to establish a body that would bring together Muslims and Christian activists and intellectuals: the National Justice Committee (NJC).

The NJC was the general council, and the various sub-committees. These were to include sub-committees on early warning and rapid response, the legal aspects, education and the media. However, the education and media sub-committees were never activated. The general council included several Christian and Muslim intellectuals and representatives of both al-Azhar and the Coptic Church, together with representatives from movements like the Maspero Youth Union and the Revolution's Youth Coalition.

The legal sub-committee identified two key problems as the main source of religious tensions: the procedures for building churches, and the discrimination against Christians and other minorities in Egypt. Its members started working on two pieces of legislation on these two issues, to be submitted to the prime minster. The early warning and rapid response sub-committee worked on identifying potential religious tensions before they develop into actual clashes.

The committee faced two main challenges: an internal one with regard to the dialogue between Christian and Muslim youth, and an external one concerning the resistance of state institutions to its activities. Internally, some NJC members acted as representatives of their religious communities, which created tensions during committee discussions. Given what they saw as 'years of discrimination', some Christian youth were driven by feelings of humiliation and injustice that sometimes rendered constructive discussion difficult. The main challenge of the dialogue within the Committee was that some members could not distinguish between their personal religious adherence and their role within the NJC. Christian and Muslim intellectuals insisted that Committee members should not represent their religious communities, but should act as Egyptian citizens trying to reach a solution to religious tensions. Externally, state institutions refused to cooperate with the NJC, seeing its work as an interference in their own spheres of influence. The security apparatus perceived it as a parallel institution that sought its own role in managing religious tensions. Moreover, the NJC failed to persuade the prime minister to allocate it headquarters or a budget. Its meeting were held in the Council of Ministers, and its members themselves financed its activities.

The attack on the church in the village of al-Marinab in September 2011 came as a serious test of the NJC and its ability to contain sectarian violence. A fact-finding committee that included Christian and Muslim activists was established to go to the village. After talking to the involved parties, this committee wrote a report and presented it to other NCJ members. The Committee discussed the report and adopted two recommendations aimed at ending the crisis: to remove the governor of Aswan for his role in escalating the crisis, and to license the churches that had been allowed to be built by the state security under the Mubarak regime but without official permission. However, both recommendations were ignored by the prime minster.

Disappointed at the attitude of the government, the Maspero Youth Union withdrew from the NJC and joined the Christian protesters in the streets. The crisis escalated further until it reached the deadly night of 9 October. After the violent repression of the protesters on 9 October, other members of the NJC froze their membership. The judge Noha El-Zainy blamed the government for the escalation of the crisis, maintaining that if the government had adopted the Committee's recommendations, the crisis would have been contained (El-Zainy 2011).

The incident of al-Marinab showed that the NJC succeeded in overcoming its internal challenges. The fact-finding report on the religious tensions and their causes was written by both Muslim and Christian activists, and was discussed with all members of the Committee. Report discussions were very constructive, seeking an end to the crisis rather than just blaming one party. However, the committee failed to resolve the external challenge of dealing with state institutions, and did not manage to get the government to adopt its recommendations for ending the crisis.

While the NJC tried to continue its work after the violence in October 2011, it came under growing pressure from state institutions, until it was *de facto* dissolved.

The House of the Egyptian Family

The idea of the House of the Egyptian Family came after the attack on the Syriac Catholic Cathedral of Our Lady of Salvation in Baghdad, Iraq, in December 2010. Ahmed al-Taib, the Grand Imam of al-Azhar, feared that Christians in Egypt might be a target of terrorism that could endanger relations between Christians and Muslims there. He proposed the creation of a national independent body, to be named the House of the Egyptian Family, aimed at preserving the national fabric of Egyptian society. After the events of 25 January 2011, the Supreme Council of the Armed Forces (SCAF) approved its creation under the leadership of both Grand Imam of al-Azhar Ahmed al-Taib and the Coptic Orthodox Pope Shenouda III. The House of the Egyptian Family is composed of a Board of Trustees and an Executive Council. The Board of Trustees is presided over by the President of the House of the Egyptian Family, the Grand Imam of al-Azhar in alternation with the Pope of the Coptic Orthodox Church. The Board also includes a general secretary and an assistant general secretary. It meets monthly, with responsibility for deciding on the policies of the House and overseeing their implementation. The Executive Council is responsible for achieving the policies adopted by the Board, and is divided into eight committees: education, religious discourse, youth and societal development, family, media, observation and suggestions, emergency, and monitoring committee. The membership of the House of the Egyptian Family includes al-Azhar, the Coptic Orthodox Church, the Egyptian Catholic Church, the Evangelical Church and the Episcopal Church, as well as Christian and Muslim figures with expertise on religion, history, sociology, law, jurisprudence and education.

The aims of the House of the Egyptian Family are as follows: to preserve the Egyptian personality, restore important Muslim and Christian values, help in understanding the differences, enhance citizenship, and strengthen the several Egyptian cultures. To these ends, it employs three main approaches: first, monitoring the religious discourse, focusing on improving the religious discourse of Muslims and Christians by stressing the principles of moderation and respect for diversity, and working on school curricula to eliminate anything inciting to hatred, division or mistrust. Second, to remove the religious façade from 'religious' tensions that are often due not to religious differences, but to political and economic reasons. Third, to support the activities of NGOs and other independent actors in rebuilding the nation.

For financing, the House of the Egyptian Family depends on donations from its founding members: al-Azhar and the three Egyptian churches, as well as civil society organizations and individuals. For greater outreach, it has established branches in four Egyptian governorates – Assuit, Menya, Luxor and the Red Sea – and is working to establish branches in Beheira, Alexandria and Port-Said.

While one of its aims is to replace the informal reconciliation sessions by its own networks of religious and civil society actors, the House of the Egyptian Family has not been able to avoid becoming involved in day-to-day tensions. It took part in the reconciliation sessions between Muslims and Christians in Khosoos in April 2013.

Types of Dialogue, and Determinants of Success and Failure

The case of religious tensions in Egypt points to two types of dialogue: outcome-oriented and process-oriented dialogues. The cases of the reconciliation sessions and the National Justice Committee are examples of outcome-oriented dialogue, whereas the case of the House of the Egyptian Family is an example of process-oriented dialogue.

Reconciliation sessions often tackle only one specific incident, with the aim of containing the crisis and avoiding further escalation. The balance of power is crucial in this type of dialogue. The weaker partner has limited negotiation power, and will often be willing to accept the terms of the agreement, knowing that further escalation will bring a higher price. The cases of Sol (March 2011) and al-Ameriah (January 2012) have shown how the Christians were willing to accept the deal offered to them by the mediators, as they know that they could not afford to let the crisis escalate. However, in the case of Imbaba (May 2011), where the Christians were in a stronger position, they felt no pressure to reach an agreement through the reconciliation sessions, and preferred to wait for a court decision. While these reconciliation sessions succeeded in preventing the violence from escalating, they failed to consolidate social cohesion among the two communities, leading instead to further social alienation (Tadros 2013).

The NJC is also an example of an outcome-oriented dialogue. However, it has sought to introduce legal changes to resolve the underlying causes of religious tensions. It has aimed at achieving institutional change through discussions among various stakeholders. Unlike the first type it has not sought to solve only one specific crisis, but has tried to examine the roots of the problem, and to draw up new institutional rules that would treat the causes of the problem and prevent it from happening over and over again. While the members of the NJC managed to achieve agreement on the causes of the sectarian problem in Egypt and on measures for solving it, they failed to get their recommendations taken up by the political authorities. Unable to introduce any institutional change, this experiment came to an end.

The third type of dialogue seeks to build confidence among the parties to the conflict, and tries to change elements in the cultural environment that might promote conflict. The House of the Egyptian Family exemplifies this type of dialogue, as it emphasizes confidence building by working with religious actors both Muslim and Christian, together with civil society organizations involved in the areas of tensions between the two religious communities. Unlike the National Justice Committee, the House of the Egyptian Family does not seek to get legal changes introduced: it focuses on confidence building between Muslims and Christians.

These dialogue initiatives for resolving the religious tensions between Muslims and Christians in Egypt indicate five main factors that determine to what extent dialogue will succeed or not:

1. The Value of Comprehensive Approach

While the informal reconciliation sessions often succeeded in preventing an escalation of the religious violence, the tensions remained. Insistence on focusing solely on preventing the escalation of violence through reconciliation sessions came at the cost of deepening the gaps between Muslims and Christians rather than bridging them. In the cases of al-Ameriah and Sol, while the reconciliation sessions prevented further escalation of the conflict, they also served to deepen feelings of humiliation among the Christians, who felt forced to renounce their rights in order to save their lives, thereby sharpening the alienation between the two communities. Both the NJC and the House of the Egyptian family have sought to go beyond merely ending the violence, offering a comprehensive approach that takes the social and economic factors into consideration. However, a challenge facing both bodies is their inability to remain aloof from day-to-day crises. For example, the House of the Egyptian Family had to take part in informal reconciliation sessions in order to prevent further escalation of violence in Khosoos in April 2013.

2. The Importance of Involving Legitimate Actors

The three dialogue initiatives show that religious actors that enjoy legitimacy in Egyptian society have played an important role in ending religious tensions, especially after the Revolution of 25 January 2011. While under the rule of Mubarak the security forces could put pressure on the parties to the conflict to reach a compromise, more recently the SCAF has often asked the help of religious leaders who enjoy religious legitimacy in order to convince the conflicting parties to accept reconciliation. The roles played by Sheikh Mohammad Hassaan in the crisis of Sol (March 2011) and Sheikh Sherif Hawary in the crisis of al-Ameriah (January 2012) were essential in putting an end to the crises and preventing escalation. The House of the Egyptian Family also works with imams and priests, recognizing their degree of influence within their local communities.

This determinant can also explain why no international actors could succeed in mediating between the Muslim and Christian communities. International actors did not enjoy the legitimacy needed to play a mediatory role: they were accused by the Muslim community of supporting the Christians, whereas the Christians were afraid of allowing international actor to intervene, as that might confirm the accusations of being 'agents of the West'. The Coptic Church has often rejected attempts by Western governments to intervene in sectarian crises, insisting that this is an internal problem to be solved by the Egyptians themselves.

3. The Importance of State Institutions

State institutions play an essential role in any attempt to end religious tensions in Egypt. These tensions are caused not by religious ideas, but by issues of rights and duties – the right to freedom of worship, for example. Measures for building trust between the two communities are essential, but not sufficient. The failure of the NJC was due mainly to the resistance of state institutions to its activities. The security sector perceived the committee as its rival, and refused to cooperate with it.

4. The Importance of Information

The different dialogue processes show that if the dialogue cannot build on complete information about the origins of the crisis and the parties involved, it will often fail. The NJC tried to intervene in several crises between Muslims and Christians over the construction of churches. However, the Committee found that disputes over the construction of churches are often a manifestation of longer-term hostility between the Muslim and the Christian communities over different issues. The NJC adopted a strategy that started with sending a fact-finding committee to the area of tension to find the real causes of the crisis and the parties in order to enable constructive dialogue over the real causes of the conflict, and not only the consequences of the conflict.

5. *The Role of Emotions*

A major challenge facing all dialogue initiatives are the feelings of humiliation felt by the Christians. In the case of the NJC, a main internal challenge was the humiliation felt by Christian youth that pushed them to take extreme positions in discussions. The same feelings represent one of the obstacles facing the House of the Egyptian Family in its efforts to build trust between the two religious communities. Regardless of whether these feelings are based on real incidents of discrimination or not, they endanger all dialogue initiatives. Such negative emotions have accumulated through what are seen as years of humiliation and discrimination against the Christians in Egypt. These emotions of humiliations and discrimination have often led the Christian actors today to refuse to compromise, arguing that they have suffered for years, even centuries, and will not accept any more compromises.

Conclusions

While some Christians and Muslims thought that the end of the Mubarak regime in February 2011 would also put an end to the tensions between the two religious communities, time has proven them wrong. Although Mubarak stepped down, his policies that deepened the differences between both communities have remained in power.

The three types of dialogue initiatives analysed in this chapter represent different approaches to addressing these tensions. While the informal reconciliation sessions emerged under the Mubarak regime, the National Justice Committee and the House of the Egyptian Family represent two new approaches. The aim of each dialogue initiative has differed. While the first aims at only preventing the escalation of violence, the second focused on dialogue among activists and intellectuals, both Christian and Muslims, on measures to be taken by state institutions, and the third has aimed at building trust among local-level religious actors.

This chapter has identified five main factors that determine the degree of success of dialogue initiatives: *a comprehensive approach towards religious tensions, engaging legitimate actors, access to information about the roots of each religious crisis, the attitude of state institutions*, and fifthly *the role of emotions*.

While the informal reconciliation sessions often engaged legitimate actors, had access to information related the tensions between the two communities, and enjoyed the support of the state institutions, this approach failed to offer a comprehensive approach, or deal with the negative emotions involved. Moreover, these reconciliation sessions often deepened the feelings of humiliation among the Christian population. The NJC succeeded in overcoming the obstacle of negative emotions among its own members, and was able to offer a comprehensive approach to the religious tensions – but it failed to gain the support of state institutions or legitimate local religious actors, and hence did not have access to full and relevant information. When it failed to get state institutions to adopt its recommendation, the NJC experiment came to an end. Also the House of the Egyptian Family has worked towards offering a comprehensive approach towards religious tensions, and has succeeded in engaging local religious actors. However, the persistence of state policies has repeatedly jeopardized its progress in building trust among Muslims and Christians. Feelings of humiliation among the Copts and lack of access to full information remain two main challenges to the activities of the House of the Egyptian Family.

Taking these five factors into consideration is essential for any dialogue initiative that seeks not merely to contain the violence but to achieve a durable solution to the religious tensions in Egypt.

References

Brownlee, J. 2013. *Violence against Christians in Egypt*. Beirut: Carnegie Endowment for International Peace.

EIPR 2010. *Two Years of Sectarian Violence: What Happened? Where Do We Begin? An Analytical Study of Jan 2008–Jan 2010*, Egyptian Initiative for Personal Rights (EIPR).

El-Zainy, N. 2011. *Ashera Masaan [Ten pm]*. Dream TV.Cairo: 11 Oct. 2011. Television [Online]. Available at: http://www.youtube.com/watch?v=RK5yaMk82h0 [accessed: 11 August 2014].

Heikal, M.H 1983. *Autumn of Fury: The Assassination of Sadat*. New York: Random House.

Human Rights Watch 2013. *Egypt: Mass Attacks on Churches*, Human Rights Watch. [Online, 22 August]. Available at: http://www.hrw.org/news/2013/08/21/egypt-mass-attacks-churches [accessed: 11 August 2014].

Iskander, E. 2012. *Sectarian Conflict in Egypt: Christian Media, Identity and Representation*. Abingdon: Routledge.

Shoukry, N. 2009. *Lijan al-sulh wa-l-Aqbat* [Reconciliation sessions and the Christians]. Cairo: Watani Publ.

Tadros, M. To be Published. *Decentralisation and Social Cohesion in Religiously Heterogeneous Societies in Transition: A Case Study from Egypt* [Online]. Available at: https://www.ids.ac.uk/publication/decentralisation-and-social-cohesion-in-religiously-heterogeneous-societies-in-transition-a-case-study-from-egypt [accessed: 11 August 2014].

Personal interviews

Interview with Beshoy Tamri, member of the Maspero Youth Union and the National Justice Committee, Cairo, 16 November 2013.

Interview with a member of the reconciliation session in Imbabe, Giza, 6 November 2013.

Interview with Nagwan al-Ashawal, head of the early warning and rapid response sub-committee of the National Justice Committee, Florence, 3 June 2014.

Interview with Mahamoud Azab, coordinator of the House of the Egyptian Family, 1 April 2014, Cairo.

Chapter 11
Conclusions

Pernille Rieker and Henrik Thune

What is the best way for people to deal with their differences? That question is the point of departure for one of the most celebrated books ever published on the subject of dialogue and negotiation processes, the multimillion-copy bestseller *Getting to Yes*, written by Roger Fisher and William Ury in the early 1980s.[1] We mentioned this work in the introduction, arguing that the book – covering a wide spectrum of negotiation processes from individuals who would like to keep their friends, to businesspeople looking for a win–win outcome of a company merger, or a statesman seeking to keep the peace – is still the most refined and clear-minded formulation of the 'integrative approach' to negotiating agreements between political actors on the international scene.

The answer given to the opening question is indeed not only common sense: it is also universally shared. According to a large online survey initiated by the UN in 2014, with more than 2.5 million participants worldwide, peaceful resolution to protect against crime and violence is the sixth most important value to the entire world population, surpassed only by such as basic needs clean water, food, health as well as education and political leadership.[2] We humans wage wars and set countries and societies on fire, but we are also keen to celebrate peace and diplomacy. Huge amounts of funding and other resources are invested in this, and we tend to elevate the legacy of figures like Nelson Mandela, Abraham Lincoln and Mahatma Gandhi because of their documented ability to resolve conflicts and settle disputes and conflicting interests peacefully. In this way, dialogue retains a widely accepted position as the main remedy for countering some of the worst menaces known to humans – collectively and individually – like warfare and the bitter break-up of close, personal relationships. As pointed out by Ole Jacob Sending in the second chapter of this anthology, dialogue is both a method of change and a tool for maintaining order and permanence. 'Dialogue makes diplomacy the institutional vehicle for the public use of reason that can temper and transform international politics' (p. 15).

This book has examined the potentials and limits of dialogue as a political tool for solving deep-rooted conflicts in international politics. Through three

---

1 For full reference to this book, see reference list in Chapter 1.
2 See United Nations, 'Have your say', http://data.myworld2015.org/.

conceptual chapters and six case studies, we have sought to answer the following questions:

1. What is the role of dialogue in diplomacy?
2. How may we explain the outcome (success or no success) of mediation efforts and dialogue?
3. What has dialogue accomplished, as tool for preventing, limiting or ending recent international conflicts?

The analyses and empirical findings presented in the chapters here cannot offer any final answers to these wide-ranging, general questions about conflict resolution and foreign policy. However, taken together, the contributions do offer some fresh nuances and insights for broader understanding.

This concluding chapter briefly synthesizes and highlights what we, the editors, see as the main contributions to the debate about the effectiveness of dialogue and peace processes on the international stage. We turn first to the meaning of dialogue as applied by states; next, we note two apparent blind spots in the academic literature; and, finally, drawing on the individual case studies presented here, we formulate some lessons that can serve as a point of departure for making engagement and dialogue an even more effective tool in the future.

The Meanings of Dialogue in Diplomacy

Despite the almost universal popular conviction that dialogue is the best way to settle disputes in international politics, it is far from clear what is meant by words like 'dialogue' and 'negotiations'. The strict etymological denotation of dialogue is fairly straightforward: from the Greek *dialogos* meaning 'conversation' related to *dia-* ('across'); an early use of the word in English is found in the thirteenth century referring to 'literary work consisting of conversation between two or more persons'.[3] However, the cultural connotations of dialogue as a term and ethos are many. The same is true for the actual practice of dialogue as a tool of foreign policy. In a European or Scandinavian setting dialogue tends to imply something rather transformative, describing a deep-rooted process of inter-subjective communication, closely linked to the idea of dialogue as used in the Socratic philosophical tradition. Within the recent and more pragmatic US tradition, the term often implies something more along the line of conventional diplomatic contact or straightforward interaction and talks between parties. The question therefore remains: What is the meaning of dialogue in diplomacy?

---

3 http://www.etymonline.com/.

Is dialogue, as is often suggested, contingently linked to diplomacy? or it is a particular method of operating applied at certain times to solve specific problems and policy challenges? And if so – what kind of diplomatic method are we talking about?

Ole Jacob Sending proposes five ways of understanding dialogue as a tool for diplomacy: dialogue as *communication*, as *problem-solving*, as *transformation*, as *justification* and finally as *mediation*. As he argues, these categories can help us to move away from a generic and normatively charged conception of dialogue towards one that is empirically researchable. This categorization also helps to clear up much of the debate because it brings out how the very meaning of diplomacy hinges on what role and aim we attribute to dialogue. If dialogue is seen as communication, we stay close to the idea of diplomacy as a system for the representation of and negotiation between states. By contrast, if we view dialogue as transformational, diplomacy emerges in a different light, now seen to be capable of changing the interests of states. One implication of this is that we should not take at face value diplomats' (and politicians') own descriptions of their diplomatic efforts: there is often a substantial symbolic or political profit to be gained from presenting diplomatic efforts as involving 'dialogue processes'.

Two Blind-spots

In this book we have used dialogue interchangeably as both a core tool and a transformative process of state and non-state diplomacy aimed at resolving, liming or preventing armed conflicts. We have also suggested that dialogue can broadly be defined as a meaningful exchange of ideas and world views related to a conflict, between external non-party actors and parties in a conflict, or between representatives of two or more contending parties. Thus, dialogue is understood as being present at all stages of conflict resolution – from confidence-building, informal dialogue seminars and capacity-building to shuttle diplomacy, as well as formal state-to-state negotiations. As discussed by Henrik Thune and Frida Nome in Chapter 3, these steps are often meshed together in an integrated and intricate back-and-forth movement, with the process aim of getting contending parties to accept the idea of a peaceful resolution and to speak with each other, and with the outcome aim of resolving or easing a conflict. But when are these different processes of dialogue successful? When does dialogue work? – And is it a rational process based on interests, as for Fisher and Ury, or are other elements relevant as well?

The Peacemaking Apparatus

Starting from an interest in real-world diplomacy Thune and Nome identify several weaknesses in the literature, and hold that the current conceptual underpinning of much of the recent research does not live up to its own ambition of real-world correspondence and relevance. The often-employed distinction between the different 'Tracks' (I, II, III) that international actors can pursue in their involvement in conflict resolution provides an ordering typological device and a language that can simplify communication about mediation processes. However, Thune and Nome argue that these distinctions are not 'analytical constructs' but merely popular (and easily recognizable) linguistic markers. The concept of 'tracks' gives a sense of clearly distinguishable tools or strategies that actors can choose between with different aims or measures – but most current mediation efforts are in fact both Track I and Track II at the same time. They are not separate initiatives or processes – one official and the other unofficial – but are often deliberately combined. Placing activities into a rigid Track I/Track II scheme, therefore, exaggerates the sense that there are separate strategies and measures for activities at different levels, and it fits poorly with how peaceful attempts to ease and solve conflict are actually conducted. Instead, Thune and Nome maintain, today's conflicts have become arenas for 'swarms' of third-party actors and a multitude of integrated mediation efforts and channels that fall outside current terminology: they are better described as a new and global peacemaking apparatus. In order to understand the achievements and failures of third-party mediation, it is necessary to study the structure and modus operandi of this *apparatus*. They conclude by identifying five factors, or what they refer to as 'dysfunctions of the global peacemaking apparatus', important for understanding the success or failure of international third-party intervention missing, but that are missing from the current academic research and policy debate. These factors, or 'dysfunctions' (referred to as the swarming factor, the international competition factor, the process dependency factor, the visibility factor and the (mis)information factor), may be seen both as warning signs which states, diplomats and other international actors should look out for in designing, funding and conducting third-party involvement in concrete conflicts, as well as variables that should be included in scholarly attempts to explain the failure or success of international mediation.

Emotions

What would a proper understanding of emotions mean for how we think about the practice of dialogue in international politics? According to Thune and Saurette in Chapter 3 this is a question that has gone virtually unasked. Focusing on the central role that emotions play in international politics, they explore the implications for how we understand the potential and the limits of the practice of dialogue. Many scholars and practitioners of international politics have systematically ignored the role that emotions play in global politics – tending either to dismiss dialogue as a legitimate foreign policy option, or to view it as a relatively straightforward tool whose success depends on being able to focus on core interests while excluding all emotional and other 'peripheral' investments.

These approaches, Thune and Saurette believe, are misguided. Through an examination of the Cuban Missile Crisis in 1962 and the Western political and military response to the Middle East after 11 September 2001, they show how emotions impact on decisionmaking at all levels and how the ways that policymakers and decisionmakers understand and respond to these emotional dimensions have a significant impact on whether moments of tension and conflict can be successfully resolved. They find that once we acknowledge the central role that emotions play in global politics it becomes clear that many Western foreign policy choices of recent decades have been particularly misguided, serving only to heighten the emotional stakes of certain tensions. That is not to say, however, that once we understand the role of emotions and the importance of processes of dialogue, it will be possible to navigate easily, and resolve all crises and tensions in the world. But a better understanding of the importance of the emotional dimension of international politics – and how dialogue processes can address these elements – may help practitioners to resolve conflicts more successfully.

Lessons for the Future: Dialogue as a Tool

The six case studies in the second part of the book show how the role of dialogue differs according to the type of the conflict. The first three chapters are cases of more traditional backchannel dialogue between states and their official diplomats, whereas the final three offer examples of more complex dialogue settings. Let us begin with the main findings in these two groups of cases, before presenting some more general lessons for future policy.

Although there are some obvious similarities between the first three cases of Libya, Iran and the Russo-Georgian/Russo-Ukrainian cases, they differ in terms of *type of conflict*, *duration* and *outcome*. In Libya, the conflicts were (temporarily) settled through the military intervention authorized by the UN Security Council in 2011. Prior to the fall of Muammar Gaddafi, Western powers had held a series of secret talks on issues such as the Lockerbie bombers and lifting of the sanctions, the abandonment of the WMD programme, and the imprisonment of the Bulgarian health personnel. All these talks fit well with elements of the integrative approach mentioned in the introduction. Despite Gaddafi's somewhat original and unconventional personality and approach, the process of secret talks between the delegates appeared constructive, and resulted in some kind of trust between the parties. The talks were therefore also a test in handling different emotions on both sides.

The case of Iran concerns the country's nuclear programme, but on a deeper level it is a manifestation of a more fundamental conflict over the future political landscape of the Middle East. Until recently, there were few signs of genuine common interest in finding a solution to the dispute on either the Iranian or the US side. Mutual mistrust reigned, and the dispute seemed to fall squarely in the 'five per cent' category of conflicts that are extremely difficult to resolve. However, recent changes in the domestic and regional context seem to have generated a new willingness to talk and have spurred a more integrative and result-oriented type of dialogue, with both sides showing interest in reaching an agreement. As Lodgaard argues in Chapter 6, the diplomatic modalities that broke the ice were dual track. On the one hand, bilateral US-Iranian talks conducted in deepest secrecy, which was necessary to get the process started. On the other hand, Iran launched a public confidence-building campaign that conveyed a sincere interest in reconciliation with the West. Even though the parties failed to reach an agreement by the self-imposed deadlines of 20 July and 24 November 2014, they agreed to continue the talks. The fact that other important events in the region (ISIS and Gaza) have shifted the political focus away from the Iranian problem may in fact facilitate a solution, since it may lead to less attention and fewer negative reactions.

The Russo-Georgian and the Russo-Ukrainian conflicts concern deep-rooted territorial issues. While dialogue and negotiations brought an end to the armed phase of the conflict in Georgia, the situation in Ukraine is still ongoing and characterized by uncertainty. And although the prospects for a negotiated solution between Russia and Ukraine seem weak as of this writing, it is difficult to believe that there can be a military solution to this conflict. As in the case of Georgia (as well as Libya and Iran), progress will probably not take place until there is a window of opportunity where a win–win solution is in sight. And then it might be useful to have the possibility of launching talks among the parties, with discretion.

There are *elements* of an integrative approach at work in all three of these cases. However, we do not necessarily find a sustained effect of dialogue, other than as a precondition for the application of other policy tools. Dialogue is important as a diplomatic tool, but the conditions needed for an integrative approach to succeed are seldom present in such deep-rooted conflicts. Any rapprochement and agreements that are achieved may provide temporary stability, but these can also easily be undone. This was the case in Libya in 2011 as well as in both the Russo-Georgian and Russo-Ukrainian conflicts. It remains to be seen whether the case of Iran will be different, and whether an agreement may be reached soon.

The final three cases in this book concern dialogue situations of a very different kind than the first three. While the first three are all examples of diplomatic processes between formal state representatives, the last three involve less formal dialogue processes undertaken by non-diplomats. The Afghanistan case in Chapter 8 shows that pursuing dialogue initiatives was justified despite the massive costs of the war and the fairly modest achievements. But it also indicates numerous lessons of a more sobering kind. As Semple argues in his conclusion:

> Those who promoted dialogue failed to take adequate account of the nature of the Taliban as an organization. They were also slow to reconcile the competing imperatives of the main parties to the conflict – the desire of the Afghan government to control dialogue processes versus the desire of the Taliban movement to keep its distance from the government. Similarly, no actor succeeded in using relationships cultivated during the low-key dialogue of the early years to enhance the dialogue when it became a higher political priority in the later phases of the conflict. (pp. 164–6)

Similarly, in Chapter 9 on Sudan, Ashworth concludes by arguing that dialogue processes has been important despite the modest achievements. He focuses on the role of the church in these processes because it 'was the only one to remain present on the ground with the people during an era when there was no government, no civil society, no NGOs and no UN presence, and even the influence of traditional chiefs and elders had been eroded by the young comrades with guns' (p. 167). In this way the church gained credibility for taking on an important role in the peace process. It established the original People-to-People Peace Process, which brought the protagonists together in an uneasy alliance for more than a decade, until massive violence re-erupted in December 2013. It can be debated whether the dialogues have been successful. However, Ashworth points out, these are long-term processes with ups and downs; perhaps their success should be judged in terms of whether they can continue in new incarnations, to keep people talking despite new conflicts and other challenges which may emerge.

Finally, Georges Fahmi's study in Chapter 10 of the role of informal dialogue processes in dealing with religious tensions between Christians and Muslims in Egypt during the first three years after the Revolution of 25 January 2011 analyses three types of dialogue initiatives: the informal reconciliation sessions, the National Justice Committee, and the House of the Egyptian Family. The chapter concludes that success is dependent on five factors: *a comprehensive approach towards religious tensions, engaging legitimate actors, access to information about the roots of each religious crisis, the attitude of state institutions,* and *the role of emotions.* According to Fahmi, taking these five factors into consideration is essential for any dialogue initiative that seeks not merely to contain the violence but to achieve a durable solution to Egypt's religious tensions. Egypt as well as the other cases studied in this book clearly shows that comprehensive, long-term and home-grown processes are important, even if the concrete achievements may be few and the setbacks many. Thus, the overall conclusion in all of these chapter is also sobering: in no instance did dialogue itself result in progress defined in terms of an agreement or a reduction of tensions. When progress was made, it was because the interests of one or more of the key players had changed.

Lessons Learnt for Future Policies

All cases analysed here support the view that dialogue can be a useful tool, but that there is little in dialogue as such that promotes mutual understanding and enduring, peaceful agreements. Dialogue may be deliberative and serve to change actors' interests and behaviour, but this seems to presuppose trust and a shared communicative horizon or a process of harmonizing deeper interests. The types of conflict analysed here are characterized precisely by the lack of such trust. Below, we highlight seven lessons that can serve as a point of departure for possible ways of making engagement and dialogue more effective tools.

1.   *Behaviour and positions tend to change as a result of changing international or domestic circumstances rather as a result of dialogue itself.*

In the case of Iran, for a long time there was scant willingness for dialogue; the few attempts were motivated by the desire to avoid war (or perhaps to legitimize war at a later stage), rather than any deep-felt belief that negotiation would serve to promote understanding between the parties. Mistrust and internal constraints on both sides have put massive constraints on the negotiations. And then, things started to happen in 2013 when there was a window of opportunity for realizing common interests. While Iran was trying to get out of its isolation, the USA was lowering its military profile in the region in order to concentrate on the Asian pivot. The fact that the focus of interest has now shifted from Iran to the situation in northern Iraq and in Gaza might also facilitate a solution. Perhaps the confluence of national interests and regional developments has created a unique opportunity to solve one of the most difficult conflicts in today's international affairs.

In the case of Libya, we also see that both geopolitical and domestic factors are at play in all the different dialogue situations. Dialogue has been a facilitating mechanism, but not a mechanism that can change the fundamentals in the conflict or solve the underlying conflicts. Dialogue was indeed a central tool and the various negotiated results were real and important, but the reasons for the breakthroughs lie primarily elsewhere – sometimes internationally, sometimes domestically. In Libya, the underlying conflict was not solved. That explains why Libya could shift so rapidly from being foe to friend and then, in the end, a foe again.

Similarly, the conflicts between Russia and Georgia and Russia and Ukraine are of the enduring kind, where the underlying conflicts have prevailed. With the Russo-Georgian conflict, there are important factors other than the dialogue itself that explain the outcome. In fact, Russia could accept the conditions set by France and the EU since it had beaten Georgia on the ground. By contrast, in the Russo-Ukrainian case, the talks in Geneva on 17 April 2014 led to the formulation of principles for solving the conflict – but these were not followed. After this initiative came several rounds of telephone contact between Poroshenko and Putin, that resulted in Putin's reluctant support for Poroshenko's peace plan for Ukraine that was announced in June 2014. A first round of direct talks between the separatists and the Ukrainian central authorities took place under new strategic circumstances caused by Russian direct military intervention in September 2014. The talks resulted in the first Minsk agreement on ceasefire signed on 5 September 2014, but this ceasefire turned out to be short-lived. On 11 February 2015 a new Minsk meeting in the so-called Normandy format – state leaders of Ukraine, Russia, Germany and France – managed to negotiate a new agreement on cessation of hostilities and political process that is to put an end to this conflict. As of this writing it is however too early to say whether the several rounds of talks have led to anything, but the mere fact that the parties have agreed on the principles of political settlement of the conflict. It is also possible that the impact of other factors (like the worsening of economic situation in Russia and fear of losing energy markets) than the dialogue itself can explain this modest (and perhaps only temporary) progress.

While all these cases show that other factors than the dialogue itself has been crucial to the outcome, the situation different for the three other cases presented in this book. In Afghanistan, Egypt and Sudan, the various initiatives for dialogue and reconciliation are seen as important even though the achievements so far, in terms of peace and reconciliation, are few. It is worth noting that these three case studies all emphasized that the dialogue may lead to peace and reconciliation only if there is a bottom-up, neutral, home-grown and long-term process. That said, also in these cases other factors seem to have influenced attempts at dialogue and prevented them from succeeding thus far.

In Afghanistan, an initiative for opening a dialogue with the Taliban was proposed by Karzai, and the parties did meet in Shahwalikot. Here, the Taliban actually agreed to relinquish Kandahar without a fight and Karzai guaranteed the security and dignity of Taliban leaders, who would be free to return to their homes. However, as Semple notes, 'Karzai soon abandoned the agreement, unable either to persuade his US allies to honour it or to rein in Afghan allies who had scores to settle' (p. 144). Further: 'the few Taliban leaders who tried to reintegrate peacefully in their home areas were soon targeted by the new authorities or US forces. The USA tried to detain Taliban leaders in Afghanistan and encouraged the Pakistan authorities to do likewise on their side of the border – exactly the opposite of what had been decided in Shahwalikot' (p. 145). All of this indicates that factors other than those linked to the dialogue as such prevented the dialogue attempt from succeeding.

The same also seems to hold for the process in Egypt. As Fahmi argues, 'measures for building trust between the two communities are essential, but not sufficient. The failure of the National Justice Committee was due mainly to the resistance of state institutions to its activities. The security sector perceived the Committee as its rival, and refused to cooperate with it' (p. 204). Likewise the persistence of state policies has repeatedly jeopardized the progress made by the House of the Egyptian Family in building trust among Muslims and Christians.

Finally, Ashworth's chapter on Sudan indicates that dialogue has not brought the governments of Sudan and South Sudan any closer; it merely helped them to end their armed conflict and to divorce fairly peacefully. External factors and pressure also played a role here. 'Due largely to external factors, Jonglei State descended back into conflict less than a year after the dialogue ended. The original People-to-People Peace Process brought the protagonists together in an uneasy alliance for more than a decade, until massive violence re-erupted in December 2013' (p 189).

2. *Diplomatic dialogues rarely transforms actors' values and identity and is therefore seldom sufficient to solve deep-rooted conflicts, even though it may affect both the timing of events and the nature of the measures that are adopted.*

Dialogue is primarily an opportunity to build trust so that – over time – pragmatic solutions may be found, if there is sufficient willingness to compromise. While the 'integrative' approach may have added analytical and practical value in general or perhaps in negotiations over specific issues, it appears to have its limits when the aim is to find a solution to long-term, deep-rooted conflicts, or as an approach to negotiations between regimes that differ radically in their normative bases. Such an approach requires mutual confidence and trust – and, as we have seen, the conflicts analysed here include parties that do not readily lend themselves to such an approach. The reason may be that these particular conflicts are in part about the actors' identities and attendant foundational values, as well as issues that are considered to be existential. The (admittedly limited) success achieved by dialogue in the Georgia-Russian and the Georgia-Ukrainian conflict and between Libya and the West is interesting, but also in these cases the underlying conflicts were not addressed. In the case of Iran, the underlying conflict seems to have, until recently, prevented dialogue from taking place at all. For long periods, any talks were limited to exchange of positions, until some results could be identified in 2013/2014. Also in the Russian case, timing seems to be important: it could help to explain the successes of the dialogue with Georgia, although it is too early to offer any conclusions concerning Ukraine.

While some success can be identified in relation to the first cases, the success stories are few in the final three cases. However, we should note that the perceived *potential* of success can be more important than actual success. In the case of inter-religious dialogue in Egypt, the lack of results is probably also due to lack of willingness on both sides to make real concessions. While a change of interests or identities is not required for such a process to succeed, mutual respect and tolerance are. None of these initiatives have managed to convince the broader population of the importance of this point. The case study of Sudan and South Sudan also highlights how complexity, with conflicts pitting different actors against each other at different times and in different circumstances, complicates the dialogue processes.

3.   *Lack of enforcement mechanisms in international politics makes any negotiated agreement fragile. As a result, agreements based on dialogue need enforcements mechanisms.*

Dialogue may result in agreements and breakthroughs. However, because dialogue in and of itself seldom contains enforcement mechanisms, any breakthrough or agreement is inherently unstable: it can easily unravel without an anchor or enforcement mechanism, which rarely exist at the international level. Many peace agreements and breakthroughs have unravelled at a later stage precisely because consensus/agreement at Track I can be undone at Track II by a shift in domestic interests or international conditions. Libya is clearly an example of that, as are also the various failed negotiation attempts between Iran and the West. The same holds for the successful Georgian-Russian process of 2008, even though the underlying conflict has not been solved and there is no guarantee that the agreement will hold. The situation is different with regard to the three final cases, since there has been no agreement of this type, although they all seem to indicate that the lack of enforcement mechanism was one factor that contributed to this lack of a lasting outcome.

4.   *The character of the dialogue seems to differ, depending on whether the negotiation is facilitated by a neutral third party.*

As all the cases have shown, it is often advisable to have interlocutors that are either pragmatic and/or have a certain distance to the conflict. In the Iranian case, constructive explorations of common ground were made when Ali Larijani, a pragmatist, and Javier Solana were negotiating. This remains interesting, even though there were no concrete results, and Ahmadinejad replaced Larijani with a less pragmatic negotiator. In the Libyan case, more neutral parties were often chosen to transmit the message from the regime, and the dialogue succeeded when the more moderate forces were representing the regime. The Russia-Georgian conflict also underlines much of the same point; and in the Sudan case, the Church managed to build up high credibility among most parties and then played a vital role in the various dialogue processes. As Ashworth explains:

> In the dialogue between the two rival leaders and their liberation movements in southern Sudan, there was no meaningful interaction between the protagonists before the People-to- People dialogue began. The same can be said of David Yau Yau and the government of South Sudan. In the main civil war between the government of Sudan and the SPLM/A, there was ongoing political dialogue of sorts encouraged by the international community, but with little progress until around 2002 – which is the point where the churches also became involved in the informal dialogue. In the currently ongoing civil war in South Sudan, there has as yet been no meaningful dialogue, despite efforts by IGAD. (p. 187)

Attempts at dialogue with the Taliban in Afghanistan between 2001 and 2014 have been characterized by the lack of international mediation. This is an example of dialogue undertaken without any real mediation of a neutral third party – perhaps with the exception of Qatar and a few non-US diplomats. Still, the failure of these initiatives can be explained by the lack of understanding of the nature of the Taliban as an organization. Fahmi's case study on inter-religious dialogues in Egypt also shows that neutral third parties like the National Justice Committee and the House of the Egyptian Family may play roles that are important, but are clearly not sufficient.

5.   *The character of negotiations differs, depending on the level of secrecy and confidentiality.*

In the introduction, we noted the negative and positive sides of secret negotiations. While secrecy may facilitate the initiation of talks and prevent popular interference in the process, talks undertaken in public make it easier for achieving arguments with commitment. Even though such negotiations are seldom transparent, it is often known that they are being conducted. This was the case in the dialogue with Iran and in the Georgian-Russian conflict. While the Iranian talks have shown few concrete results yet, the recent progress and prospects for an agreement seem to be partly linked to the fact that these talks have been undertaken in secrecy. Sometimes the fact that the parties meet at all is also kept secret. This was the case in most of the negotiations between Libya and the West, which were at least partially successful. Still, all this varies with the conflict in question: after all, negotiations in the Georgian-Russian conflict succeeded even thought they were public. In the three final case studies in this book, that point is less relevant since these are informal processes undertaken on lower levels. All this makes is difficult to draw conclusions. What is important is to bear in mind that the level of secrecy may influence the result in some way or other, that and the choice of procedures should therefore be considered carefully from case to case.

6.   *Western states often adopt a top-down approach, making it more difficult to generate trust and establish a genuine dialogue.*

Armed with a sense of supremacy anchored in a combination of material preponderance and a claim to universal values, Western powers often demand concessions from others as a precondition for starting negotiations. As seen in both Iran and Libya, the 'imperial' or top-down attitude of Western states can generate tensions that undermine the effectiveness of dialogue. It is scarcely a coincidence that Turkey and Brazil managed to broker a deal with Iran while EU3 or the USA could not. Libya, Iran and Russia all have wanted to be recognized as significant players in their respective regions, a recognition that is often not forthcoming from significant others (the USA, the EU, the 'West'). Herein lies a paradox: While great powers are generally needed to guarantee and make parties commit to an agreement, they are often not the best mediators, because of their tendency to try to universalize their particular interests. Conversely, small and medium-sized powers may be good mediators, but they are often unable to get the parties to adhere to an agreement because they lack the resources for imposing sanctions against them. While Western states as such did not have an important role in the Sudan peace processes or the confidence-building measures in Egypt, US involvement was explicitly avoided in the Afghanistan case, where German diplomats came to play an important role.

7.   *Dialogue is more effective at preventing conflicts than resolving them*

From the assessment of the nature and effects of dialogue in the three first cases, we may conclude that dialogue is most effective when it is part of a larger array of diplomatic tools. On the other hand, it is quite certain that *not* having a dialogue may heighten the risk of misunderstandings and push actors further toward positions that preclude any possibility of an agreement.

All the cases presented here have shown that dialogue appears to be most effective in preventing tensions from becoming manifest conflicts. Fundamentally, all these conflicts stem from historically received and politically nurtured ideas about the other side. If anything, dialogue can help nuance and transform understandings of others, and promote the capacity to recognize and tolerate difference.

As this volume has shown conflict resolution seem to be dependent first and foremost on contextual changes at the international, regional and/or national level. It has also shown that even though diplomatic dialogues are rarely sufficient to solve deep rooted conflicts, it can initiate important processes that lead to solutions. This is particularly true if the processes are facilitated by a neutral third party, if top-down approaches are avoided and if the choice of having secret or public talks are carefully evaluated. The main challenge, however, is that there are often no enforcement mechanism that can ensure long-term commitment by the parties in case of an agreement. As a consequence of this, different types of dialogue processes seem to be more effective at preventing conflicts and escalation of conflicts, than resolving them.

Index